REVOLUTION

Volume 28

THE RUHR AND REVOLUTION

THE RUHR AND REVOLUTION

The Revolutionary Movement in the Rhenish-Westphalian Industrial Region 1912–1919

JÜRGEN TAMPKE

LONDON AND NEW YORK

First published in 1979 by Croom Helm Ltd

This edition first published in 2022
by Routledge
4 Park Square, Milton Park, Abingdon, Oxon OX14 4RN

and by Routledge
605 Third Avenue, New York, NY 10158

Routledge is an imprint of the Taylor & Francis Group, an informa business

© 1979 Jürgen Tampke

All rights reserved. No part of this book may be reprinted or reproduced or utilised in any form or by any electronic, mechanical, or other means, now known or hereafter invented, including photocopying and recording, or in any information storage or retrieval system, without permission in writing from the publishers.

Trademark notice: Product or corporate names may be trademarks or registered trademarks, and are used only for identification and explanation without intent to infringe.

British Library Cataloguing in Publication Data
A catalogue record for this book is available from the British Library

ISBN: 978-1-032-12623-4 (Set)
ISBN: 978-1-003-26095-0 (Set) (ebk)
ISBN: 978-1-032-16352-9 (Volume 28) (hbk)
ISBN: 978-1-032-16355-0 (Volume 28) (pbk)
ISBN: 978-1-003-24816-3 (Volume 28) (ebk)

DOI: 10.4324/9781003248163

Publisher's Note
The publisher has gone to great lengths to ensure the quality of this reprint but points out that some imperfections in the original copies may be apparent.

Disclaimer
The publisher has made every effort to trace copyright holders and would welcome correspondence from those they have been unable to trace.

The Ruhr and Revolution

The Revolutionary Movement in the Rhenish-Westphalian Industrial Region 1912–1919

Jürgen Tampke

Croom Helm London

© 1979 Jürgen Tampke
Croom Helm Ltd, 2-10 St John's Road, London SW11

British Library Cataloguing in Publication Data

Tampke, Jurgen
The revolutionary movement in the Rhenish - Westphalian region, 1912-1919.
1. Revolutionists—Germany—Rhine Province —History—20th century 2. Revolutionists— Germany—Westphalia—History—20th century.
I. Title
322.4'2'094343 DD491.R4

ISBN 0-85664-976-7

Printed in Australia at Griffin Press Limited, Netley, South Australia.

Acknowledgments

I am grateful to the many friendly people in the libraries and archives[1] of both the Federal Republic of Germany and the German Democratic Republic. Thus I would like to thank the staff of the *Hauptstaatsarchiv* in Düsseldorf and the *Staatsarchiv* in Münster, the *Zentrales Staatsarchiv* in Potsdam and its historical division II in Merseburg, the *International Instituut voor Sociale Geschiedenis* in Amsterdam, the Westphalian Economic Archive in Dortmund, the archive of the SPD in Bonn *(Friedrich Ebert Stiftung),* the archive of the DGB in Düsseldorf and the Coal Miners Union archive in Bochum as well as the *Stadtarchive* in Bochum, Bottrop, Castrop-Rauxel, Dorsten, Dortmund, Düsseldorf, Duisburg, Essen, Gelsenkirchen, Hagen, Herne, Lünen, Mülheim, Oberhausen, Remscheid, Solingen, Wanne-Eickel, Witten and Wuppertal. I am thankful to all people who gave advice but I am indebted especially to Bruce Kent, Chris Cunneen, Michael McKernan and my wife Jane.

[1] The only archive at which I was refused access was the Gute Hoffnungshütte Archiv in Oberhausen. This was regrettable as access might have given me more insight into the policies of the leaders of German heavy industries. On the other hand a number of relevant documents from this archive have been published recently and nothing in these suggested that more thorough research at the Gute Hoffnungshütte would have altered any argument presented in this book (G. D. Feldman, 'The Origins of the Stinnes-Legien Agreement, *I.W.K.,* Vol. 9, no. 19/20, 1973, pp. 45–103).

Contents

Tables

Plates

Illustrations by courtesy of the Stadtarchiv Dorsten, Essen and Düsseldorf

Abbreviations

AfS	*Archiv für Sozialgeschichte*
AfSS	*Archiv für Sozialwissenschaft und Sozialpolitik*
AK	*Generalkommando des siebten Armeekorps* (Supreme Command of the Seventh Army Corps)
ASL	Auxiliary Service League
AZE	*Arbeiter-Zeitung,* Essen
BAS	*Bergische Arbeiterstimme,* Solingen
BAZ	*Bergarbeiter-Zeitung,* Bochum
Bl.	Blatt (page)
BVS	*Bergische Volksstimme,* Remscheid
Diss.	Dissertation
DMV	Deutscher Metallarbeiterverband (German Metal Workers Union)
GA	*Generalanzeiger*
GAZ	*Gelsenkirchener Allgemeine Zeitung*
GDK	Gewerkschaft (colliery) Deutscher Kaiser
HSTAD	Hauptstaatsarchiv Düsseldorf
IdR	Informationsstelle der Reichsregierung (government information office)
IHK	Industrie-und Handelskammer (chamber of industry and trade)
IISG	International Instituut voor Sociale Geschiedenis (Amsterdam)
IWK	*Internationale Wissenschaftliche Korrespondenz zur Geschichte der deutschen Arbeiterbewegung*
JCH	*Journal of Contemporary History*
JMH	*Journal of Modern History*
KPD	Kommunistische Partei Deutschlands (German communist party)
LA	Landratsamt
MB	*Mitteilungsblatt,* Berlin
OBA	Oberbergamt (government mining office) (Dortmund)
RdI	Reichsamt des Inneren (office for the interior)
Reg.	Regierung (government)

RWZ	*Rheinisch-Westfälische Zeitung*
SPD	Sozialdemokratische Partei Deutschlands
STA	Stadtarchiv
STAM	Staatsarchiv Münster
USP	Unabhängige Sozialdemokratische Partei Deutschlands (Independent German Social Democratic Party)
VBB	*Volksblatt,* Bochum
VfSW	*Vierteljahreshefte für Sozial-und Wirtschaftspolitik*
vol.	volume
VZD	*Volkszeitung,* Düsseldorf
WAVZ	*Westfälische-Allgemeine Volkszeitung,* Dortmund
WWA	Westfälisches Wirtschaftsarchiv, Dortmund (Westphalian economic archive)
WZ	*Walder Zeitung*
ZfG	*Zeitschrift für Geschichtswissenschaft*
ZStA, Po	Zentrales Staatsarchiv, Potsdam
ZStA, M'burg	Zentrales Staatsarchiv, Historische Abteilung II, Merseburg

Note on administrative terms

In 1918/19 the Ruhr was part of the Prussian western provinces of Rhineland and Westphalia. At the lowest level of the Prussian administrative system was the *Amt,* an amalgamation of several parishes the head of which was the *Amtsrat,* and the town, headed by the *Bürgermeister* (mayor). Several *Ämter* and towns combined to form the *Kreis (Stadtkreis* or *Landkreis).* The chief administrator of the *Kreis* was the *Landrat. Grosstädte* (cities with a population of more than 100,000) were taken out of the *Kreis* and became self-governing under the leadership of an *Oberbürgermeister* (lord mayor). Several *Kreis* and *Grosstädte* combined to form the *Regierungsbezirk* (government district) which was headed by the *Regierungspräsident* (government president). The latter was responsible to the *Oberpräsident* (Supreme President) of the province and at the top of the pyramid was the Prussian Minister for the Interior.

Parallel to the administration was a system of representative institutions to which delegates were elected *(Gemeinde* or *Stadtverordnetenversammlungen, Provinziallandtage).* These assemblies had responsibility for important local policies and election to them was based on a class franchise system.

With the exception of the terms mayor, lord mayor, government district, and government president, the German terms mentioned above are used throughout this book.

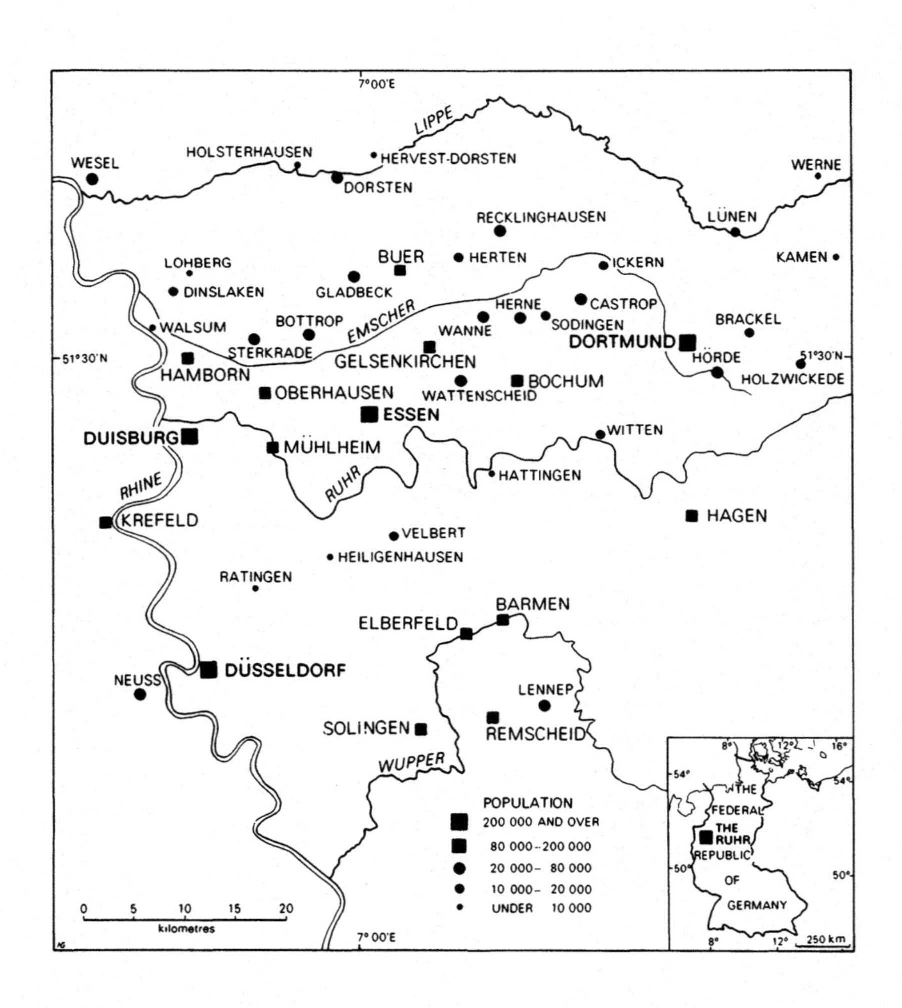
7°00'E
LIPPE
WESEL
HOLSTERHAUSEN
HERVEST-DORSTEN
DORSTEN
WERNE
RECKLINGHAUSEN
LÜNEN
BUER
HERTEN
ICKERN
KAMEN
LOHBERG
DINSLAKEN
GLADBECK
CASTROP
HERNE
SODINGEN
BRACKEL
WALSUM
BOTTROP
EMSCHER
WANNE
DORTMUND
STERKRADE
GELSENKIRCHEN
HÖRDE
51°30'N
HAMBORN
WATTENSCHEID
BOCHUM
HOLZWICKEDE
OBERHAUSEN
ESSEN
DUISBURG
MÜHLHEIM
WITTEN
RUHR
HATTINGEN
RHINE
KREFELD
HAGEN
VELBERT
HEILIGENHAUSEN
RATINGEN
BARMEN
ELBERFELD
DÜSSELDORF
NEUSS
LENNEP
SOLINGEN
REMSCHEID
WUPPER
POPULATION
200 000 AND OVER
80 000 - 200 000
20 000 - 80 000
10 000 - 20 000
UNDER 10 000
0 5 10 15 20
kilometres
THE FEDERAL REPUBLIC OF GERMANY
THE RUHR
250 km

Introduction

The German November Revolution has been studied closely both in the east and in the west for the last fifteen years and it is probably not exaggerated to claim that for a time at least the revolution and its aftermath, the period of the Workers' and Soldiers' Councils, became the leading topic of debate in modern German history. The last fifteen years then remedied a long time of lack of interest and silence on the German November Revolution. There were a few personal accounts from participants in the revolution in the early 1920s but soon the topic fell into oblivion.[1] During the Weimar Republic the official attitude was to play down the revolution. Historians and politicians referred to it as a period of general unrest, such as might be expected to follow defeat in war and the overthrow of the monarchy and avoided the term revolution. It stood for something opposed to the German tradition of obedience and law and order. Historians, at best, credited the Majority Socialists leaders for having averted the grave danger which was said and believed to have faced Germany at that time. This official attitude is seen for example in O. Stollberg (ed.) *Zehn Jahre deutsche Geschichte* (Berlin 1928). Gustav Noske wrote the chapter on the November Revolution which he titled, as was to be expected 'The defense against Bolshevism'.[2]

Although this interpretation of the revolution survived until the 1960s there was one noticeable exception in German historical writings. Arthur Rosenberg in his two books on the birth and the history of the Weimar Republic[3] was the first historian to argue that the November Revolution offered the chance to introduce far reaching social, political and economic reforms which could have been brought in without having to turn to Bolshevism. Rosenberg claimed that the SPD leaders panicked by making an agreement with the reactionary military and administrative establishment and thus prevented progressive reforms which would have put Weimar Germany on a more stable political path. Similar conclusions were also reached by the American scholar A. J. Berlau in his study of German Social Democracy 1914–1921 and by the Englishman R. Coper in his book *Failure of a Revolution.*[4] But these were exceptions and Rosenberg received scant attention in the works of the West German historical establishment. By about 1960 things were beginning to change, in both East and West Germany.

Not unexpectedly large-scale research work had begun earlier in East Germany.[5] The first revolution in a fully industrialised country would obviously attract Marxist historians. Its closeness in time to the Russian October Revolution encouraged comparison and led to explanatory studies of why the German Revolution had failed. Moreover, the linking of the November Revolution with the foundation of the Communist Party, and its history to the present day, is of vital importance in East German historical tradition.

By 1960 in West Germany too, three interesting works had appeared. First there was Walter Tormin's *Between Soviet dictatorship and Social Democracy: The History of the Council-Movement in the German Revolution 1918/19.* The second major work of the 1950s was Wolfgang Sauer's dissertation about the pact between the Social Democrat leader Ebert and the old army establishment concluded before the revolution was 24 hours old. Finally there was Hans Schieck's dissertation on the struggle about which economic system would emerge from the revolution.[6] Schieck admits that a basic change in the economic system would not have been possible, because of the high level of industrialisation in Germany. He nevertheless concludes that the diffident and indecisive policies of the SPD and union leaders thwarted the chance to at least achieve some changes in favour of the workforce.

Such as socialisation of the coal-mining and other mining industries. Then came Eberhard Kolb's work which showed the comparatively moderate character of most of the Workers' and Soldiers' Councils. Next was Peter von Oertzen's book on the Works' Councils. Von Oertzen, who is now a prominent left-wing politician in the SPD federal caucus, stressed the importance of democratisation of the economy, of socialisation of key industries and of economic codetermination as key concepts in a genuine democratisation of the state.[7] A vital part of von Oertzen's argument is his discussion of the attempt of the Essen Workers' and Soldiers' Council to socialise the coal-mining industry in the Ruhr. His findings on this issue have been challenged recently and are the subject of a considerable debate.[8] After von Oertzen there was a large number of publications dealing with a whole range of topics associated with the revolution. Its causes were again investigated as were its main events, its institutions and the reasons for its failure. The question was asked to what extent was the term revolution applicable and many regional studies were published. More emphasis was now placed upon the orthodox or centrist wing of the Independent Socialists and the overall view of these studies confirmed Rosenberg's original argument: that there was a third way. The revolution offered a genuine chance to alter existing inequalities, to lay the basis for social, economic and constitutional reconstruction of German society. The argument is that the SPD leaders failed to realise the revolution's potential and were in part to blame for exposing the Republic to the political extremism which proved so fatal for Weimar Germany. Of course their failure in 1918/19 was not the sole cause for Hitler's rise to power but substantial social reforms might have arrested the deep division in the labour movement which was one of the more important factors crippling Weimar Germany's political life. The overall findings of these years of research work were published in 1972 under the title *From Empire to Republic (Vom Kaiserreich zur Republik)* edited by Eberhard Kolb. The latter summarises:

> investigations of the council movement . . . led to a discussion of whether there was a real possibility during the revolutionary months to initiate thorough changes in the political as well as in the socio-economic order, . . . changes which in no way need to have led to a 'bolshevik' solution, but which would have put the first German Republic on a more solid democratic footing. Because the sources show that there was a great deal of democratic potential within the workers councils. The common view that the Workers' and Soldiers' Councils were dominated by communists is wrong. Instead these councils were under the influence of moderate social democrats and union leaders who supported democratic and social changes but who rejected the notion of 'the dictatorship of the proletariat'. The communists on the other hand, were numerically weak, in the months between November 1918 and January 1919 in no position to undertake effective action. Thus the bolshevists revolution during the winter weeks was at best fictitious but not a real alternative.[9]

Kolb's findings were supported in a large study of Soldiers' Councils published shortly afterwards by Ulrich Kluge and in a series of essays on the revolution in the Rhenish-Westphalian Industrial Region which was edited by Reinhard Rürup.[10]

It did not take long before this new interpretation was challenged from both left and right. The traditional German historical school had kept quiet for a while but when the new interpretation was gathering momentum, almost establishing itself as the accepted interpretation, they started to hit back. Their replies stated in general that the new view of the November Revolution lacked substance. Of course there had been the Bolshevists threat; one cannot get an impression of the strength of the extreme left by just looking at the election statistics, and consequently Ebert and Scheideman did the only thing they could do.[11] This critique on the part of the conservative West German historians has become quite savage recently. Henning Köhler, in reviewing Kluge's *Soldatenräte und Revolution* has this to say:

> So by way of conclusion this book does not seem to be an attempt to clarify historically an important chapter in the November Revolution but it pursues

primarily the goal to support the thesis of the missed chances of the council movement. And by so doing it develops a concept which rests on unproven assumptions and on the preposition of legitimacy provided by revolution, . . . a concept which lacks any substance and which is historically completely untenable.[12]

The East German historians too would have little of the third way. They acknowledged that at last some bourgeois historians made an effort to look seriously at the November Revolution but the findings, in their opinion, were of course still wrong, the only way to success was the one advocated by Karl Liebknecht and Rosa Luxemburg, but with no strong organised German Communist Party, the revolution and socialism was doomed from the start. Perhaps the most friendly evaluation of a West German's work was Dieter Baudis' review of Peter von Oertzen's study on the Works Council. 'Even if we have to describe von Oertzen's position still as reformist' writes Baudis, 'and even if von Oertzen, as supporter of social reform, does not show any far reaching ambitions, his work nevertheless must be evaluated as a symptom of a more realistic assessment of certain social exigencies.'[13]

This briefly summarised is the state of the debate today and it is likely that the stage of intense interest in the German November Revolution is over. That the German November Revolution had such a renaissance recently is largely the product of the exciting political climate of the late 1960s and the fact that the Brandt government made possible a so-called 'Offnung nach Links', 'An Opening to the Left'. The discussion about codetermination and other far reaching reforms encouraged research into the German Revolution. Now this renaissance is largely over and if we are to believe foreign observers there is now a return to the right, a moderation and cooling off in the political climate, which extends throughout all sections of the German community.[14] The previously favourable climate has now changed and of course there has always been a strong subjective element in the debate of which the historians are aware. Their evaluation and their willingness to accept new evidence depends on how they stand on such issues as codetermination, social democracy and worker participation. If the debate is to continue it would be up to the 'third way' historians to make the next move and counter the various criticisms made recently. Their replies would have to shift emphasis from pointing to the missed opportunity, the mistakes and failures, to more concrete suggestions of what in practice the SPD leadership could have done. As this would involve a considerable degree of speculation it is probably not attractive to the historians involved. But notwithstanding the future of the debate on the German November Revolution the past fifteen years have been most productive. By entering social, ideological and labour history they have opened up a whole new field in German history, which had hitherto not attracted major attention.

The Rhenish Westphalian Industrial Region—or the Ruhr as this area is commonly called[15] was one of the parts of Germany in which the revolutionary conflict during the months of November 1918 and April 1919 was especially pronounced. In subsequent years too there were strikes, battles between paramilitary forces, uprisings, indeed civil wars, which all bears witness to an inexorable shift to the extreme political left through the fourteen years of the Weimar Republic. By the time of Hitler's takeover the Ruhr had become a communist stronghold.

An industrial area of great importance, the Ruhr has frequently attracted the interest of historians covering the German Revolution of 1918/19 and the trouble-stricken years of the Weimar Republic.[16] The most noteworthy recent treatise in addition to the collective publications of R. Rürup and Jürgen Reulecke[17] are the works of Erhard Lucas. Lucas's findings, which run into several volumes already,[18] contain a massive amount of detailed material and his writings must rank among the most informative on the labour movement and on German social history. His comprehensive account of the November Revolution in the Ruhr is yet to be published. Non-German publications on the other hand are virtually non-existent. Although some regions in Germany have attracted historians from Anglo-Saxon countries,[19] the Ruhr, the largest industrial region in Germany, receives only brief mention in recent publications on the November Revolution.[20]

This book then sets out to give a comprehensive account of the history of the revolutionary period in this part of Germany. It also seeks to explain why the revolution took such a variable course in the Ruhr. Why did some places remain quiet throughout the period, why in others did opposition and strikes persist? How was it possible that within weeks of the collapse of the old order not only left-wing socialists but also communists and syndicalists could present a challenge to the Majority Socialists and the state, which was based on ever growing support? This is not only to be explained by the course of events from November 1918 to April 1919. To find an answer to these questions it is necessary to place the revolution in its wider historical context and investigate a series of long-term trends which go back to the outbreak of World War I and beyond. By doing so the study has moved into a field of history in which—as was stressed in some of the chapters written for the recent international symposium on the industrial system and political development in the Weimar Republic—there is still plenty of room for further research but little has been done so far.[21] It is hoped that this work will contribute to knowledge about European urban and working-class history.

Part I describes the economic, social and political background of the region up to the time of the coal-miners' strike of 1912 and illustrates that by the time of this strike the seeds of division within the socialist movement which were to bear fruit in 1918/19 had already been sown. Part II examines how the war aggravated social hardship and accentuated the rift in the workers' party. The third part discusses the revolution during its most hopeful period between November 1918 and early January 1919. As a case study of the revolution under the leadership of the Majority Socialists, events in the eastern Ruhr will be analysed. The quiescent course of the revolution here is contrasted with that of the Lower Rhine area, with its powerful working-class tradition, where the left-wing USP led the revolution along much more radical lines. The book then turns to the trouble-stricken western Ruhr and to the attempt by the Essen Workers' and Soldiers' Council to halt the rapidly growing polarisation of the Ruhr's workforce. The collapse of the attempted socialisation of the coal industry in Essen and the government's failure to introduce proposals aimed at altering the *status quo* in the coal industry and heavy industry set the stage for the final act, the confrontation between the disappointed workers and the government. We will investigate the tragic events which occurred in the region between February and April 1919 and will show how these clashes completed the division within the socialist movement and gave the extreme left the support of the majority of the working class.

The conclusion will raise the question of the extent to which a study of the revolution of the Ruhr throws light on the various points of controversy which have been discussed recently in the debate on the German November Revolution.

I

Seedbed of revolution: the Ruhr to 1912

Chapter 1

Social and economic background

At the time of the collapse of the Second German Empire the country to the north of the river Ruhr had passed through half a century of rapid industrial expansion and was a leading example of Germany's industrial development.[1] Following a tradition going back to the middle ages a small amount of coal-mining was undertaken here by the middle of the nineteenth century. The miners were normally *Kötters,* which meant that they also worked small farm holdings. The industry then employed about 12,700 men.[2] The old Hanseatic trading cities of Duisburg, Essen, Bochum and Dortmund around the Hellweg[3] accounted for the region's few urban settlements but up to the mid 1850s the Ruhr, like most of Germany, was predominantly rural. At this stage a handful of entrepreneurs encouraged industrial development by financing coal-mining.[4] The rise in coal output in turn encouraged the establishment of iron- and steel-works. Liberal trade laws enacted in Prussia from 1850 onward, the introduction of coke for smelting and the improvement of the railways fostered the process of rapid industrialisation. The invention of the Thomas process of steel-making in the 1870s was a milestone in the history of the region. It led to a vast increase in steel production and consequently an increase in the demand for coal. Coal-fields now began to spread to the north, first into the valley of the river Emscher, until they reached the river Lippe, where mining development came to a halt.

The expansion to the north was accompanied by the growth of larger companies, speedier exploitation and deeper shafts, all of which contributed to a sharp increase in production. Coal output grew from 1.6 million tons in 1850 to over 20 million tons in 1880, 60 million in 1900, and thence to 114 million tons by 1913. In 1850 there had been 190 mines. The average mine produced 8,500 tons of coal annually and employed a staff of 64. Although the number of mines had only risen to 214 by 1900, the average output was 280,000 tons and the average number of employees about 1,400 in each mine. Both figures doubled again during the next fourteen years.[5] The growth of the iron and steel industries was equally impressive. The first Thomas steel was smelted in September 1879 at the Hoerde works and at the Rheinische Stahlwerke at Ruhrort. In the next five years plants inaugurated the Thomas process at Bochum, the

Oberhausen Gute Hoffnungshütte, at Phoenix in Ruhrort and at Dortmunder Union and Hoesch in Dortmund. By now Germany was making more than half of the world's basic steel.[6] Iron production, which in 1870 was still below one million tons, rose to over nine million in 1914. By the last decade of the nineteenth century only the Rhine could provide the cheap transportation for such a bulky commodity as iron ore, which was demanded in ever increasing amounts by the steel smelting industries. Hence at the turn of the century eleven iron and steel works were established between Oberhausen and Mülheim, the largest being the Thyssen works at Hamborn. Founded in 1890, the latter embraced by 1900 five blast furnaces with basic Bessemer and open hearth steel works and rolling mills. The Thyssen complex also included the coal mining company Deutscher Kaiser, the largest coal-mine of the Ruhr in the pre-war years. In 1900 Deutscher Kaiser employed about 4,000 men on three shafts, producing 1.2 million tons of coal. A fourth shaft was sunk and coal output rose to 4.5 million tons by 1913. In addition a large battery of coking ovens was established at the third shaft in 1895. Altogether the Thyssen works employed at that time about 24,000 men.[7]

Thus, before the war, the western part of the area was already the centre of a large-scale iron and steel industry, which in terms of manpower and production was outstanding even for the Ruhr. The east of the area, centering around Bochum, Dortmund, Gelsenkirchen, Herne and Recklinghausen remained as the actual 'Kohlenpott', the coal and coke producing part of the Ruhr. Situated in the centre is Essen, then—as it is today—a coal-mining city, but above all the seat of the Krupp dynasty with its heavy industries. Parallel to and benefiting from these developments, the cities to the south of the Ruhr also passed through a period of marked industrial growth, with a series of steel-making and steel-processing firms spreading from Hagen in the east to the tool and cutlery centres of Solingen and Remscheid, and to the Rhenish steel metropolis of Düsseldorf in the west.[8] In less than fifty years the Ruhr had developed from a minor rural province to one of Europe's largest industrial regions. The population for the region in this study had risen from about 350,000 in the middle of the nineteenth century to almost four million in 1914. To resettle such a number of people within less than two generations would have been difficult under any circumstances. However, growth in the Ruhr occurred at a time when Manchester liberalism was at its zenith in Germany. Not unexpectedly, the over-rapid industrialisation and population growth led to many social problems. There was a considerable deterioration of working conditions, as shown in longer hours, poorer health, higher accident rates, victimisation and inadequate government supervision. There was an overall drop in real wages and a vast decline in the standard of housing.

Since these social problems explain the explosive situation which had arisen before the outbreak of World War I, they need to be described in more detail.

In terms of population the country around the Ruhr was in no way equipped to meet the demand for manpower brought about by the new growth.[9] The indigenous population did not even suffice to man the first wave of industries in the 1850s. Migration was thus needed to provide the manpower. This set in on a larger scale in the 1860s, first from the surrounding provinces and states in the west. From the 1870s but particularly in the 1880s and 1890s the bulk of immigrants came from Prussia's eastern provinces, the Polish parts of the empire.[10] Dortmund, for example, in 1850 a small town with an estimated population of 13,000, had grown to 58,000 in 1875 and to 214,000 in 1914. The corresponding figures for the other Hellweg cities were Essen 10,000, 55,000, 295,000; Duisburg 20,000, 37,000, 229,000 and Bochum 8,000, 28,000, 137,000.[11] Yet these growth rates of the Hellweg cities were low compared to that of the Emscher Valley city of Gelsenkirchen, where industrialisation set in later and was more intense. Gelsenkirchen did not exist as a city until 1903 when it was formed by an amalgamation of seven villages and the country market town of Alt-Gelsenkirchen. At the time the first shaft was sunk here in 1855, the total population of the seven parishes was 6,834. This had risen to 25,000 by 1870 and to 155,000 by 1907.[12] But even this was surpassed by the north-western city of Hamborn, already referred to because of its record industrial growth. Hamborn, in 1870 still a village with approximately 2,000 people living in the region, increased its population from 28,000 in 1890 to just over 100,000 two decades later.[13]

The Hellweg cities in general benefited from the more gradual growth. W. Köllmann in his investigation into the occupations of *Nahwanderer* (immigrants from the neighbouring regions) and *Fernwanderer* (immigrants from the distant provinces and from abroad) in the 1907 census notices that there are many *Nahwanderer* in middle-class groups such as public servants, clerks and self-employed. This leads him to suggest that the greater part of the *Nahwanderer* had good qualifications and were attracted to the cities by the improved opportunities in the public service or industry. On the other hand the majority of *Fernwanderer* who left their homes without qualifications, often having been forced out by poverty, tended to occupy the lower positions. Köllmann's tables show that the middle class made up almost a quarter of the population in the Hellweg cities but only one-sixth in Gelsenkirchen.[14] The earlier start no doubt favoured the Hellweg cities. They contained the service industries, the administrative offices of industry and commerce and the major departments of the public service, all of which provided white-collar employment. The average size of companies indicates the existence of a broader middle class too. In Dortmund there were 3,642 registered firms in 1910 employing a total workforce of 47,260. The figures for Bochum and Duisburg are similar. Gelsenkirchen in contrast had a workforce almost equal to that of Dortmund (44,437), but only 1,987 registered firms. The situation was the same in the smaller cities and rural mining municipalities of the north.[15] Here too Polish immigrants often accounted for more than 50 per cent of the workforce and up to 40 per cent of the population.[16] Thus the north experienced the great bulk of the migration from the east and was much more prone to proletarianisation, the ingredients of which will now be described.

The miners of the middle of the nineteenth century, indeed even as late as 1865, in many ways enjoyed a privileged position.[17] Working conditions were regulated by the *Revidierte Clevisch-Märkische Bergordnung* of 1776.[18] The laws, which originally had exempted the coal-miners from tax and military duties,[19] restricted the working time to eight hours, guaranteed a fixed income, the *Normallohn,* a salary rather than a wage, and gave the miners the right to work. Although most of the mines were owned privately, the influence of the owners upon working conditions was limited. Unlike the clothing industry or the newly developing metal industries, the coal-mining industry had no female or child labour or Sunday shifts. A series of supervisory offices set up by the Prussian government, the *Berg-* and *Oberbergämter,* ensured that the rules were upheld. Above all, the privileged position of the miners was emphasised by an advanced insurance system, the Knappschaftswesen (Coal Miners' Benefit Scheme) which gave the miners free *Kur* (course of baths) and medical treatment in case of illness or accident, sick payments during the whole period of illness and invalid payments in case of permanent disablement. Not unexpectedly under these favourable circumstances, the miners saw themselves as privileged craftsmen. They were noted for the pride with which they regarded their position and for their religious devotion,[20] which was strengthened by the perpetual threat of death through accident. Hence until 1865 the *Bergmann* in the Ruhr had little in common with the fourth estate, the urban wage earners, whose numbers were quickly growing.

After 1865 the position of the miners changed for the worse. Notwithstanding the conservative character of the Prussian government and the failure of the liberals to gain constitutional reforms in 1848, the economic liberals succeeded in 1851 in passing the first of a series of laws which by 1865 had established the *freie Arbeitsvertrag*[21] for German industrial relations. In the coal industry the laws culminated in the *Allgemeine Berggesetz* of 1865, which finally placed production and working conditions under the control of the mine owners, although the government's mining departments reserved themselves some control function, particularly in the field of mine security.[22] Thus at a time when a major assault upon the depressed working conditions in the newer industries was being staged inside and outside parliament, the social position of the miners began a period of continuous decline.

It took little time for the men to feel the effect of the change brought about by the new laws. The miners' long struggle to recover their former privileges began in 1872 with the first major strike in the Ruhr.[23] The grievances at this time foreshadowed those of the great strikes of the twentieth century. The main complaint was about the increase in working time. With the growing depth of the shafts and the increase in staff the travelling time to the actual place of work in the mine increased. Working time in many collieries rose to nine hours and in some mines to ten. The miners demanded to be paid for the extra time or to have it included in the normal shift.[24] Compulsory overtime and special shifts also caused complaints. Refusal often resulted in dismissal, accompanied by reports which endangered future employment. Finally the miners reacted against having become wage-earners and demanded a return to the *Normallohn*. Or, if this was impossible, they asked for a wage rise of 25 per cent. The strike did not succeed and three decades later the complaints had snowballed into a vast number of issues.

The miners' health was hardest hit by the new developments. There was a direct correlation between the increasing depth of the shafts and the decline in health.[25] The greatest threat to health was bad air and high temperatures. The air in the mines (which was polluted with choke-damp, carbonic acid, carbon monoxide, coal dust and nitrogen), the extreme heat, particularly in the deeper mines, and the moisture left the miners subject to rheumatic pains, eye complaints, chronic lung and trachea illness and, especially, skin diseases.[26] The miner rarely worked standing up. For most of the time he was bending or lying down. This placed a great strain on breathing and circulation, and hence added to the harshness of the occupation. The unnatural posture in which the underground worker found himself at most times also made extraordinary demands upon the muscles during the hewing and transporting of the coal. As the unionist Otto Hue remarked, only men aged between 20 and 35 were able to work under such 'murderous' conditions.[27] That this is an accurate observation is shown by the decline of the age at which the underground workers retired as invalid from 54.2 in 1865 to 46.2 in 1905. The extent to which mining was taking a larger toll on health than other industries is shown by the annual claim figures as reported by the health funds. Around the turn of the century the Knappschaftsvereine had about 75 per cent more illness to report than did the average health fund in Germany.[28] To counterbalance this, the trade unionists and other social reformers demanded more government inspection of the mines, better regulations with regular checks that they were being adhered to, and the introduction of various inventions to improve conditions. The complaints indicate how much the official inspection of the *Bergämter* had lapsed since 1865.

During the late 1890s and the early years of the new century, the Ruhr was struck by a worm disease of epidemic proportions. Exact figures have never been established but as many as half of the miners might have been affected by the malady at one stage. To challenge the frequent claims made by the administration and the mine owners that the disease was imported by Italian workers and that the numbers of people affected were on the decline, the coal-miners' union, the *Alte Verband,* made a survey of hygienic conditions. Of the eighty-seven shafts which were investigated, toilet facilities at twenty-six were described as 'repulsive', 'completely covered in dirt' or 'pigsty'. In these cases the men had to excrete in the *Strecken* (galleries). Cleaning and shower facilities at thirty-four shafts were ranked as 'completely insufficient' and 'disgusting'.[29]

Nothing, however, illustrates the waning influence of government control on working conditions as much as the accident rates. In the middle of the nineteenth century the English government sent a commission to Prussia to study the methods by which the Prussian government achieved its low accident figures. Thirty years later the Prussian government returned the compliment. The following table covering fatal accidents illustrates what had taken place.[30]

Table 1
Fatalities per thousand miners

England		Belgium		Prussia	
1840/65	3.431	1841/50	2.974	1841/52	1.650
1883/92	1.810	1881/90	1.992	1867/80	2.465
1891/95	1.705	1886/95	1.708	1886/95	2.555

In the decade between 1894 and 1905 reported accidents in the coal industry rose from 38,241 to more than 80,000. The following causes were given for the accidents in 1905:[31]

Dangerous nature of work	68.51%
Fault of the company	0.90%
Fault of other workers	3.73%
Injured by their own fault	26.86%

This means that in more than two-thirds of the cases an act of God was to blame. In a further quarter it was the fault of the miners. Not even in one percent of all the accidents was the state of the mines held responsible. Admittedly, there is a danger of accidents in mining which is outside men's power to control completely. Admittedly too, carelessness would have taken its toll. However, the haste with which the companies recruited thousands of new men to put them into production with a minimum of preparation and training and the lessening of concentration caused by the long working hours would account for a large share of the row 'Injured by their own fault'. The statistics also show the laxity of the government departments. In the year 1904, for example, the *Oberbergämter* controlled 3,055 shafts. In 205 of these there was no inspection at all. Of the remainder, 919 were inspected once, 607 twice and 1,324 three times and more.[32] Thus most of the mines did not have an inspection for months, and, often enough, the inspectors announced their visit so far in advance that the worst deficiencies could quickly be covered up. This certainly throws doubt on the authenticity of the first row, and in view of the major mine disasters,[33] the question remains how many lives would have been saved by acceptable and thorough inspections.

Of the 80,000 reported accidents in 1904 compensation was paid in only one-twelfth of the cases.[34] In all other claims the benefit funds found reason to reject either sick payments or invalid pensions. This raises the question of what had happened to the Knappschaftskassen which were described above as the pride of the coal-miners. Changes here were brought about by the law of 10 April 1854. Up to that stage the Knappschaftskassen were owned and run by the miners. The new law compelled the mine owners to contribute at least the same amount as was paid in by the staff. In turn they were given equal say in the administration of the funds. That was how the law read in theory. In practice, however, it meant that the mine administrators were in control of the expenditure while the workers still paid for the major part of the contributions.[35] Soon illness payments were reduced to half of the normal daily wage, the period for which sick payments were made was limited and old age, widow and orphan benefits were kept low as the following table illustrates:[36]

Table 2
Decline in welfare payments, 1875–1902
(marks)

	1875	1902
Annual retirement payments for miners	261	236
Widow pensions	192	156
Orphan payments	45	35
Daily sick payments	2.50	2.12

Only membership dues had risen from 23 marks in 1875 to 52 marks in 1902.[37]

There was no reduction of working hours, which were a major source of complaint after 1865.[38] A massive strike in 1889 centred in particular around long hours, overtime and extra shifts. Although the chairman of the mine owners' association, Hammacher, signed an agreement which limited the miners' time underground to eight hours and restricted the descent and ascent to half an hour, the strike proved unsuccessful. The association soon dismissed Hammacher and made no effort to keep to the agreement.

A further source of complaint was the ill-treatment the miners often experienced from their superiors. Pieper refers to a series of court cases which show that even corporal punishment was used.[39]

Finally there was the malpractice of 'zeroing' *(Nullen)*. Wagons which were not filled enough or which contained too many stones were 'zeroed', which meant that the miner received no pay for the load. The companies did of course still profit from the sale of the coal. The miners saw this practice, against which they had no right to appeal, as a particularly grave injustice as circumstances made it often impossible to produce a wagon filled with pure coal only.[40]

Attempts were made to improve conditions but nothing substantial had been achieved by 1914. The most sincere effort to halt the process of decline in the coal-mining industry came in the early 1890s from the Prussian Minister of the Interior, Berlepsch. The latter had made a name for himself already as Government President of Düsseldorf when, after the 1889 strike, he advocated the creation of a workers' board, an arbitration court *(gewerbliches Schiedsgericht)* and a mining industry council *(Bergbau Gewerbekammer)*.[41] The workers' board was to have formed a link between employers and employees and improved relations between them. The arbitration court was to provide speedy and cheap jurisdiction without the distrust characteristic of the existing legal procedures. The council was designed as a permanent institution to guard the interests of the miners.

These forthright suggestions earned Berlepsch the Ministry of the Interior soon after Wilhelm II's accession when improvements in the conditions of the working classes were widely debated in parliament and public. As minister he introduced the *Berggesetznovelle* which, in addition to the proposed creation of workers' boards, arbitration courts and mining councils, tried to reassert government control over working conditions. The new law also contained clauses which gave the miners some protection against 'zeroing' and abolished compulsory extra shifts. Finally Berlepsch hoped to make the state-owned mines an example of how a responsible owner should run his company. The opposition of the *Bergbauliche Verein* and of the reactionary wing in his own Conservative party, however, thwarted Berlepsch's plans.[42] The only improvement introduced in his term of office was the *Berggewerbegericht* (mining court) at Dortmund, which adjudicated on differences arising from the existing laws. It was seldom used, however, and one may question Kirchhoff's claim that the new court at least gave the miners an increased feeling of legal security.[43]

Some of Berlepsch's plans were implemented after the 1905 strike. A law finally passed which restricted a normal shift to eight and a half hours. The descent was limited to half an hour and if it took longer, extra travelling time had to be deducted from the eight hours the miners' were compelled to work underground. The unions attempted to make extra shifts illegal but this failed. 'Zeroing' was now abolished and replaced by a system of monetary penalties. Finally Berlepsch's idea of workers' boards was put into practice although the law ensured that they remained most moderate.[44] To qualify for representation a worker had to be thirty years of age. He was also required to have worked without interruption for the last three years and, finally, he had to speak German fluently. As most miners had participated in the 1905 strike the second clause excluded them from standing for the first elections to these boards. The workers' boards were given a say in the running of the insurance funds and the penalty system. Above all, the representatives were to be the spokesmen for complaints raised by the staff. Moderate as these improvements were, they were at least a start. Unfortunately, no effort was made to progress further.

Unsatisfactory working conditions were not confined to the coal industry, although the latter's decline was unique in the industrial history of Germany before 1914. The second major employer in the Ruhr was the metal industry. It encompassed a large variety of enterprises ranging from the huge steel-producing and iron-smelting plants to the smaller manufacturing industries, and the small workshops in the county of Berg. Conditions varied from branch to branch and place to place. The metal workers are generally regarded as the first urban proletarians, the victims of Germany's early industrialisation. Their situation improved with Bismarck's welfare legislation and the social legislation of the early 1890s.[45] In the years before 1914 the industrial climate, especially in the smaller and medium sized plants, had steadily become better. The unions were more likely to be recognised and wage agreements and collective works contracts between unions and employer associations increased in number. By 1913 almost 200,000 metal workers were covered by collective agreements.[46] This was only a fraction of the total workforce; but the situation compared favourably with that in the coal-mining industry. In general the social status of the metal workers was better than that of the miners in the Ruhr. Successful miners prided themselves that their sons were working in the metal industry rather than following in their footsteps.[47] Of course the majority of metal workers were not to be found in the more advanced light metal and manufacturing concerns but in the huge steel plants of Krupp, Stinnes or Thyssen, and here a different situation prevailed as regards union recognition and collective bargaining. Still the workers here too seemed to have been conscious of a higher social standing. At least part of their political and industrial conservatism can be related to this. The metal workers in the coal-mining district had a very different outlook from their fellow workers in Hagen, Remscheid, Solingen and Düsseldorf, the cities south of the Ruhr, who, as will be shown, were among the more radical of the German workers.

The annual records of the Metal Workers' Union and the works inspectors show excessive working hours heading the list of complaints in the metal industries in the decade following the turn of the century.[48] Although steady progress towards the reduction of working time was made before 1914 the statistics for 1913 show that in the Rhenish-Westphalian Industrial Region only 4 per cent of the workforce worked less than 9 hours. (The corresponding figure for the whole of Germany was almost 20 per cent.) About 25 per cent worked between 9 and 10 hours (36 per cent), 50 per cent for ten hours (30 per cent) leaving about one-fifth with a working time of more than ten hours a day. The worst conditions, twelve hours and more of working time, prevailed at the large rolling mills and foundries as well as in the tool and cutlery workshops in Solingen.[49] Added to this was the overtime which was often compulsory on pain of dismissal. In 1912 the 220,000 metal workers in the government district of Düsseldorf worked a total of 24.6 million extra hours. The works inspectors refer to cases in which workers did up to 24 hours a week overtime for the length of a full year.[50] Other means by which the employers tried to increase production were special awards in the form of cigarettes, pea soup or ham,[51] or by cutting into the workers' lunch and tea breaks.[52]

As in the coal-mining industry, the hard conditions took their toll on health. The number of illnesses reported to the metal workers' insurance funds was 35 per cent above the average of German health funds.[53] Accidents increased in the years 1885 to 1910 50 per cent faster than the growth of the workforce.[54] Inspections here too were inadequate. Before the war the 33,580 plants in the metal industry were controlled by 58 works inspectors, requiring each inspector to make an average of 340 inspections a year.[55] Assaults upon workers by superiors,[56] lack of hygiene and proper cleaning facilities[57] and, finally, misuse of insurance funds by the administration[58] were complained of as frequently by the metal workers as they were in the coal industry.

The unsatisfactory conditions in the mines and heavy industry were generally recognised by open-minded contemporaries and have rarely been challenged since. The employers rejected the complaints as unfounded and distorted. However, the genuine figures which the unionists and other reformers[59] collected from inspections and insurance data readily disproved the industrialists' claims. The regularity with which the subject of working conditions was brought up in the Reichstag shows the widely-felt concern. To counterbalance this drive for reform, the Ruhr industrialists advanced as their main weapon the high level of wages.

The cost of living and its relation to income has been the subject of controversy since Bernstein's claim that the improvement in living conditions justified a revision of Marxist theory. Although contemporaries stressed the absence of reliable statistics on working hours, wages and comprehensive food prices,[60] it is not unusual to find references to an improvement in living conditions for the workers during the last two decades before 1914. This optimistic approach is found in writings on the Ruhr too.[61]

The claim is hard to sustain. Despite the vast literature on the topic, no comprehensive study of living conditions comparable to the works of Charles Booth was undertaken in Germany.[62] The few studies of working-class families were based on too small a number of cases to be statistically significant. All these surveys agree that, for the majority of families investigated, the balance between expenditure and income was extremely precarious. They reveal an upper crust for whom conditions were good at all times, but a majority for whom income was insufficient to pay for the basic necessities of food, clothing and rent.[63] To balance its budget a family could either take in a lodger and hence add to the overcrowding, or it could send the wife to work. As Fürth points out, the income figures for working wives are in inverse proportion to the income of the husband.[64] The income of the wife is highest where the man earns the least and decreases as his wages become larger, with most working wives being married to husbands in the lowest income bracket. This undermines any assumption that wives worked to bring in 'a little extra money' for special commodities. It is certain that they were forced to work so that the family could obtain the basic necessities. Wages in the Ruhr coal-mining industry were high, above average; still it is wrong to infer from this that living conditions here were not a source of serious complaint in the pre-war years.[65] Koch, whose work on the Ruhr miners in Wilheminian Germany enjoys a great deal of authority, derives his evaluation of prices and income from poor statistical material.[66] A much more careful analyst of living conditions was R. Calwer, whose work is often referred to in studies of real wages in Germany before 1914. Covering a number of larger cities, Calwer used a multitude of wage statistics and price tables. He worked out the food ration needed by a family of four, and accounted for heating, clothing and rent. Calwer worked with great care. He doubted that a rise in living standards had taken place in the late 1890s[67] and he correctly analysed the adverse trend which set in during the last years of peace.[68]

Modern research has confirmed the scepticism of more critical contemporaries. G. Bry in his study of wages in Germany arrives at the conclusion that the average weekly real earnings appear to have reached their upper peacetime limit as early as 1900. Bry claims that although money earnings increased by about one-third between 1900 and 1914 these gains were largely offset by increases in prices of consumer goods.[69] For the miners and metal workers this is a conservative estimate. Their income rose by only 22 per cent, hence they would have belonged to that minority of workers which Bry believes experienced an actual decrease in real earnings.

Housing constituted a further problem which by 1914 had assumed grave proportions in the Ruhr as well as in other industrial centres of Germany. Originally the miners were *Kötters*. In 1850 almost all miners would have possessed their own house with a smallholding of land and stock adding to their share of social security. By 1870 house owners had fallen to 26 per cent of the total number. The great majority of miners at this early stage of Ruhr industrialisation already lived in privately owned or company flats. It seems that the building rate up to this stage did not fall too far behind the demand. Flats then were still described as containing three to four rooms with pigsty, chicken houses and facilities for other small domestic animals. From 1870 onward, however, the building rate fell quickly behind the migration intake.[70] The *Kolonie* became the predominant form of housing for migrants from the east. The colonies were built by companies. They consisted of a block of houses which were usually placed close to the mines away from the normal township or village. They varied in size and quality of accommodation. The smaller colonies accommodated several hundred people, the larger ones might swell to the size of whole suburbs. The following description of a colony gives an indication of what could have been done in the field of housing if the company were willing to make an effort:

The *Erlenkamp* is the largest of the colliery's settlements planned and built by the mine in a tree-filled valley. The idea of a garden city was realised here for the first time. In its disposition and shape the settlement is adapted to its natural surrounding. The main roads are not long and straight but lead in attractive curves *(lebendige Biegungen)* from north to south. Smaller streets branch off, connect with each other and lead to small court yards. The houses are low with overhanging eaves and inhabited attics. They are built in groups of four or six. There is only one flat in each house. Only in the north, along the old country road, are a few multistorey houses with several flats. There are small decorative gardens at the front of the houses and in the back are facilities for small-scale husbandry and gardens with vegetable patches, fruit trees and shrubs. As far as possible existing trees were kept and shapely newly-planted trees have grown over recent decades. If one looks down on a summer's day from one of the high mine towers to the settlement one sees that the houses are hidden by the foliage. Because of its shape many visitors justifiedly like to compare [the *Erlenkamp*] to a village.[71]

At first sight, then, the colonies do not seem to give an unfavorable impression. The mine companies and writers close to them readily pointed out that unlike the *Mietskasernen* in the cities the colonies consisted of single-storey, or at the most, double-storey buildings. The houses had gardens and facilities for small animals attached to them so that the tenants could provide for themselves in times of economic hardship. The final attractive feature usually referred to is that the people in the colony were able to enjoy their common ethnic and cultural heritage.

Of course the company landlord did not provide such favourable accommodation only for altruistic reasons. In almost all cases the tenancy agreement contained clauses which bound the worker to the company.[72] Pieper, a contemporary critic of social conditions in the Ruhr, pointed out that company flats could often mean more difficult work, less pay, harsher treatment or additional overtime and extra shifts.[73] Many leases also included participation in strikes as a reason for the immediate giving of notice. The creation of a barrier to the spreading of social democracy was a further advantage the employer saw in the colonies. Malicious literature and newspapers could be kept out more easily and possible dissident cells could quickly be removed. This, however, proved a two-edged sword for, although it was extremely difficult for socialists and free unionists to gain support here for a long time, the colonies eventually became radical strongholds.

Far from being an advantage to them, the fact that the migrants from the east were being housed together in one block proved a great social stigma. The indigenous population often treated the new settlers with arrogance and disdain. *Polacken, Gesox, Mistzeug aus dem Osten* and *hergelaufenes Pack* were the derogatory words commonly used.[74] Alcohol was believed to flow freely here and there were rumours of constant brawls. Enough to keep the decent citizen away. Social intercourse between the two groups remained extremely limited. Croon describes that marriage of an *Alteingesessene* into a colony was seen as a social disgrace by the former's family.[75]

In addition to this, a great many of the colonists, the Poles, were victimised by a series of discriminatory laws which resulted from the strong nationalism of the German government's policies at the time. By 1910 the Poles accounted for one-third of the total workforce employed in the mining industry.[76] They lived, as did most migrants from the east, in the northern parts of the region. In 1904 an amendment to the settlement laws *(Novelle zum Ansiedlungsgesetz)* made it impossible for the Polish workers in the Ruhr to buy allotments in the eastern provinces.[77] As many settlers had come with the intention of acquiring enough money to secure a smallholding at home, this placed the Poles at a great disadvantage, particularly as the German migrants from the east were still able to return and perhaps buy a small allotment for their retirement.

The *Reichsvereinsgesetz* was passed by Bülow in April 1908.[78] Paragraph 12 of this law was a severe blow to the Poles, as it forbade the use of any other language but German in club and association meetings. The *Reichsvereinsgesetz* probably greatly strengthened the feeling of solidarity among the Ruhr Poles, sharpened the national differences, and thus delayed the process of assimilation.

It even appears that the advantage of small-scale husbandry was enjoyed only by a few. In a government study of the number of animals held by the miners shortly before the outbreak of the war it was shown that the notion of the average mining family having one pig in the pigsty and several chickens in the hen house was largely illusory.[79] The figures show that in the southern mining districts a family usually had a pig, a goat and some poultry. In the north it would have at best a few chickens and perhaps a goat, but to have a pig would have been abnormal.[80] As the public servant who conducted the survey in Recklinghausen county wrote, to have more than the smallest number of animals would have been impossible for hygienic reasons.[81]

The least satisfactory housing took the form of multi-storey blocks of tenement flats, the *Mietskaserne.* Contemporaries, and later writers too, at times argued that the Rhenish-Westphalian industrial region was spared the degradation of *Mietskaserne* living.[82] In this they relied on a very favourable interpretation of what constitutes a *Mietskaserne* by setting a minimum height of five storeys. Admittedly the average population per house was lower in the Ruhr than in Berlin, Breslau or Hamburg. But the facts are that the evils associated with living in *Mietskasernen* were found in a three-storey house, in a suburban one-storey cottage or in a colony. And these evils were extremely poor conditions in relation to hygiene, space and light, high rates of child mortality, tuberculosis and alcoholism and, above all, overcrowding.[83] The difference then between the Ruhr and Berlin, for example, was merely that of one floor.

Table 3

Percentage of multi-storied dwellings in 1910[84]

Number of stories	3	4	5	6 and more
Berlin	11.0	31.5	31.4	2.2
Düsseldorf	49.4	29.5	0.1	
Essen	36.0	41.1	2.7	

More important than the average house population was the room density. Here the Ruhr cities did not compare favourably. The number of persons per room was in Berlin 1.28, Dortmund 1.52 and Düsseldorf 1.46.[85] The reports of the government inspectors,[86] home-building societies and private critics confirm the appalling picture of housing in the Rhenish-Westphalian Industrial Region. Statistical surveys of housing in Essen showed that one-fifth of the population was living in very overcrowded conditions. A further 45 per cent, the report reads, 'does not live under satisfactory conditions even if one applies a modest interpretation for the living-space needed per person'.[87] A study undertaken by the *Westfälische Verein zur Förderung des Kleinwohnungswesens* in Western Westphalia arrives at similar conclusions.[88] A survey undertaken by the administration of Hörde near Dortmund shows that the average flat accommodated 5.5 dwellers. In 5 per cent of all the households surveyed the flat consisted of one room, in a further 57 per cent of one bedroom and kitchen. Sixty per cent of all bedrooms had an area of less than 10 cubic metres, 10 per cent even less than 5 cubic metres. On the whole only 30 per cent of all flats investigated were of satisfactory standards.[89]

The rate of population growth was largely determined by the uncontrolled rate of industrial expansion. It is true that there was a population explosion in the eastern provinces, that land reforms might not have been the answer to this[90] and that the industries in the west might have had to absorb the population surplus from the east, and with it the social problem.[91] Still, a more moderate growth rate of industry would have allowed for better housing. The fact that Thyssen, Stinnes and other industrialists relied upon such devious practices as misleading promises and *Kopfprämien* seems to confirm that there was still room for slower industrial growth. The government also failed to intervene effectively. In 1911, for example, the Duisburg city council built 40 flats, industry and private builders in the same year 3,463. In Düsseldorf the council built 250 out of 4,422.[92] This was not enough to combat profiteering.

Perhaps a more gradual industrial expansion or a more effective government policy on housing would have prevented the worst features of overcrowded living. As it was, vast *Mietskasernen* slums like Oberbilk in Düsseldorf, Segeroth in Essen, Obermarxloh in Hamborn emerged, which, like the colonies, were to become the breeding ground for radicalism. The gloominess of the pre-war Ruhr was relieved by some pockets of wealth. In the southern parts of the Hellweg cities and in the rural mining parishes just north of the Ruhr there were still a considerable number of house owners, and rents tended to be lower as the demand for housing was never as acute as in the north. As rents alone took between 15 and 25 per cent of income, this could mean the difference between living on the poverty line and being fairly comfortably off. For the newcomers, too, life in the Ruhr was not always a worrying and hopeless struggle. If the family was not harrassed by a major illness or accident, if the elder children, instead of establishing their own home as early as possible, stayed with the parents and contributed part of their income, and if the family was able to withstand the adverse social conditions, then there was the chance of improvement. They might have acquired a house, enhanced the educational opportunities for their children, or returned to the homeland in the east for their years of retirement.

The general trend, however, was against these favourable exceptions. Evidence for the deterioration of social conditions in the Ruhr lies in the fact that in 1905 it was the scene of the largest strike in Germany before 1914. The demands made by the workers reflect all the major complaints listed above: wage increases, reform of the wage system, improvement in working conditions, more say for the employees in the administration of their contribution funds, reform of the Knappschaftswesen, improvements in the system of tenancy agreements and more humane treatment by the superiors. The strike of 1905 has been well covered by contemporaries and historians. The most explicit account given at the time was A. Brust's 'Der 1905 Streik'.[93] Newer historical evaluations are to be found in Koch and Kirchhoff.[94] Both have questioned whether deterioration of living conditions played a major part in the miners' life before 1914.[95] For the outbreak of the 1905 strike Koch blames above all the worm disease and the closing down of some unproductive mines in the south, whilst Kirchhoff claims that it was the recognition of the unions which really stood at stake. Yet the worm disease had reached its peak in 1903 and was on its decline by 1905.[96] The closing of the mines, too, had occurred early in 1904 and its impact would have been diminished. The recognition of the unions was certainly of importance to the growing union bureaucracy and to some members of the rank and file more conscious of trade unionism. It is, however, hard to determine how important union recognition was for the average miner. In the list of demands this point was included last, almost giving the impression that it has been included as a last minute concession to secure stronger backing for the strike from the unions' leadership. Both Kirchhoff and Koch fail to produce evidence why the accounts given by the contemporary observers should be discounted. And these descriptions, as well as government officials,[97] certainly saw the strike as the culmination of the long-standing grievances brought about by the deterioration in living conditions. Although the 1905 strike was unsuccessful it led the government to inquire into some of the issues raised and a small amount of legislation was passed subsequently.[98] But these did not deal effectively with the multitude of problems and consequently did not stem the socialist tide.

Chapter 2

Working-class politics

By 1914 in the Ruhr, as in all major industrial areas of Germany, the SPD was the leading working-class party. The history of the party in the district followed two main trends. The long-established cities to the south of the Ruhr in the Berg district provided the core of the Lower Rhine *(Niederrhein)* party branch, which was one of the more radical of the SPD. In contrast, the provincial, semi-rural social background of the coal region to the north of the Ruhr encouraged early revisionism and reformism. These were also fostered by the growth of a moderate union movement. But by the time the party had established itself in the coal region under revisionist leadership, the social basis of reformist labour movements—a comparatively well-to-do workforce—had given way to mass settlements of workers who always lived close to subsistence level. The conflict which resulted from this between the SPD and union leadership and the bulk of the rank and file was fought out during the November Revolution but it was foreshadowed for the first time in the strike of 1912.

The early strength of the SPD in the Rhenish-Westphalian Industrial Region was in the Berg district, the geography of which presents a striking contrast to the fertile Hellweg region. The mountains in this area are distinguished by their steepness and the soil, rich with slate and lacking calcium, is too barren to allow for productive farming. Hence there was no semi-rural industry which was associated with the early coal-mining industry. Instead the towns on the bank of the river Wupper had always concentrated upon manufacturing and trade. In the nineteenth century Solingen was producing knives, forks, scissors, razor blades and other household accessories and Remscheid axes, hammers, tongs, scythes and other tools. To the north of Solingen and Remscheid were the textile manufacturing centres of Barmen and Elberfeld. Craftsmen in these towns had long since formed associations and guilds to protect their interests and to provide insurance against hardship. The Berg district was one of the first regions in Germany to industrialise.[1] Following the introduction of modern equipment and new production methods, especially steam power, the number of larger workshops and factories rose rapidly. In Solingen, for example, there were three factories in 1816 but forty-two in 1856.[2] In the wake of industrialisation urban population began to rise much earlier than in the coal region to the north of the Ruhr. While the Prussian population increased by 86.1 per cent in the years between 1816 and 1861, the corresponding figure for Solingen was 142 per cent.[3] Remscheid's growth rate too is well above the Prussian average and Elberfeld and Barmen became the first industrial cities in Germany.[4]

By the early nineteenth century the average manufacturer in the region was a merchant who commissioned a number of craftsmen to produce his goods. The latter worked on their own or with the help of, at the most, a handful of assistants in his industrial cottage workshop *(Schleifkotten).* As the *Kotten* had to rely upon water power they were situated on the bank of the river Wupper or its tributaries. By the end of the nineteenth century the number of these independent artisans had fallen because of the steady growth of factories. The conflict between the threatened small workshops and the new factories was the reason for the early radicalisation of the workforce in the Berg district. The textile industries in Barmen and Elberfeld as well as the steel industry in Remscheid and Solingen were highly susceptible to economic fluctuations and the greatly expanded workforce was not equipped to endure any period of economic hardship without great suffering. The double or multi-storey *Arbeitermietshäuser* which were so characteristic of proletarianisation in Germany sprang up here well before they were built elsewhere in the region of this study.[5] Finally, the Berg district was predominantly Protestant. The fact that the Protestant churchmen[6]—unlike their Catholic colleagues—failed to make a concerted effort to remedy the precarious living conditions of the workforce was a further reason why it was here that Lassalle found his earliest following. Wuppertal was the first city in the west of Germany to return a socialist to the North German Reichstag, when in September 1867 von Schweitzer won an outright majority on the second ballot. Less than a year later Lennep-Remscheid also elected a socialist.[7] In Solingen it was not until 1884 that the SPD was able to gain an absolute majority. In general these three electorates were safe for the SPD in the years that followed, although middle-class candidates were at times able to achieve a surprise victory in all three seats.[8] In the last decade before 1914 the SPD even threatened to overcome the handicap of the Prussian franchise system and endanger the hold of the middle classes upon the city and town assemblies. In Höhenscheid, a small town near Solingen, the SPD did indeed win the local council election, a unique occurrence in Wilhelminian Germany and an event which caused considerable concern.[9]

The conflict between factory and small workshop extended to the local party and the unions. Solingen especially was noted for its severe *Bruderzwist* between the traditional smaller craft associations, which were united in the *Industriearbeiterverband,* and the newly founded German Metal

Trade Workers Union (DMV).[10] The conflict was not fully resolved by the outbreak of World War I; but, far from harming the cause of the SPD in Solingen, it seems to have helped. At election time the factions always united and the discussion and arguments which followed in the wake of the conflict encouraged an active party life in Solingen. The party and union leaders in the Berg district—unlike their associates in the eastern Ruhr—enjoyed a radical reputation. As the voting on political and ideological motions showed, the delegates to the party's conventions stood left of centre.[11] Strong anti-revisionist statements show that this was the case with the local branches too. Still, the exact political position of the bulk of the SPD voters is not clear. The reports of the secret police are valuable here. The police officers in the Berg district, unlike their colleagues in the local government regions of Münster or Arnsberg, had learned to live with social democracy. They were able to distinguish between the various factions and their reports stressed that some of the socialists were less dangerous than others. Their judgment on the political situation wavered but in general they felt that the average worker tended towards revisionism.[12] The degree of radicalism among the rank and file probably depended upon the economic situation and this was relatively unstable in the early twentieth century.

The capital of the dukedom of Berg was Düsseldorf, which from 1806 onward was the centre of the regional Prussian administrative district. By the middle of the nineteenth century Düsseldorf was a prosperous town with a multitude of public parks and gardens, distinctive buildings and rich mansions. Its status as a capital and its location made it attractive to trade and commerce. Düsseldorf became the entrepôt for a large number of commercial firms, and a multitude of banks and the growing industrial combines of the Ruhr were persuaded to establish their administrative headquarters there. The shipping facilities provided by the Rhine encouraged the establishment of huge steel plants in the second half of the nineteenth century. The factories of the Rheinische Metallwarenfabriken, Mannesmann, Rheinstahl or Klöckner, rose on the outskirts of the city and in the neighbouring towns. By the turn of the century Düsseldorf was a city of striking contrasts. On the one hand there were still prosperous mansions situated in well-to-do suburbs around the Zoo and Grafenberg, while on the other hand there were blocks of multi-storey tenement flats around the big factories in Oberbilk or Flingern. The population growth during the second half of the nineteenth century was the most rapid in the region of this study. It more than quadrupled from 50,000 in 1850 to 213,000 in 1900, only to double again in the next fourteen years, partly through the incorporation of neighbouring towns, and partly as a result of further immigration.[13]

As was to be expected, this growth caused extremely overcrowded living conditions. A small study of seventy-two working-class households in Düsseldorf which was undertaken in 1897 had shown that only two of the families in the survey had a bed for each member. In thirty cases two persons had to share a bed; in another thirty-one the rate was 3:1, in eight families four people were sleeping in one bed; and in one case there were five to a bed.[14] By 1900 the average house in Düsseldorf accommodated 20.55 dwellers, but the figures for the working-class suburbs surpass the average by 50 per cent.[15] This social background and the influence which was spreading from the eastern parts of the Berg district (Remscheid, Solingen, Elberfeld, Barmen) had ensured that the history of the SPD here would be relatively radical.

Although the earliest support for the socialists goes back to Lassalle's time the party's history from 1890 onward was very impressive here.[16] After the repeal of the anti-socialist's laws in 1890 the party won 28.25 per cent of the total vote. In 1894 a workers' secretariat was founded; in 1898 the socialists erected their own union and party premises, the *Volkshaus;* and in 1901 they founded their own newspaper, the *Volkszeitung.*[17] The party scored its first major success at an election in 1903 when the SPD received 40 per cent of the votes, only 4 per cent less than the *Zentrum.* Thus Düsseldorf had become one of the first German cities with a predominantly Catholic population (71 per cent) where the socialists established themselves. In 1903 Peter Berton was elected *Kreisvertrauensmann* (party secretary) of the SPD. Only thirty years of age, Berton had proved himself a capable agitator and during the next ten years he set up a network of branches and stewards throughout the district which greatly helped to bring about the party's success at a by-election in 1911 when it finally defeated the Catholics.[18]

By 1914 party membership in Düsseldorf had become the largest in the Lower Rhine district. The socialists had their strongest following in the industrial suburbs of Oberbilk, Flingern, Derendorf, the old town and Eller as well as in the newly incorporated suburbs of Rath and Gerresheim.[19] Again, as in the Berg district, the conflict between the rival factions within the SPD had not crystallised before 1914. The radical language of the *Volkszeitung* stands out in the police reports of the pre-war years and is claimed to have been enjoyed by the workers.[20] The party leadership, chairman Wilhelm Schmitt, Pfeiffer, Berton and also Lore Agnes, did not speak at any of the party's pre-war conventions although they did vote against the revisionists.

Urban background, early industrialisation and high density living were the basis for the radical tradition in the Berg district. In the coal region, by contrast, the SPD found it much more difficult to gain a footing and displayed clear revisionist tendencies. The rural, conservative origin of the local and the immigrant working population provides the main reason for this. Another reason was the *Herr im Hause* standpoint of the industrialists[21] and the firm action taken by government administrators. The Government President of Münster, whose area of responsibility included many of the northern mines, was distinguished by his efforts to curb the SPD. He caused his subordinates to interpret the *Reichsvereinsgesetz* so rigidly that in 1907 he had effectively barred the socialists throughout the region from all halls or other rooms they wanted for their functions.[22] The first gains were made by the socialists during the 1890s in the electorate of Dortmund and Bochum, that is in the Protestant south-east of the coal region. In Dortmund the SPD increased its share of the votes from 5.7 per cent at the 1887 election to 26.7 per cent in 1890 and reached 34.7 per cent by 1898. (The figures for Bochum were 2.1, 15.0 and 26.2 per cent respectively.)[23] This illustrates again that the Evangelical Church, probably because of its stronger link with the conservative Prussian establishment, failed to match the concerted efforts of the Catholics to halt the desertion of its working-class members to the Social Democrats.[24] The real breakthrough for the SPD, amounting to a political landslide, took place in the 1903 Reichstag election. In Dortmund and Bochum the share of the vote rose to 42.8 and 35.5 per cent respectively. In the electorate of Duisburg/Mülheim it rose from 14.7 to 31.1 per cent and in Essen from 13.0 to 28.3 per cent. These figures only hint at the progress which had been made throughout the northern parts of the Ruhr. The greatest increase occurred in the electorate of Recklinghausen/Borken where the votes rose from 2,000 to 8,900, thus by almost 450 per cent. Increases of up to 300 per cent are reported for a belt of towns and mining parishes stretching from Hamborn in the north-west through Oberhausen, Gelsenkirchen, Wanne, Eickel, Herne to Castrop in the north-east.[25] The strength of the SPD reached its peacetime peak in 1912, when in all industrial electorates, except Essen, the SPD became the strongest party.[26]

The tendency of the SPD towards revisionism is perhaps best illustrated by its history in the eastern Ruhr. By 1900 Dortmund and Bochum still had few of the characteristics of a city. 'The large population', wrote a contemporary around the turn of the century, 'has been achieved by the incorporation of a few parishes which today still have the character of villages and the old town has retained its provincial life'.[27] The early SPD voters were migrants from the neighbouring hinterland of the region and Protestants.[28] They still remembered better times in the past and they voted SPD because the party for which they had normally voted, the right-wing National Liberals, showed no concern for the growing burden of their occupation. As they were Protestants they of course could not vote for the Catholic *Zentrum*. The Reichstag candidates for the two electorates were always firmly on the right wing of the party. The first SPD member of the Reichstag from the Dortmund electorate, Lütgenau, for example, demanded capital punishment for the anarchist who had attempted to assassinate the Empress Elizabeth of Austria. Lütgenau lost pre-selection when it was revealed that he had close contacts with the local *Zentrum* candidate and the editor of the Catholic daily newspaper *Tremonia*.[29] His successors in Dortmund until 1918, Theodor Bömelburg and August Erdmann, were both committed revisionists.

For a few years during the first decade of the new century an active left-wing group challenged the moderate party leaders in Dortmund. Radical agitators had emerged at some of the larger collieries to the east of Dortmund, especially at Brackel where the miners Besser, Schlisio, and Schirmer were steadily spreading their influence. The position of the left wing in the Dortmund party branch was strengthened by the appointment of Konrad Hänisch as the editor of the Dortmund *Arbeiter-Zeitung*. In the years between 1906 and 1908 the revisionists were relegated to a minority at district branch meetings. The 1908 district convention in Dortmund passed a resolution in favour of the general strike and against the revisionists, in response to the stand taken by the South German SPD members of state parliaments.[30]

The radical voices which were heard in Dortmund in those years caused a conflict with the Bochum branch where the leadership and influence of the revisionists were never challenged.[31] The radicals also brought about a division in Dortmund itself. Their demise came when the leading personalities on the left wing began to sympathise with the syndicalists. In autumn 1908 Besser, Schlisio and Schirmer invited the German syndicalist leader Fritz Kater to speak to the miners. This led to their expulsion from the SPD at the 1909 Western Westphalian party convention on the ground of displaying anarcho-syndicalist tendencies.[32] In response the expelled miners founded the syndicalist *Freie Vereinigung der Bergarbeiter Deutschlands*. This proved to be an unwise decision as they exchanged their influential party position for what was soon to become political oblivion. The only occasion on which they attracted attention over the next few years was when they led a spectacular, but unsuccessful, strike at the Lucas colliery in Brackel.[33] In 1910 the right wing finally managed to push Konrad Hänisch out of the *Arbeiterzeitung*.[34]

Now the revisionist union and party establishment was in full control in the eastern Ruhr. As Michels had discerned the bureaucratisation of the party in the years preceding 1914 had ensured that the real power was in the hands of a few professional *Funktionäre*. Their leaders, who included Max König, Fritz Husemann, Bredenbeck and Ernst Mehlich, held all vital party positions and controlled the newspapers. The typical characteristics of SPD bureaucracy began to emerge. Winning votes for the elections became the primary goal. To achieve this an image of strong party unity had to be presented. Hence the controversial ideological intra-party discussions of the last years of peace received little comment either in the newspapers or at regional party conventions.[35]

A further reason for the dominance of the revisionists in the coal region was the growing strength of the unions. By the first decade of the twentieth century the Free Unions[36] had become the great moderating factor in Germany's industrial life. Their gradualist policies had given them considerable influence on the right wing of the party by 1900.[37] The organisation in the pre-war years could provide its members with legal support and financial aid. The unions were recognised by an increasing number of industries and collective wage agreements increased year by year. Success helped to strengthen their cause and the leaders became even more careful to avoid conflict with the Imperial establishment.

There were three major unions in the Ruhr's coal region before the war, the Christian, the Polish and the Free Unions.[38] The Christian Miners Union *(Gewerkverein Christlicher Bergarbeiter für den Oberbergamtsbezirk Dortmund)* was founded in 1894 and by 1914 had attracted about 80,000 members.[39] The *Gewerkverein* was originally set up as a non-denominational association but their main support in the Ruhr came from the indigenous Catholic population in the northern districts, especially Oberhausen, Recklinghausen East, parts of Essen and the north of Dortmund.[40] There are no studies of the living conditions in this area. It seems probable, however, that having migrated from nearby regions, the people's standard of living was above that of the eastern immigrants. They still would have had contact with the land and many would have entered urban life with some support. It seems reasonable to assume that, like the more prosperous Protestant miners in the south, many of the local Catholics were not subjected to economic fluctuations like their fellow workers from the east.[41] The major problem which faced the Catholic Union was caused by the discrepancy between the views of the upper level of the Catholic hierarchy, who were on favourable terms with the industrialists and demanded *wirtschaftfriedliches Verhalten* (peaceful economic policies), and the working-class members who favoured stronger action. Up to the 1905 strike the Catholic Union participated in industrial action but in subsequent years the moderate wing gained the upper hand, and in the last years of peace their stand differed little from that of the yellow unions. This was shown for example by their boycott of the 1912 miners' strike.

The Polish Union, founded in 1902, proved much more radical when it came to industrial action.[42] Its forthright demands for social reform led to a rapid rise in membership, which reached 75,000 in 1913, just below the number of the Christians. On the political scene, however, the Polish union leaders were too occupied with nationalist problems to become involved to a major extent in local matters.

The largest group, as elsewhere in Germany, was the Free Unions.[43] In the Ruhr their strongest associations were the *Alte Verband* of the coalminers and, to a lesser degree, the local branches of the *Metallarbeiterverband*. The history of the union movement here runs parallel to its development in the rest of Germany. Starting from moderate beginnings, membership grew rapidly during the 1890s, which enabled the unions to widen the scope of their benefits. In the first decade of the twentieth century, workers' secretariats *(Arbeitersekretariate)* sprang up in all Ruhr cities. These were staffed by members who had acquired by painstaking work sufficient legal know-how to support the workers and their families in their fight against injustice. Their task in the Ruhr was extremely difficult. The enemy was not only big capital with its *Herr im Hause* attitude but also a hostile judiciary and public service. The worst incident occurred in 1895 when three leading union officials were sentenced to long gaol sentences on what proved to be false charges based on the testimony of perjured witnesses. Well into the new century the average rank and file member was threatened with being arrested on charges of infringing paragraph 13 of the *Reichsvereinsgesetz*.[44] Notwithstanding this, the unionists' standing in the party steadily rose. Their insistence on 'practical politics' and short-term goals without indulging in too much revolutionary talk helped to make the party look respectable in its early years. As with the party, the unions' increase in membership and financial strength was accompanied by a growing bureaucracy and a rising number of officials *(Funktionäre)*. There were occasional aggressive articles in the *Bergarbeiterzeitung* or the local party newspaper. However, union leaders were moderate men, who tried up to the last moment to prevent the 1905 strike, and when this failed, attempted at least to keep it locally confined. In subsequent years more advanced district administrators referred to union stewards as the 'sensible element' among the miners.[45] Konrad Hänisch, editor of the *Arbeiter-Zeitung*, Dortmund, often complained about the difficulties he had with the union establishment.[46] Otto Hue, editor of the *BAZ* and probably the most outspoken critic among the leaders of the coal-miners' union, did not shrink from defending colonialism at the 1911 Western Westphalian party convention.[47]

The favourable social conditions for unionism in the late nineteenth century had enabled the SPD right wing and the unionists to control the party in the eastern Ruhr. But by the time the party moderates had established their hegemony the social picture of the region had greatly changed. The eastern Ruhr was no longer a *gesunder Gewerkschaftsboden* (fertile field for unionism).[48] The bulk of the workers were no longer living in semi-rural towns but in vast blocks of *Mietskasernen* in the north of Dortmund and in Gelsenkirchen, as well as in enormous colonies which were spreading around the mines in the north of the electorate. Wanne, for example, a village with a population of 2,500 in 1871, had become a mining colony with a population of 53,000 by 1914. The number of inhabitants in Herne rose from 4,500 to over 60,000 in the same period. Buer, a small town of mediaeval origin, had 5,738 citizens as late as 1880, but by 1914 almost 70,000. The social effects of these immense growth rates—a large percentage of Polish migrants, overcrowded living conditions, inability to grow one's own food—were such as to cause the conflict within the labour movement which was to emerge with the revolution.

The bulk of the miners in the north differed in character from those in the south who had switched to the SPD in the 1890s. It had taken them longer to break off from their conservative tradition but, having made the break, they would, given adverse social and economic conditions, go further and not be content with the revisionists' goals and policies. This conflict within the socialist miners' movement was foreshadowed by the strike of 1912.

The miners' walk-out of 1912 has attracted considerably less attention from historians than the strikes of 1889 and 1905. In contrast to the 1905 strike that of 1912 was much shorter, participation was lower and it ended in a complete defeat. Koch sees the strike as the product of agitation by the Free Unions who, in their conflict with the Catholic union movement, and seduced by the favourable situation created by the English miners' strike, almost forced the strike upon a reluctant workforce.[49] Although Gladen allows for the decline in real wages, he stresses, with Koch, that the fundamental reason for the strike was the demand for union recognition.[50] The arguments of these historians are not convincing. The *Alte Verband* with its moderate, even conservative leadership would not have plunged headlong into such a dangerous undertaking. In 1912, with millions of marks of membership funds at stake, mass strikes were to be avoided.

The relation of wages to prices is of great importance for an assessment of the background to the 1912 strike. Price rises for the major food items over the preceding five years amounted to 25 per cent and more,[51] with wages remaining steady. Even if allowance is made for the comparatively high wages in the industry, this would have hit hard at most miners. A small stock of animals and a garden would have lessened the impact of rising food prices and explains the cool reception given to the strike by *Alte Verband* members in the south and by the well-to-do Catholic union members in the north. But most other miners could not rely upon home grown food to any great extent.[52] Not surprisingly then, from the autumn of 1910 onwards wage demands were made by all unions.[53] The year 1911 saw the *Dreibund*, a triple alliance between the Free, Polish and Hirsch-Duncker unions, present numerous demands for wage increases to the mine owners' federation. Throughout the year there was also a continuous quarrel between the *Dreibund* and the Christian Union. The *Dreibund* demanded that the latter should join them in threatening strike action. This the Christians refused. Although they agreed with the necessity of combating price rises, they claimed that the policies of the *Alte Verband* were directed at the destruction of the Christian Union.[54] In general, there was plenty of talk during 1911 but no commitment to any definite industrial action. By February 1912, 16 months after the first efforts to improve wages were made, pressure from below became too strong and forced the leadership to act. Some mines had already started to walk out.[55] On 8 March a union delegates' conference decided in favour of strike action by 507 votes to 74.[56] Three days later the *Dreibund* issued their demands. They included the usual points on long-standing grievances and union recognition and on 12 March the strike began.[57]

To judge from the documents there was a keen desire among a large section of miners to walk out. Reports of meetings held by the unions shortly before the strike refer to *Kampfstimmung* in Hamborn and Dinslaken,[58] *scharfe Stimmung* in Dortmund[59] and of overflow meetings with thousands being locked out throughout the northern region.[60]

The strike statistics are of great interest. On the first day 50 per cent of the employees walked out and the figures rose to just over 60 per cent two days later. They stayed between 50 and 60 per cent for the next few days and dwindled after nine days. The members of the Christian union seemed to have followed their leadership, which meant that about half of the strikers did not belong to any union at all.[61] Of the Free Union's strongholds only the mining districts Dortmund I and Dortmund II had a high strike participation. The figures for such traditional areas of the *Alte Verband* as Bochum South and North were only around 40 per cent, for Wattenscheid 45 per cent and for Hattingen just over 50 per cent.[62] Local leaders and the rank and file in these southern parts were reported as having been in disagreement with the decision to walk out. The centre of the strike was clearly not in regions which can be termed traditional union strongholds but in mining districts where the unions had made gains only recently. Figures of strikers were the highest (up to 75 per cent) in Dortmund III, Recklinghausen West and East, Gelsenkirchen and Duisburg.[63] Here too the strike was carried out with a fervour unheard of in the Ruhr. The worst clashes between the police and striking miners occurred in Hamborn,[64] Buer,[65] Herne and Gelsenkirchen.[66] In the first three cities the police fought the demonstrating miners with sabres *(Säbelhiebe)* causing serious injury to many. In Gelsenkirchen two men were shot dead by a policeman. Frequent unrest was also reported from Dinslaken, Herten, Horst, Sodingen and Castrop and troops were moved into the region to support the police. Police were supposed to have been impartial enforcers of law and order. How they handled their duties in this situation can be judged from the fact that during the strike the mine owners paid them bonus money in gratitude for their good work. The government president objected to such practices but allowed the policemen to keep the reward.[67]

The mine owners also did their best to ensure public support by publishing a leaflet titled the *Untaten der Streikenden (Misdemeanours of the strikers).* The police investigated the accusations levelled against the striking miners and found not only that the bulk of the brochure was exaggerated and distorted, but also that victims of manhandling were to be found mainly among the striking miners.[68]

The union chiefs failed to give any leadership to the strike and hurried to bring it to an end. They called for a conference after the first week of the strike which decided by a small margin to return to work.[69] The worst fears of the Free Unionists had come true: total defeat, a strengthened position for the industrialists, the waste of two million marks of strike payments and the start of a decline in membership. Some left because they regarded the action by the leadership as too radical. But the bulk would have left because of disillusionment with the apparent weakness of the movement. The miners, of whom 155,000 had a penalty of five days' pay taken out of their wages, were left in a state of bitter resentment.[70]

'The union movement might reach great strength', wrote August Bebel two decades before, 'but once big capital becomes as powerful as Krupp or the *Dortmunder Union,* then unionism will not provide the answer anymore, then we are left only with the political struggle'.[71] Bebel's prediction had proved accurate. The *Herr im Hause* standpoint of the industrialists and the social consequences of the uncontrolled industrial expansion, deterioration of working and living conditions and overcrowded housing, had brought about an explosive situation. To avert the danger steps should have been taken to curb the growth of discontent. Instead the war which broke out two years later hurried the Ruhr towards revolution.

II

The war and the ripening revolutionary situation

Chapter 3

Social conditions

In the Ruhr, as elsewhere in Germany, the war was greeted by large demonstrations in support of the Kaiser and the Empire. The peace marches which took place on the eve of the war were isolated events. In the Rhenish-Westphalian Industrial Region the largest anti-war demonstration occurred in Düsseldorf where over 10,000 workers marched along the street, the *Königsallee*, sang the socialist *Internationale* and demanded the solidarity of all workers against the Imperialist war. Their protest march was met by counter-demonstrations organised by student fraternities and other right-wing groups and was soon dispersed by the police. From the outbreak of the war Germany was placed under a state of siege. Power passed into the hands of the military, which in the region covered by this study was represented by General von Gayl, head of the Seventh Army Corps[1] stationed in Münster. As the new authorities issued their first decrees—which curbed the activities of fortune tellers and warned the population not to overreact to rumours about enemy spies and saboteurs—the problems created by the situation began to take shape.[2]

There were three basic reasons for the accelerated radicalisation of the workforce in the Ruhr during the war. First, there was a substantial change in the composition of the workforce, as women and juveniles played a more important part in German war production, and forced labour was introduced. There was, secondly, a deterioration in working conditions which was shown on the one hand by the growth of huge impersonal factories and on the other by a sharp increase in accidents. Finally, and above all, there was a worsening of living conditions, especially in respect of food supply.

The German Empire was not prepared for a long war. The nation depended heavily upon international trade, having to import almost half of its raw materials and about one-third of its food before the war. Almost two-thirds of its manufactured products were sold abroad[3] and the imposition of the Allied blockade deprived Germany of all but 20 per cent of its export markets.[4] Moreover, with the exception of coal, Germany lacked minerals. Procurement for the forces caused great difficulties during the first months of the war.[5] The government was soon forced to interfere in the economy and gradually took control of Germany's whole economic system.[6] But by 1915 the change from peacetime to war economy was largely completed and the impact made by this transformation upon the industrial scene had become evident.

The reports of the local administrators in the Ruhr show that of the tradesmen, many of whom had been forced to close down their business by the call-up, builders and carpenters were the worst affected.[7] The textile, furniture, porcelain, decoration and luxury goods branches of the retail trade also suffered badly.[8] The coal industry from the start of the war faced a shortage of manpower.[9] As the war ministry paid little attention to professional qualifications and the possibility of having workers replaced, 100,000 miners, almost 25 per cent of the total workforce, were called up.[10] These men could never be fully replaced. The coal-mining industry tried to make up for this loss by employing juvenile labour—which had been illegal in peacetime—and by increased overtime.[11] A section of the workforce returned with the Hindenburg program but the majority had to be replaced by prisoners of war and by labour recruited from occupied countries.[12] In other industries, the immediate impact of the war upon the labour market was even harsher. The lack of raw materials and the loss of markets abroad forced the textile and steel manufacturers in Düsseldorf and the Berg country to dismiss many employees.[13] However, the metal industries, too, soon revived. Large orders for war material had ensured that in this industry also unemployment was overcome before the end of 1914.[14] The textile branches never fully recovered during the war. It was not until ammunition production absorbed a great part of the workforce that the war economy in the valley of the river Wupper reached its full strength.[15] Once the initial difficulties were overcome the industries in Düsseldorf, Solingen, Barmen and the other towns south of the Ruhr, like their counterparts in the collieries to the north, had to face lack of manpower.

In the ammunition, textile and metal industries the men called up were replaced mainly by female labour. By 1918 women constituted 51 percent of the total workforce in Germany.[16] The percentage of male juveniles (16 years and under) rose from 7 in 1914 to 11 in 1918.[17] These were supplemented from 1916 onward by Auxiliary Service Law men but thereafter the Germans had exhausted their supply of manpower and foreigners had to be employed. Prisoners of war were mainly slated for the coal-mines. For the ammunition and metal industries workers from occupied territories had to be recruited. If they came from the west, especially from Belgium, they were, in general, treated as fairly as could be expected under the circumstances. They normally came on a one-year contract, could return to their home on completion, were paid normal wages and had only limited restrictions on their movement.[18] Those who came from the east, however, were living under virtual slave labour conditions. About their recruitment in and around Lodz, the Polish parts of the Russian empire, little is known, although evidence suggests that the devious practices of signing up workers in the east, which have been referred to already, were employed again.[19] On their arrival in the industrial region they found that, notwithstanding their contracts, they were not allowed to return to Russia before the end of the war, either for holidays or for any other reason.[20] Their movements were confined to the boundaries of their place of work,[21] in some cases they were almost totally confined to their barracks.[22] They were often ill-treated and underpaid.[23] Not surprisingly, many Russian Poles tried to escape, normally into Holland.[24] As this was difficult to accomplish they became increasingly rebellious and by 1918 were regarded as a source of constant unrest.

In addition to the change which was brought about in the workforce by the war there was a change in the size of the factories. Lack of markets and the necessity to ration the available raw materials had forced whole branches of industry to close down or to cut output to a fraction of its pre-war level. The number of companies with ten or less employees in Prussia, for example, fell from 75,012 in 1913 to 53,583 in 1918.[25] On the other hand the number of people employed by the Krupp works in Essen grew from around 40,000 to 130,000 and at the Rheinische Metallwarenfabriken in Düsseldorf from 11,000 in 1913 to 48,000 in 1918. The Thyssen works at Mülheim employed over thirty thousand people by the end of the war, to quote only the major examples. Thus, as Peter von Oertzen points out, the conversion to the needs of the war had greatly altered Germany's industrial scene. Where before the war the small workshop and the medium-size factory—which in principle still followed craftsmanlike methods of production—was the chief source of employment, now the bulk of the German labour force was found in the *Grossbetrieb* with its mechanised assembly lines. The type of worker also changed. Skilled craftsmen made way for semi-skilled factory workers. Huge plants arose and the new forces which poured into the big industries had little in common with the tradition of the German working-class movement.[26]

Working conditions and security precautions were far from satisfactory before 1914 and the war soon aggravated the situation. Moderate as their impact had been, work inspections after 1914 decreased even further. The government also permitted a relaxation of the restrictions on overtime and on juvenile and female labour. Lack of manpower and material had led to a sharp decline in the transport system. Wagons, engines and other equipment had progressively deteriorated causing havoc to public transport and industry. Derailment or failure of brakes caused a series of fatal accidents.[27] Lack of wood increased the accident danger in the mines.[28] So did the shortage of dynamite which was often replaced by much more dangerous gas.[29] An extremely hazardous state of affairs was caused by the deteriorating condition of the miners' lamps. These and faults in the ventilation system help to explain the never ending series of *Schlagwetter* (fire damp) explosions which from 1917 onward took the lives of several hundreds of people.[30]

The main danger in the munition factories came from contact with highly explosive and poisonous chemicals whose properties were still relatively unknown. Explosions caused the major accidents.[31] Very high, too, were the figures for gradual death or permanent disablement brought about by poisonous gases.[32] The metal workers' complaints centered again around the excessive working hours, which were made more difficult to tolerate by the lack of food. Pressure to shorten working time was brought upon the industrialists and the government from 1917 onward but it was not until autumn 1918 that some metal plants in Duisburg, and especially in and around Solingen,* introduced 56 and 54-hour shifts. This success was probably greatly helped by the fact that here the union movement, under the influence of radical opposition forces in the metal workers' union, presented a strong front.[33] The orthodox union establishment in the steel industry, as well as in the coal-mining industry, was content with petitions and did their best to hinder more drastic action.[34] Their own attempts at improving working hours were fobbed off.

In addition to these health hazards, there were physical exhaustion, mental fatigue and lack of concentration caused by perpetual undernourishment. As all industries associated with war production had also to rely on a large intake of unskilled women and juveniles, the rate of accidents caused by negligence and inexperience soared. The figures for mass fatalities rose almost ten times between 1914 and 1917.[35] In 1917 alone 3,000 miners died in the mines.[36]

Penalties and maltreatment also became more frequent. Most miners never regarded the penalty system as an acceptable replacement of the 'zeroing' which had been abolished after the 1905 strike. During the war years, however, penalties were imposed so frequently that there was scarcely a grievance column of the *WAVZ*, the *Bergarbeiterzeitung* or the Bochum *Volksblatt* which did not make special reference to harsh fines. This was also the case with misdemeanours of the pit foremen and other superiors: lack of consideration for the difficulties of the men, beating, negligence which in some cases led to fatal accidents, were also frequently the subject of complaint.

Of the numerous factors which combined by autumn 1918 to bring about the collapse of the Second German Empire the food problem was the most important.[37] As with industry, German agriculture was not prepared to withstand the impact of prolonged warfare. In pre-war years meat, wheat, poultry, eggs, fish and various kinds of vegetables had to be bought on a large scale from abroad, predominantly from nations which were cut off by the blockade.[38] This was also the case with concentrated fodder and most artificial manures, especially Chilean saltpetre and raw phosphates. German agriculture moreover was extremely handicapped by the lack of labour. In Westphalia 40 per cent of the male agricultural workforce was drafted into the army.[39] This large-scale call-up of farmers and agricultural labourers could not be compensated for by female labour or prisoners of war.[40] When it became obvious in 1915 that the war was not going to end quickly, the government attempted to deal with the problem of food production. However, inexperience and an element of panic caused by the realisation that a catastrophic food situation might arise in the near future clouded its judgment. The famous pig slaughter of 1915, which had grave consequences for the food production in the region covered by this study, was perhaps the clearest example of the haste and thoughtlessness characteristic of the government's early decisions on food supply. In the *Landkreis* Recklinghausen, for example, the number of pigs fell from 70,000 in 1914 to just below 30,000 after the pig slaughter.[41]

By 1916 the government had overcome its initial organisational difficulties. A complicated system of food distribution was established, which functioned as well as could be expected, given the extremely adverse conditions. To ensure that the food produced in Germany's surplus regions would reach heavily industrialised areas, the Ministry of the Interior had set up a series of control and advisory departments. In the beginning the *Kriegsgetreidestelle* (War Wheat Board) was set up as lack of wheat was the first outcome of the Allied blockade to be felt in Germany. This was soon followed by the establishment of national boards for the acquisition and distribution of potatoes *(Reichskartoffelstelle)*, sugar *(Reichszuckerstelle)*, meat *(Reichsfleischstelle)*,[42] fodder *(Reichsfuttermittelstelle)* etc. By now, too, all food items were rationed and subjected to price control. The bulk of the work of distributing food rations was undertaken by the local council administrations. The authorities here in conjunction with the central offices had to buy the items and arrange for transport, they then had to hand it out to the public by means of an extensive card system, the *Lebensmittelmarken*.[43] Finally, a whole new department was introduced, the *Kriegsernährungsamt*. The creation of the War Food Office which followed demands for a 'food-dictator' from an increasingly hungry and desperate public illustrated how critical the food situation had become by 1916. Right from the outset of the war the three *Regierungspräsidenten* of the region had called for monthly meetings of all lord mayors, *Landräte*, and other officials connected with the procurement and distribution of food.[44] The meetings lasted for the duration of the war and discussions covered all aspects of the food problem. The urban and rural municipalities of the industrial region also formed non-profit-making procurement companies which had their headquarters in Dortmund[45] for the eastern region and in Düsseldorf for the west.[46] Notwithstanding their benevolent aims—to protect specially the poorer sections of the community from possible shortages—the nationalisation of food soon made their existence superfluous. On top of this the administration of the larger cities tried to build up stocks, as long as this was possible.[47]

Of course administrative zeal could not avert starvation in a nation which had not been self-sufficient in peacetime. There was not enough food to go around any more, and the regions which were to suffer most were the heavily industrialised parts where the neighbouring rural hinterland could not cope with the demand. The situation in the Rhenish-Westphalian Industrial Region was among the most precarious.[48] In spring 1916 a person in the Ruhr on average was still receiving 1.5 kg of bread, 4.5 kg of potatoes, half a kilo of meat, approximately half a kilo of vegetables, cheese or fish, 250 grams of butter and 200 grams of sugar per week. To these were occasionally added an egg or a small amount of fruit. Children were given half of these rations. Special rations of up to 250 grams extra meat were given to workers in the steel and mining industries. Pregnant women, babies and sick persons were cared for with extra amounts of milk—which was becoming ever scarcer for the public—eggs or other high protein items. A year later, after the ill-famed turnip winter of 1916/17, the potato ration had declined to between 500 gm and 1 kg, to be supplemented by about a kilo of turnips. Meat had fallen to 400 grams, butter was replaced by margarine. Potatoes had recovered to three kilos by 1918 but by now everything else had become scarce. Meat in particular began to fall below the prescribed minimum which was now 250 grams. By the summer of 1918 the weekly food rations in the Ruhr had decreased to between 100 and 140 grams of meat, margarine rarely reached the prescribed 62½ grams, marmalade had become the main spread, though sometimes artificial honey *(Kunsthonig)* was distributed instead. A small portion of barley, semolina or other meal might have provided an occasional break in the menu. Worse was yet to come. The potato ration in the last months of the war fell from three to two kilos and the authorities had great difficulty in maintaining the official bread handout of 200 grams per day.[49] Meagre as these rations were their allocation was by no means guaranteed.[50] There are regular reports of vegetables, corn or potato deliveries which went astray or did not arrive in full quantities.

It is commonly presumed that the cities suffered most from the food shortage. This is generally correct. Yet in the Ruhr some of the smaller towns and rural mining communities in the north fared worse. At least the problems of the cities were recognised and the urgency of their position clearly established. Also the *Grosstädte* with their comparatively powerful administrative apparatus could press their claims with more vigour and could even participate in the black market. In the smaller mining towns and rural municipalities basic food rations were set lower than those of the cities as they were regarded as *Selbstversorger* (self-sufficient) or at least partly so. To establish self-sufficient regions was necessary as far as Germany as a whole was concerned but it placed the heavily populated settlements north of the river Emscher and south of the river Lippe in a hopeless situation.[51] The administration in Wanne, for example, throughout the war never had sufficient potatoes to issue the population with rations for storing. They had to be distributed week by week.[52] Reports from these areas in fact mention settlers going to the cities to purchase extra food,[53] since in the places where they lived the rations handed out in times of crisis had reached an all time low.[54] The majority of the hunger strikes—and with few exceptions all strikes in the Ruhr during the war were hunger strikes—occurred in these districts. Of approximately 130 strikes which were analysed by Spethmann in his extensive account of miners' strikes in the Ruhr during the war,[55] about 40 per cent took place along the Hellweg. The number of strikes in the southern mining districts was insignificant. The rest were in the north. Spethmann's figures only register the number of strikes. If allowance is made for the size of the mines and the number of participants the figures would show up the strike predominance here even further. Regularly listed are a series of names which were soon to become famous. GDK in Hamborn, the Prosper collieries in Bottrop, Ickern and Viktoria in Lünen.

Strikes were the more peaceful way of protesting against the conditions created by the war. There were demonstrations by women against the food situation throughout the whole region of this study from 1916 onward.[56] Riots were reported from Barmen and Gelsenkirchen,[57] and the largest occurred in Düsseldorf in June 1917.[58] Throughout May and June turnips had been the predominant food items for the poorer classes in Düsseldorf. When by the end of June the vegetable farmers from the neighbouring village of Hamm demanded prices which were above the official price level, a number of irate housewives marched on the Town Hall and demanded improvement of the food situation. As their action met with little response, rioting and looting spread. The sentences which were meted out after this affair were noted for their unnecessary severity. One hundred and eighty persons were sentenced to a total of 118½ years gaol and 145 years detention. The official version which the Düsseldorf police chief Dr Lehr demanded to be given to the public was that the riots were caused by Belgian workers who were enemy agents, employed to undermine the morale of the German people. This helps to explain the large number of foreigners gaoled (55) and the harshness of some of the sentences. Three Belgian workers, for example, caught in an attempt to break into a baker's shop, were charged with high treason. Although the men asserted their innocence and no document to the contrary could be tabled, they were sentenced to three and five years gaol. The prosecution had demanded the death penalty. Also excessive were the sentences of three or more years gaol for minor thefts during the rioting, which were imposed upon men and women with dependent families.[59]

The entangled system of federal, state and municipal departments which controlled the distribution of food never functioned well; nevertheless most public servants by discipline and selfless hard work fought against the insurmountable obstacles and at least prevented a total breakdown. But not all *Beamte* fell into this category. A serious food scandal occurred at Bochum which involved 5,000 tonnes of flour and thousands of bread cards. Before the fraud was detected a racket of more than a hundred people, among them many public servants, had sold flour valued at more than one million marks to wide circles, especially to 'upper-class citizens'.[60]

That title and responsible position were no obstacle to indulgence in fraudulent activities is also seen by the Düsseldorf food scandal. After the collapse of the Empire, the Workers' and Soldiers' Council there found documents in the local food departments which revealed that leading public servants, including the lord mayor, had received extra rations out of public stores.[61] Public servants were not involved in the massive fraud at the Essen central market, but the neglect of the authorities helped the wholesale dealer Gusdorf to defraud them of goods valued at three million marks.[62] Embezzlement of public food stocks on a minor scale was reported throughout the region.[63] Added to this were offences which were perhaps not always the product of deliberate fraud but might have been caused through overwork or other deficiencies the war had imposed. There was for instance mismanagement of sauerkraut in Dortmund and of meat in Benrath and Ratingen.[64] The most fatal of these lapses occurred at the Dortmund slaughter house where the blunder of a veterinary officer led to 35 deaths and to serious food poisoning for several hundred workers.[65] However, most unscrupulous racketeers were to be found outside the public service. The court cases list every week butchers whose liverwurst and bakers whose bread contained too much water, shopkeepers who overcharged and coffee-house owners who sold short. The following extract of a report of the *Chemische Untersuchungsamt* (Chemistry research department) in Düsseldorf indicate what a person might expect in his food.

> . . . Thus they used, to quote only a few examples, a slimy, boiled mixture of corragleenmoss with 98% water as a substitute for salad oil, yeast preparations as a

substitute for flour and a mixture of butter-fat and starch-paste as a substitute for butter. At least these [products] were still edible but they also offered and sold goods which were injurious to health as for example salad oil which contained petrol, flour which was made up of gypsum and barite and pudding mixtures which contained lime perfumed carbon dioxide.[66]

The authorities acted swiftly against the countless small offenders but were not always as decisive with the big racketeers. The whereabouts of 300,000 cattle and 1.3 million pigs (a third of total holdings in 1917/18) which disappeared without trace in the books of the *Viehverbände* was never established. Small in comparison (three months prison) was the sentence imposed on a Bochum marmalade producer whose marmalade was found to have contained 25 per cent turnip, 12½ per cent fruit peels and cores, 12½ per cent rhubarb and 50 per cent syrup. The product was described as spoiled, nauseating and adulterated with dead flies. According to the report of the local food inspector it had become mouldy. A veterinary surgeon claimed that the marmalade was dangerous, if not fatal, for horses. At best it could be boiled and be given to pigs.[67]

These large-scale frauds added to the already existing hardship. There was heated argument both during and after the war between representatives of the workers and sections of the middle class about who suffered the most from the lack of food, the blue- or white-collar workers.[68] With the levelling of the incomes the social gulf between the middle class and the workers undoubtedly narrowed. While there was still food in 1915 many workers might have enjoyed for a short period the rising wages which stemmed from the labour shortage. But by mid 1916 at the latest, conditions quickly became worse than in the leanest pre-war years. In fact, the gap between wages and prices widened substantially during the war. Average wages in Germany for men rose by 152 per cent between 1914 and 1918 and for women by 186 per cent. Both rises were less than the price index figures as worked out by Quante for the Rhenish-Westphalian Industrial Region which had increased by 245.7 per cent.[69] Neither the coal-miners' nor most of the metal workers' wages could keep up with that development. To match the rise in prices a worker had to earn 100 marks a week or more in 1918. A survey done by the Metalworkers' Union shows that only 2.5 per cent of all male employees in the metal industries received that amount. A further 22.5 per cent earned between 75 and 100 marks, 44 per cent between 50 and 75 and the remaining third received less than 50 marks.[70] The corresponding figures for the coal industry were slightly lower.[71] Moreover, incomes of 3,000 marks and above were subject to increased taxation.

The special food ration for miners and metal workers was scarcely enough to provide the extra calories needed. The companies had to provide extra rations from the black market. If this could not be done—which was the case in the closing months of the war when food began to run out in the black market too—workers collapsed at their jobs.[72] Lack of food was the central issue in the endless series of strikes in the coal and metal industries which began in summer 1916.[73]

The majority of the German people then, as Skalweit put it, 'hat schlecht und recht gehungert'. Yet not all were hungry, or at least not all were equally hungry. There was the contrast between the city and the country. The common picture presented in the urban working-class newspapers of greedy farmers flourishing at the expense of the starving workers was as much an exaggeration as was the industrialists' claim of the rich profiteering workers. The farmers and peasants had to give their horses to the militia, they saw their land stripped of manure and ravaged by desperate attempts to provide food for the nation. But since they were producing the food, they were less likely to suffer from the lack of nutrition which plagued the urban dwellers. Similarly the *Kötters* and the workers who owned an animal pen and a decent piece of garden were better off than their associates in the *Mietskasernen* and most of the colonies. However, what caused ill-feeling with the suffering common people were such food orgies as that given by an Elberfeld munition manufacturer who invited sixty guests to his silver wedding anniversary. The guests were offered a seven course meal which included various birds, trout in butter, asparagus, ham and roast beef. The meal was accompanied by a selection of seven exquisite wines.[74] The bill for an industrialist who entertained two lady friends with wine and food for a night in Gelsenkirchen amounted to 1,000 marks.[75] Leading hotels in Düsseldorf and Dortmund offered as late as autumn 1918 rich and delicious meals to those who could afford them.[76] Middle-class newspapers, like the *RWZ*, carried many advertisements for sea-side resorts which stressed 'good air' and the availability of 'gute Küche'. Advertisements also offered participation at high prices in hunts in which plenty of game was to be shot. The big-time racketeer and the tycoon in profitable war industries had no need to suffer.

The key to better eating lay in access to the black market, or as it became known in Germany, in *hamstern* (scrounging).[77] This was a dangerous activity. Farmers' houses were subject to frequent searches, and if the police found stores of meat or—still worse—if a farmer was caught in the act of selling food privately, he faced court charges and severe penalties. The person seeking the goods, however, faced a much greater chance of being caught. As most of the scroungers had to use the trains, a sudden raid upon a village railway station could leave many hungry urban dwellers poorer than when they had arrived. Being caught would not only mean loss of the travel expenditure and of the money paid for the goods, but also serious legal charges. Moreover, as the German railway system had fallen into disrepair by the later stages of the war, the *Hamsterer* literally risked his life in the overcrowded trains.

With the increasing inflation and the shortage of items money could buy, the farmers and peasants sought bartered goods. For obvious reasons these could not be too large. Ornaments, jewels and smaller commodities were most valuable bartering items. Since these were more likely to be found in better-off middle-class homes than in a working-class household, the workers were still at a disadvantage, even if their wages kept abreast of prices. To scrounge effectively a person had to be smart, needed to be well informed about the right places to go to and certainly was helped if he could speak the broad accent of the Westphalian peasants.[78] If he had these qualifications and provided he was not caught at the railway station, he might bring home a good piece of ham or several pounds of sausages.

But even the skilful operator of the black market could only provide for occasional relief. He was competing with the great industrialists who took the largest share of the market and who were difficult to outbid. The companies, particularly in mining and heavy industry, needed extra food as the normal rations for their workers did not provide sufficient nourishment. There was hardly any limit to their purchasing power. A confidential report by the Royal Meat Department for the *Rheinprovinz* in November 1917 points out that big companies like Krupp and Thyssen had monopolised the meat black market to an extent which threatened the whole food distribution of the region.[79] This became known to the public only after the war when some of the Workers' and Soldiers' Councils undertook checks upon food stocks. The control council of the Düsseldorf Workers' and Soldiers' Councils was the most active of these and large quantities of meat, fats, wheat and frozen vegetables were found at the Rheinische Metallwarenfabriken at Düsseldorf.[80] The government knew about these activities but they had no counter to the argument of the industrialists that the food was needed to prevent the workers from physical exhaustion. The government in Düsseldorf made a feeble attempt to gain some control over the black market but this met with no success.[81] Hence the *status quo*—which was that the big companies pursued their own food procurement—was maintained until the end of the war. As the black market did not provide for unlimited supplies of food, plants and mines sometimes had to discriminate in its distribution. Companies sometimes gave extra food rations to their yellow unions[82] or offered the items at high prices to the workforce. All these cases caused bad blood.

To the complaints about the food situation and working conditions were added a series of further grievances which brought about an explosive situation by the autumn of 1918. From 1916 the dislocation of industry and the lack of raw materials seriously reduced the availability of all the basic necessities of life. A severe shortage of clothing, soap and fuel prevailed. The lack of heating material was perhaps the least pronounced in the Ruhr. There was suffering in the winter of 1916–17 when mismanagement on the part of the War Office left consumers very short of coal.[83] However, the creation of the coal commission in August 1917 and the fact that the Ruhr was the main coal producer in Germany ensured that for the rest of the war lack of coal, comparatively speaking, ceased to be a major problem for the average household in the mining region.

As to clothing, a different picture presented itself. The war had wrought havoc in the clothing industry. With few exceptions only those manufacturers survived who were able to secure army contracts. Hence there was a great fall in civilian clothing production. When it realised the extent of the problem, the government permitted a few companies, which were scheduled to close down, to continue operating. But their output remained far too small to combat the shortage. The *Reichsbekleidungsstelle* called for voluntary contributions of clothes from the better-off sections of the community. This produced little result and the government, in the summer of 1918, finally ordered a 'voluntary' contribution of at least one suit.[84] Checks were to be made in households, if more than one suit was found and no donation had been made fines were to be imposed. The general reaction from a wide section of the workers was that they saw themselves eligible to be on the receiving end rather than be called upon to contribute.[85] Thus the result again fell well below expectations. In August 1918 the government established 'clothing specialists' at all War Office bureaus but the empire collapsed too soon to give the new officers their chance.

Of all clothing items, shoes were probably affected the worst. On the few occasions that the local authorities were able to acquire a shipment, housewives queued until all hours of the night to be among the lucky ones who received a pair. Here too profiteering and black marketing flourished. Large stocks of shoes were found after the war. The dealers had hidden them to avoid selling at the low *Höchstpreise.* Transmission belts were, next to food, among the most popular stolen goods. As the *Volkszeitung* points out, by sheer desperation to cater for the family's footwear, many honest family fathers were driven to stealing belts.[86]

In the last year of the war a family was given 50 grams of soap per head a month and 125 grams of soap powder of which up to 75 per cent was clay. Public baths had to be closed and the deterioration of washing facilities at work and at home had led to plagues of vermin and to numerous skin diseases.[87] The shortage of kerosene for lighting ensured that evening relaxation such as reading or outings was kept to a minimum. More impor-

I Miners' houses at Ickern

II Miners' house at Dortmund-North

III and IV   Miners' houses at Hamborn

tant, it increased the danger of accidents at night. The deterioration of equipment in the train and tram services caused a series of accidents.[88] Derailment, failure of brakes and other mechanical faults caused major tram accidents.[89] Rail passenger services had to be greatly reduced. The result was serious overcrowding of trams as well as of trains. Jumping on and off moving carriages became a widespread habit and often had to be paid for dearly.

Lack of doctors and shortages of medicine made the battle against disease more difficult. The call up had reduced the number of doctors by half and more.[90] Tuberculosis, which of all illnesses had shown itself as the greatest enemy of inhabitants of cities, tripled on average in all Ruhr cities.[91] The war also led to the spread of infectious diseases such as dysentery, diphtheria, lung and larynx tuberculosis and typhoid fever.[92]

The hardship suffered by the people was contrasted with an orgy of profit making. The war meant an end to many *Mittelstand* livelihoods. But the few who survived had the chance to improve their fortune considerably during the war years. Their shops would have held a virtual monopoly in the suburbs, and if they could manage to play the black market without getting caught, they might have survived rather well. The editor of the *VBB*, for example, notes with frustration that his baker and plumber were able to race several horses at the local racing club.[93] A list of profiteers issued by the Düsseldorf lord mayor shows that some bakers and locksmiths made 100,000 marks profit for the three years 1915–1917. A food merchant raised his earnings from 19,000 in 1916 to 240,000 marks in 1917. A producer of mourning hats topped the list of the small profiteers with 338,000 marks.[94] The real profits of the war, however, were not made by the suburban butcher but by industry. A list published by the *Bergarbeiter-Zeitung* in July 1918 of profits by thirty-eight coal and steel companies in the region showed that on average profits had risen by 100 per cent between 1914 and 1917. Krupp, the big cannon manufacturer, increased his earnings to a record 104 million marks. Klöckner, who held the scrap iron monopoly, increased the gains of his *Mannesmann* companies from 16 million in 1914 to 50 million in 1917.[95] These were real rises even when allowance is made for rapidly increasing inflation. The major tycoons used the favourable position which the war had created to strengthen their economic power—and with it their social and political strength—by buying up mines and the smaller manufacturers.

These profits proved a source of embarrassment for the government. As 90 per cent of total German revenue was raised from the wage and salary earners, demands for heavier taxation on profits were loudly put forward. Attention was drawn to England and the U.S.A. where there were laws designed to prevent excessive profit making. The government, however, always acted reluctantly on this issue for fear that a challenge to the industrialists might endanger the already precarious state of war industry. In 1916 the first plans on war taxation were tabled. The government proposed the introduction of a capital gains levy, of stamps and freight duties and an increase in the taxation of tobacco, which clearly shows the German government's dependence on indirect taxation. The chamber of commerce in Bochum asked the companies in its district for their opinion. In principle the answers welcomed the introduction of extra means to help to defend the *Vaterland* but most objected to specific points, especially to those points which would affect their own business.[96] A real war profit law was only introduced shortly before the end of the war when the difference between peace and war income was made taxable at from between 5 and 50 per cent. There was also some reluctance on the part of the courts to act against excessive profiteering. The Remscheid munition manufacturer Adels, who was charged with tax evasion worth 1½ million marks, was sent to prison for six months.[97] This was the same sentence as was imposed on two Russian Poles a few weeks earlier for having stolen one sandwich.

In autumn 1918 the Ruhr experienced a series of extraordinary catastrophes. September 13 brought the news of the Castrop poisoned horse meat affair. Due to negligence of meat inspectors at the Dortmund slaughter houses, contaminated horse meat was delivered to several mining communities in Castrop. More than 300 people were stricken with serious food poisoning and 35 died.[98] The workers were outraged. They could not fail to notice that only the miners of the town were affected, and they felt—not unjustifiably—seriously discriminated against. The outrage at this news had hardly calmed down when it was reported that thirty children of the Westphalia colony in Herne, who were spending their summer holidays in the east, had died of eating poisonous mushrooms.[99] On the same day, news arrived that forty children of the textile city of Mönchen-Gladbach were killed in a train crash on their return from holidays.[1] Only days later twenty-one people met the same fate at Krefeld.

To the stunned amazement of the SPD and many other newspapers, September was also the month in which the government introduced the 'meatless weeks'. For one week in every four the public now had to do without meat altogether. In September the first people fell victim to the influenza epidemic which eventually spread to most of the world. The initial reaction was one of cautious optimism. 'There is nothing special to worry about', the *VBB* had written in June, '. . . it is a "gutartige Krankheit" '.[2] This forecast could not have been more wrong. The physical and mental exhaustion and the increased danger of infection brought about by overcrowded transport facilities and constant queueing proved disastrous. The total who died of this epidemic in Germany was estimated to have been

170,000. This would have meant that the Rhenish-Westphalian Industrial Region accounted for about 15,000 of the victims.[3]

By now the papers noticed incidents which were unusual for Germany's law-abiding citizens. Policemen who tried to arrest deserters were mobbed and the soldiers freed to the accompaniment of loud cheers by onlookers. There was almost a state of open rebellion in the Catholic workers' movement when some of their more outspoken leaders were severely reprimanded by the church hierarchy.[4] Attempts by the AK to raise the morale of the workers with special film showings achieved as little as did the Kaiser's visit to the Krupp's works in Essen where he spoke in front of 1,000 carefully chosen and loudly cheering workers. The reports on the frame of mind of the population from the smallest *Amtmann*, the *Landräte*, the Government Presidents and Supreme Presidents all agree on the disillusionment among a wide section of the public.[5] 'The spirits of the population', wrote a police commissioner, 'are so low and depressed that we must fear the worst. There are uncontrollable rumours in the air about the intentions of the USP . . . it is also claimed that arms dealers have sold large quantities of arms. . . .'[6]

The fall in real wages and deterioration of working conditions, lack of food and a sharp decline in the standards of health had led to an extremely precarious situation for the old regime in the Ruhr and elsewhere in Germany by autumn 1918. The situation was aggravated by vast inequalities between the rich and poor and, notwithstanding the desperate efforts of some public servants, by considerable corruption. We must now turn to those who were to assume power: the revolutionary German socialists.

Chapter 4

The parties of the left

The war soon brought the tension within the German Social Democratic Party to a head. During the war and its aftermath the three strands of the pre-war years—the extreme left, the orthodox centrists and the revisionists—became separate political parties. In the Rhenish-Westphalian Industrial Region the workers' movements throughout the war were in a state of turbulence. The Majority Socialists and Free Union leaders with their pro-war, though anti-annexationist, attitude and their hopes that support of the establishment would bring social betterment to the workers, waged an uncompromising struggle against left-wing dissent. Pitted against them was the extreme left, Spartacists and syndicalists, who were the sternest critics of the imperialist warmongers and their supporters. Finally there was the USP, not as spectacular as the extreme left but never tiring in its efforts to combat the war and the sell-out of the Majority Socialists.

In the Ruhr, as elsewhere in Germany, the revisionist section of the SPD and the Free Unions welcomed the chance which the war offered to come to terms with the Wilhelminian establishment. Of the eight party newspapers that were printed in the region of this study in 1914[1] only two, the *Volksblatt* in Bochum and the *Arbeiter-Zeitung* in Dortmund (the later *WAVZ*), were controlled by the party moderates. Predictably—and in contrast to their sister papers in the region which were conspicuous by their lack of enthusiasm—articles in these two newspapers came closest to the *Hurrah-Patriotismus* of the middle-class press. The union leadership too threw itself behind the fatherland almost to a man. Only two of the younger members of the executive of the *Alte Verband* dissented from the new course.[2] The party leadership of the Western Westphalian branch admonished their comrades to 'exercise discipline' and demanded 'tact and comprehension for the situation'.[3] Still, the chauvinist excesses characteristic of some periodicals like the *Internationale Korrespondenz*, the *Korrespondenzblatt der Gewerkschaften* or the *Glocke* and of some of the members of the party, such as Heilmann, Dr David, Kolb or Noske are normally not found here. In Duisburg the chairman of the local union branch, Sevenheek, could persuade members to devote a full shift's pay to the soldiers at the front. When the objection was raised that the money should only be given to union comrades, Sevenheek recalled the Kaiser's declaration that he knew of no more parties and reminded his listeners: 'the times demand that we stand man to man, shoulder to shoulder and fulfil our duties as Germans'.[4] The leader of the *Alte Verband*, Herman Sachse, was also noted for his extraordinarily nationalistic statements at times;[5] and of the two newspapers in the eastern Ruhr the *Volksblatt* in Bochum tended occasionally to align itself with the party's extreme right wing.[6] But these were exceptions to the rule.

In general, the unionists and the regional supporters of the caucus majority and its policies remained within the boundaries of the decision of 4 August. In their newspapers and in the few public meetings which the governing general, von Gayl, permitted them to hold, they maintained that Germany was fighting a defensive war forced upon it by envious neighbours who were bent on the nation's destruction.[7] Although they agreed with Konrad Hänisch that 'not everything of course will remain exactly the same as it has been before the war . . .'[8] their papers consistently opposed annexationism.[9]

Moderate as their articles were on several occasions they provoked von Gayl, who acted very swiftly throughout the war against any left-wing violations of the *Burgfrieden*, to forbid printing of *WAVZ* for a few days.[10] Such incidents did not perturb the local SPD leaders. They never wavered in stirring up enthusiasm for the cause of the *brave Feldgraue*. They also helped to combat the disenchantment with the war which had set in by mid 1918 by arranging for community singing and theatre evenings. In return for their loyal service the regional Majority Socialists—like their leaders in Berlin—called for the reform of the Prussian franchise as a first step to parliamentary democracy and full social integration of the worker. These political demands again brought the party and unionists into conflict with the AK in Münster; so did the continuous criticism of the deteriorating working conditions, labour exploitation and war profiteering which were printed in the *Bergarbeiterzeitung*, the Bochum *Volksblatt* and the *Westfalische Allgemeine Volkszeitung*.[11]

The continuation of the war and the elusiveness of victory made it increasingly difficult for the SPD in the Ruhr to defuse the sharp criticism which was coming from the left. It became particularly hard to maintain convincingly that Germany was fighting a defensive war when the German army dictated a peace which swallowed one-quarter of Russia's (European) territory, two-fifths of its population, and three-quarters of its iron and steel. Whilst the Brest-Litovsk negotiations were still in progress the *WAVZ* quoted extensively—and approvingly—from the Austrian socialist Adler's criticism of the policy of the German government, and demanded a fair peace.[12] But once the treaty was signed their indigestion quickly settled. Mehlich, editor of the *WAVZ*, derived moral justification by drawing attention to Russia's history of over two centuries of aggrandisement. He admitted that 'we really do not feel happy with this peace' but felt inclined to endorse Friedrich Stampfer's argument 'that we will have to vote for it after all'.[13]

Embarrassed by their inconsistency which the left wing had little difficulty in laying bare, Ernst Mehlich, Otto Hue and their colleagues tried to improve their image by fiercely attacking the Pan-Germans, a small fanatical group of annexationists on the extreme right wing of the political spectrum. Perhaps Mehlich's thundering speech against the 'expansionists and warmongers whose scandalous doings undermine the peace efforts of the government and the Reichstag . . .'[14] did convince the few hundred people who turned up to the rare SPD public meetings that the party's drive for peace was just as powerful as that of their left-wing opponents in the USP. The more critical contemporary socialists, however, would have agreed with Wilhelm Dittmann's observation that the Majority Socialists attempted to divert attention from their political stand by their noisy polemics.[15]

By June 1918 the Prussian conservatives had fobbed off the final attempt to abolish the franchise restrictions in elections for the Prussian *Landtag*. Thus the record of the SPD in achieving constitutional reform was as bad as was their stand on foreign policy. In late spring 1918 the *WAVZ* attempted to do some soul searching. 'Why is it', asked the newspaper 'that notwithstanding the many setbacks—the treaty of Brest-Litovsk, the submarine warfare and its consequences, the consistent rejection of franchise reforms—and in the face of the hunger and the suffering, we still support and vote for the war credits?' Because—and the paper here draws attention to a speech given by the regional Reichstag member Max König at two local branch meetings in Dortmund—'our enemies refuse to give us peace, because they want to destroy us'.[16]

The desire to defend their threatened country and hope for constitutional reforms were two factors which kept the Majority Socialists in line with the government's policies. A further very powerful reason was the expectation that loyal service to the fatherland would bring about improvement of the social condition of the working class. It was not only in Germany that the war was recognised as a catalyst for social reforms. In England, for example, the Education bill of 1918, the establishment of a Ministry of Health, the Town and House Planning Act and the Insurance Act of 1920 all stemmed from the necessity for collectivist social legislation which the war had forced the government to pass on behalf of the lower section of the community. Thus there was nothing unusual in the fact that the chairman of the German Free Trade Unions, Carl Legien, recognised after six months of war that 'in the social field improvements have been achieved which a few months ago would have been regarded as impossible. . . . We have now learned how to travel along this road . . . and we will not be easily deflected from it'.[17]

In the Ruhr the service done by the unionists and moderate party leaders was invaluable for Germany's war effort. From 1916 onwards the complete regional establishment, Hue, Franz Pokorny, Mehlich, Sevenheek, Husemann and others undertook an enormous stint of travelling throughout the region pacifying irate and hungry workers, preventing strikes or persuading the men to go back to work. They admonished the workers at many branch and works meetings to do their duty like the soldiers at the front and to come to their union leader if they had complaints. The latter would settle any issue. The meetings were normally accompanied by angry shouting from the audience. To air one's complaint openly had proved to be dangerous. Too often a protester was presented with a call-up notice soon after.[18]

The vulnerability of the SPD's industrial policies to left-wing criticism had become apparent by the late spring of 1918. Their loyal support of the war had in June 1918 led to major embarrassment when it became known that the booklet *Tatsachen, Ein Wort zum Nachdenken für den deutschen Arbeiter* was distributed with the support of several leading regional SPD officials. The brochure was produced by the AK in Münster with the intention of strengthening the waning desire 'to hold out' among the workforce. It included appropriate quotes of well known unionists and SPD politicians and contained predictions about the bleak future of the German workers should the enemy win the war. After printing it, the military authorities asked the local party leaders for their opinion. Despite the biting comments of the regional USP, most of the SPD officials who were consulted, though not all, could find nothing objectionable and agreed to help distribute the 500,000 copies.[19]

Probably the greatest success for Legien and the union movement was the introduction of the Auxiliary Service Law.[20] The bill resulted from the severe shortage of labour Germany was experiencing by 1916. Neither the release of skilled workers from the front brought about by the Hindenburg program[21] nor the employment of prisoners of war or foreign workers brought a sufficient number of labourers into Germany to fill the vacant positions in the war industry. The result was increasing *Arbeiterabwerbung* and job changing as most workers naturally preferred the higher paid positions which were offered, especially in the munition plants. This endangered production in other industries and it threatened such important public services as the railways, where the pay was lower.[22] In short, the ASL, which was introduced in December 1916, tried to muster for war production those men and women who were able to work but had so far not been incorporated in the workforce and it placed restrictions upon the *freie Arbeitsvertrag* for the duration of the war. The employee was still able to change his position provided he could prove to an arbitration committee that his new employment would constitute a marked improvement on his previous one. The bill was severely attacked by the left-wing socialists who saw it as a further sell-out of the union leaders and the Majority Socialists to the imperial establishment. But the unions and the SPD were satisfied with the ASL.[23] It was the first time that the German industrialists, including the owners of the heavy industries in the Ruhr, were forced by law to join sittings with the representatives of labour. As G. D. Feldmann sums it up, measured in the simplest political and social terms, the ASL was an important step in the direction of parliamentarisation and the integration of German workers into the state through the recognition of their organisations.[24]

This statement needs to be qualified as far as the Rhenish-Westphalian Industrial Region is concerned. In February 1915 the four coal-mining unions had suggested the establishment of a joint employer-employee arbitration board to discuss difficulties about pay, working conditions or production problems which might arise out of the war. The suggestion had the support of von Gayl, as well as of the Düsseldorf government president, Kruse, who had written already that the patriotic stand of the workers must be rewarded and demanded that in the big industries too 'royal absolutism had to make way for constitutional monarchy'.[25] But Kruse was an exception. His colleagues in Arnsberg and Münster were most concerned about the 'very dangerous experiment'.[26] The government mining officials *(Bergräte)*, too, felt that such a step would unnecessarily strengthen the unions.[27] By August 1915—the original suggestion of the four miners' unions had since been shelved—the mine owners' association presented a memorandum to the regional governments which warned about the consequences of making any concessions to the Social Democrats.[28] While the ASL was still in its preparatory stages the Ruhr industrialists made every effort to hinder the placing of workers in the arbitration committees[29] and when the bill was finally passed, they were as obstructive as possible. The response of the Krupp works was most hostile[30] and the Thyssen works in Hamborn acted as if they had been affronted. They asked what the bill was to achieve and maintained that there was no need to create a further body where delegates of the workers would represent the interest of the workforce. 'There are six workers on the board of our company's benefit fund who have been elected by secret ballot and who have also for decades looked after the interests of the workers. . . . Not only in matters concerning the benefit fund but in all fields.[31]

Four months after the bill became law in December 1916 only a third of the companies with a workforce of more than fifty employees had taken steps to fulfil its requirements.[32] It was not until von Gayl applied pressure that the companies acted more swiftly and by August 1917 the arbitration clause of the ASL was generally established in the Rhenish-Westphalian Industrial Region. In their operation, however, the arbitration committees created by the ASL remained insignificant. In the region of this study the local courts met a few times and a number of workers were given permission to change their jobs. The Ruhr industrialists became only the more bent on maintaining the *status quo* in industrial relations, as the unions were soon to recognise when they attempted to approach the mine owners about the reduction of working hours.

The recognition which the unionists and SPD leaders received for their services to the fatherland was very limited. Admittedly a few officials were called upon to participate on local food boards,[33] but in the government district of Münster, for example, the public meetings of party branches were forbidden by the local administration as late as July 1918, just as had been the case in the pre-war years.[34] Their newspapers were under permanent censorship.[35] Such firm supporters of the government's policies as the party secretary Pokorny and the Reichstag member König had their speeches checked by the commanding general.[36] Finally, some of the high-ranking government officers in the region did not even acknowledge their anti-strike activities but blamed the hunger strikes of winter 1916/spring 1917 upon union agitation.[37]

Thus, as far as the Ruhr was concerned, the ASL did not bring the workforce any closer to integration into the system. The industrialists eventually recognised the unions in response to the threat of defeat in war and internal disorder, but the average worker in the Ruhr gained little from the negotiations in which his national leadership was indulging. When the revolution came the union and party leaders would find it difficult to justify a co-operative approach to their followers.

Perhaps the most questionable part of the Majority Socialists' policies lay in the tactics employed during the war in the course of their uncompromising struggle against the minority opposition, the later USP. The split, in the Ruhr district, did not work to the advantage of the SPD. When the final break came in Easter 1917 the Westphalia West branch voted to stay within the SPD, whereas all Lower Rhine branches except Essen and Duisburg[38] joined the opposition. These votes indicate that the following of the opposition had been growing increasingly powerful since early in the war.[39] To combat this development the SPD and unions fought a fierce battle against the left from 1915 onwards. An important aim in their struggle was to gain control of the party newspapers.[40] As stated, at the beginning of the war two of the eight regional newspapers were in the hands of loyal supporters of the majority. By the end of the war the USP was left with only two papers. In summer 1915 the state leadership of the SPD in Württemberg replaced the dissident editors of the *Schwäbische Tageswacht* with conformists.[41] The second newspaper which was to be 'stolen' from the minority, even before the *Vorwärts,* was the *Niederrheinische Volksstimme.* The *NVS,* in its opposition to official SPD policies on the war, was the most outspoken newspaper in the region. It was edited by Karl Minster and Karl Schoch. Minster had arrived in Germany just before the war, after having spent two decades in the United States. By 1916 he had begun to establish himself as a leading spokesman of the extreme left in the Rhenish-Westphalian Industrial Region. The *NVS* was frequently placed under preventive censorship.[42] After an article about German pre-war protectionist policies[43] and their impact upon relations with England—which was described by the censors to have been 'hurtful to German feelings'—the party leaders in Berlin decided to act. They ordered the local branch chairman, Schluchtmann, to replace Minster and Schoch with the moderate party official Pokorny. The affair caused a great stir in the Duisburg and neighbouring party branches. To calm the situation Braun and Ebert came to Duisburg where at a public meeting at Hotel Ganbrinus they answered charges arising from the change in editorship.[44] In general, they succeeded in winning back support and alleviating the situation in Duisburg. Minster and Schoch then founded a weekly, *Der Kampf.*

The events associated with the second newspaper take-over in the Rhenish-Westphalia Industrial Region were very tragic indeed. The *Freie Presse* in Elberfeld was run under the editorship of Otto Niebuhr, a popular party member of long standing. Like the *NVS,* the *Freie Presse* was at odds with the censors right from the start of the war.[45] An editorial against escalation of submarine warfare led the party leadership to establish an internal censor, the Reichstag member for Düsseldorf, Karl Haberland. The latter took the first opportunity to arrange for Niebuhr's dismissal, which was followed by a call-up notice. Niebuhr, who had been found physically unfit for military service, died at the front shortly afterwards.[46]

The most important take-over in the long run was that of the *Volkszeitung* in Düsseldorf. This paper was founded after the repeal of the anti-Socialist laws with the help of a loan of 25,000 marks from the national leadership of the party. The money had been repaid and the newspaper was fully owned by the Düsseldorf party branch, which had joined the USP after the division. In April 1918, when the business executive of the paper, Hans Pfeiffer, was arrested, the leaders in Berlin saw their chance. They claimed that the paper lacked effective control and applied for a writ so no items of value could be stolen or removed. Legally this step was unjustified as no money was owed to the Berlin central executive; but the move succeeded. The Düsseldorf court issued an interim order which placed the paper under the authority of Gerlach, a local SPD man. The USP lodged an appeal against the court's action but this had no chance of success during the war. For the majority this proved a Pyrrhic victory. The newspaper lost circulation and the affair left this, the largest and most influential party branch, more firmly than ever in the hands of the USP. The division within the Düsseldorf labour movement widened more and indeed had become irreversible, and this was to prove a very important factor in determining the course of the revolution in this city.[47]

Thus by spring 1918 the USP had only two newspapers in their possession, both on the periphery of the region, the *BAS* in Solingen and the *Bergische Volksstimme* in Remscheid. The *Arbeiterzeitung* in Essen, like the local party branch there, occupied a peculiar position between the USP and SPD. It was critical of the official SPD course and was sometimes opposed to it, but was not aligned with the USP. In general, however, party and newspaper here tended to be closer to the Majority Socialists, as became evident in the time of polarisation after the war.

Possession of a newspaper was of great importance in an age when newspapers were the sole news media. Berlau's point that it was the local press rather than the influence of parliamentary representatives which determined the character of the constituencies is well illustrated in the Ruhr.[48] The Reichstag member for Dortmund, August Erdmann, who before the war belonged to the right wing of the party and who joined the opposition mainly because of his anti-war sentiments, was from the time of his defection non-existent as far as the *WAVZ* and the Dortmund party establishment was concerned. His name was not mentioned in the paper and he was not allowed to speak in his constituency until the October reforms of 1918 had led to a liberalisation of Germany's political life. The SPD's monopoly of workers' newspapers in the western Westphalian branch is the key factor in explaining the moderate following of the USP here. Although there was a good deal of activity by the opposition, the reader of the *WAVZ* or the *VBB* may well have thought that the USP was virtually non-existent in the eastern part of the Ruhr. These newspapers refrained from any mention of local USP activities, refused to print readers' letters or publish criticisms of their one-sided presentation. The local USP in its frustration turned to the nearest USP paper either in Remscheid or Solingen or to the *Mitteilungsblatt* in Berlin, the national weekly of the party, but this was of course no substitute.[49]

The most unsavoury aspect of the behaviour of the Majority Socialists during the war was their actual co-operation with the political police and the AK against the USP. In September 1915 Schaal, co-editor of the *BAS*, drove to Münster and persuaded the AK to withdraw a recruiting order for Franke, a member of the newspaper's editorial staff. Instead he arranged for the call-up of Dittmann, who had recently joined the rank of the caucus opposition. Dittmann soon after was drafted into the army.[50] In Bochum letters of the gardener Woczek, an outspoken opponent of the SPD's war policies, which were addressed to the coal-miners' union executive, ended up on the desk of the Bochum police president. The 'strongly confidential source' which had passed on the letters and other material on dissidents' activities in Bochum can only be a reference to Bochum union establishment.[51]

The situation in the Ruhr did not differ from that in the rest of Germany. By 1918 the Majority Socialists had come to terms with the imperial establishment. They had supported the war, and the empire had begun to depend upon this support. The co-operation of union and party officials in curbing strikes, in calming angry workers and in the battle against the opposition to the war was invaluable to Germany's war effort. The Majority Socialists had nothing to do with bringing about the revolution of 1918. The weeks of constitutional reforms which preceded the November Revolution saw very jubilant newspaper articles about Germany becoming a genuine parliamentary democracy. The SPD papers, mirroring the opinions of local leaders, felt great satisfaction about the fact that in the region too the ancient prerogatives were crumbling. In October Düsseldorf, for example, had its first SPD representatives on the city's council. In Dortmund for the first time a member of the party was promoted to the office of city councillor. As far as the SPD here was concerned the revolution was over. Indeed it became increasingly irritated when the achievements seemed to have no impact on the bulk of the working population. The leaders tried at mass meetings to pacify the growing unrest. In private they were already sitting in conference with their life-long opponents, the coal and steel magnates, who, also frightened of a revolution, had at last joined the conference table with the leaders of labour.

Essential to a study of political opposition in Germany during the war is an analysis of that group of ardent anti-war activists and devoted revolutionary socialists which formed around Rosa Luxemburg and Karl Liebknecht and which later in the war became known as the Spartacists. Small as their number was for the whole of Germany this group was well represented in the Rhenish-Westphalian Industrial Region. At the first meeting of the SPD's extreme left wing[52] which was attended by, among others, Rosa Luxemburg, Karl Liebknecht, Franz Mehring and Paul Levi, the Rhenish-Westphalian Industrial Region was represented by Peter Berton, editor of the *Volkszeitung* in Düsseldorf, and Karl Minster of the *NVS.* The meeting decided to inform the Socialist International that not all German Social Democrats agreed with the majority of the Reichstag caucus. It was agreed to do this in form of a brochure which Berton offered to produce at the printing office of the *VZD*. *Die Internationale*, as the paper was called, was published in May 1915 and 9,000 copies were distributed throughout the empire.[53] It was outlawed soon after and Berton, together with the editors, Liebknecht, Luxemburg, and Mehring, was placed on trial.[54] Berton was acquitted. However, by this time (June 1915), he had already been called up to the army where he remained until the end of the war.[55] Whether Berton, had he remained in Düsseldorf, would have become a member of the Spartacists is doubtful. Throughout the revolution he did not move to the left of the centre of the USP and when the party finally split he remained with the Social Democrats.

There is no doubt about the authenticity of the extreme left-wing political stand taken by two of Berton's party comrades in Düsseldorf, the party secretary, Westkamp, and the sculptor Ochel, who were to play an important role in Düsseldorf during the revolution. In March 1915 both were caught distributing the anti-war pamphlets *The main enemy is in our own country* and *Under the state of seige*. They were sentenced to three months' gaol and the chief of the police in Düsseldorf had arranged for further custody for them on their release. This was rejected by von Gayl.[56] Shortly after completion of the sentence Ochel fled to Holland to swell the ranks of the German anti-war movement in that country.[57]

There was also extreme left-wing agitation in parts of the Berg district. The local archives contain lists of a small group of radical dissenters around the fitter and turner Seidel[58] and of a substantial group around the writer Issel in Remscheid,[59] although many of the latter would have been USP supporters rather than Spartacists.

The most influential activist on the extreme political left during the early part of the war was Karl Minster.[60] Minster, who was born in the Rhenish-Palatinate in 1873, had migrated as a young man to the United States where he lived until 1912. He returned to Germany, probably because of becoming involved in internal differences within the American Socialist party, and worked on the editorial staff first of the Remscheid party newspapers and then of the *NVS*. From the outset of the war Minster supported the group around Liebknecht. Under his and Julius Schoch's editorship the *NVS* came frequently into collision with the censors and his speeches at branch meetings were always bringing him to the brink of being arrested.[61] When the party leaders finally decided to take the editorship away from him and Schoch, they immediately founded the *Mitteilungsblatt des Sozialdemokratischen Vereins Duisburgs* which after four issues became *Der Kampf*. For one year this paper was the mouthpiece of the group of international socialists around Liebknecht, not only for the Rhenish-

Westphalian Industrial Region but throughout Germany.[62] In essence, *Der Kampf*, which was published weekly, concentrated its attacks not against the Majority Socialists—who for Minster and Schoch were beyond contempt—but against the *Sozialistische Arbeitsgemeinschaft* which preceded the USP. They accused the 'centrists' of being indecisive in their action of criticising the majority of the SPD caucus on the one hand and at the same time refusing to make a clear break:

> The workers' movement falls into three parts now: Social-Imperialists, centrists and left-wing radicals. The first are those workers who wait for the crumbs which fall from the table of the bourgeoisie. . . . The second are indecisive, they know that the working class will not get anything out of going with the bourgeoisie but do not know as yet how to fight against them . . . [Finally] there are those who know that the goal of socialism can only be achieved through the struggle of the masses against the bourgeoisie.[63]

The newspaper commented extensively on the fate of the extreme left throughout Germany. It reported the cessation of membership contributions to the parent party to which the branches in Bremen and Brunswick agreed in December 1916.[64] A few columns of *Der Kampf* continued to be devoted to regional branch matters but the importance of the paper in this field quickly waned. Being situated in Duisburg did not help the newspaper. Admittedly the Duisburg SPD branch in their first flush of anger against the federal leadership's decision to change the editorship of their newspaper without consulting the local branch, even talked about cutting off their membership contribution. But only a small group of the branch actually put the threat into practice, the bulk of the members having soon decided to ignore the issue.[65] Duisburg, moreover, was unsuited to become a centre of left-wing radicalism. Being one of the Hellweg cities it experienced a comparatively favourable growth rate with a low percentage of eastern migrants. By 1914 there was only one major coal-mine in the city, with the bulk of the workforce being employed by small to medium size metal plants or by the harbour facilities. Duisburg's housing figures also compare extremely well with those of the other large Ruhr cities. A few party sub-branches in Duisburg and Hamborn continued to advertise notices about their political functions in *Der Kampf*[66] and the social gatherings and outings which the paper at times announced had some response but the importance of the newspaper in local affairs went no further. Being printed only weekly it was handicapped by the fact that the normal working-class family had to buy the local dailies for information on the distribution of food rations. Finally *Der Kampf* was not a regional or local working man's paper but an informative weekly for the conscientious and educated Marxist on the extreme left-wing of Germany's socialist movement. If it is correct that *Der Kampf* had a circulation of 1,800 copies,[67] then the readership in the Ruhr must have been only small.

Minster left Duisburg in October 1916 to move to Brunswick where he took up the editorship of the *Volksfreund. Der Kampf* was continued along the lines he had established and was in part still influenced by him. In spite of its radicalism the paper suffered little interference from the authorities. Probably Dittmann's comment to the commission which investigated the causes of German defeat in the war, that the internal strife among the left-wing socialists suited the AK, provides the explanation.[68] Eventually, however, the paper went too far. It was banned one year almost to the day after its foundation, following an article on Friedrich Adler's assassination of a high ranking Austrian public servant. 'You present', wrote von Gayl in his order prohibiting further publication of the paper, 'murder as worthy of imitation and you hold the point of view that murder of a public servant to bring about social changes is justified'.[69] In April 1917 *Der Kampf* came to its end.

Minster continued his work in Brunswick for a few more months but when faced with a draft notice from the German army he joined the group of German left-wing socialists who had fled to Amsterdam. Among them were Ochel from Düsseldorf, Hammer who was to become famous during the time of the revolution in Essen, Wilhelm Pieck, the later president of the German Democratic Republic, and the syndicalist Karl Rocker. Restless as Minster was, he soon founded, with Pieck and Hammer, a new *Der Kampf* which was smuggled across the border into Germany.

Rosi Wolfstein is often associated with Minster. Like Minster, Wolfstein, who originally came from the small Westphalian town of Witten, had moved to Duisburg in the pre-war years. At that time she, too, stood on the threshold of a long association with the extreme political left in Germany. She was a leading member of the Duisburg party branch when Minster was working with the *NVS*. The notion of 'Karl and Rosi',[70] however, must be the construct of historians who have been eager to detect a local 'Karl and Rosa' relationship, as there is no evidence that the two were working closely together. There are various documents on Rosi Wolfstein's activities during the war. She participated in bringing about the spectacular food demonstrations in Barmen.[71] The records also show her agitating at branch meetings in Duisburg against the local SPD leaders.[72] She was arrested in Duisburg in May 1917 for distributing the pamphlet *War against war* and remained in gaol until the revolution in November 1918.[73] With Wolfstein's arrest the Spartacist movement in the Rhenish-Westphalian Industrial Region came virtually to an end until it was revitalised by the revolution. There are only two more documents referring to Spartacist activities after May 1917. Both relate to Essen. The first is a report of the secret agent Kölpin about the Spartacists Neumann and Deuter,[74] the second is the court case against W. T. Beuthen, who was charged with having distributed Spartacist *Flugblätter* during the strike of January 1918.[75] These documents hint that there was a small group of Spartacists in Essen until the end of the war. They confirm, however, that with all leaders arrested by 1918 the caution which is commonly applied in estimating the role of Spartacists as a causal factor in the November Revolution is justified.[76]

In the light of the course of events from November 1918 it is necessary to look at a grouping on the extreme political left which has attracted only scant attention from historians to date, namely the German syndicalist movement. Syndicalism in Germany goes back to a series of arguments which arose within the German union movement shortly after the repeal of the anti-socialist laws. A minority of the unionists—conscious of Marx's claim that society could only be transformed by violent political action—disagreed with Legien's concept of political neutrality and large-scale union federations. Instead they demanded that unionists become politically active and support the party in its struggle for a revolutionary overthrow of society. Unlike the Free Unions, which were becoming top heavy with a growing apparatus of professional *Funktionäre,* the *Freie Vereinigung deutscher Gewerkschaften* as the syndicalists called themselves believed in the importance of independent local branches as the basis for unionism. The *Freie Vereinigung* remained in the SPD until the 1907 party congress in Essen, when it was decided—under pressure from Legien—to present an ultimatum to the syndicalists either to join the free unions or to be expelled. Of the 17,000 members, 9,000 decided against amalgamating. Under the leadership of the bricklayer, Fritz Kater, they continued their activities and adopted officially the goals and tactics of French revolutionary syndicalism.[77]

Up to 1914 the following of the syndicalists declined over Germany as a whole. In the Rhenish-Westphalian Industrial Region, however, they did well in the last pre-war years. The driving force behind the first flowering of syndicalism here was the tiler Karl Windhoff in Düsseldorf. The reports of the Düsseldorf party branch's meetings in the early years of the century show Windhoff as a most bitter opponent of the revisionist tendencies which were fostered by the growth of the free unions. Like Kater in Berlin, Windhoff decided against dissolving the *Freie Vereinigung*. In the years before the war he worked very hard to overcome faction-fighting within his local branch and it was partly because of his able leadership that the decline of the syndicalist movement elsewhere in Germany did not occur here.[78] A further reason for the increasing support of the syndicalists was the social conditions in the northern Ruhr. In the autumn of 1908 the coal-miner Besser founded the *Freie Vereinigung der Bergarbeiter Deutschlands.*[79] This added an important new element to the development of syndicalism in the region, since the bulk of the syndicalists had hitherto been bricklayers and ceramic tilers. The foundation of a miners' syndicalist union in Brackel was followed by the establishment of branches in a variety of mining areas in and around Dortmund.[80] By 1910 the movement had spread throughout the north of the coal-mining region, and in 1912 Hamborn had two branches of the *Freie Vereinigung der Bergarbeiter.*[81] Admittedly, the membership of these branches was small.[82] But those who did join the syndicalist unions were the most idealistic and the most active among the workforce.

The activities of the syndicalists during the war are obscured by the absence of documents, which is partly explained by the fact that the political police was very much understaffed during the war years.[83] Most of the few documents on syndicalism during the war in the Ruhr are on the *Allgemeine Arbeiterverein* in May 1917 in Düsseldorf. As in peacetime this union was founded in protest against the policies of the free unions. It was a metalworkers' union with the bulk of its support coming from the *Rheinischen Metallwarenfabriken.*[84] As the *Allgemeine Arbeiterverband* did not shrink from publicising its existence, the police soon became aware of the union and could take the normal repressive steps. The strike of the 35,000 employees of the Thyssen works in Mülheim, the largest strike in the Ruhr during the war, was most likely the work of syndicalist agitators.[85] Finally, there are two documents which refer to syndicalist underground activities at the *Gewerkschaft Deutscher Kaiser* in Hamborn.[86] Hence, Bock's claim that 'although the pressure of the war laws made all agitation impossible, it was in these [the war] years, that the miners began to "see the light" . . . ' seems to be justified.[87] By November 1918 there was a core of syndicalists who, given the right circumstances, were ready to place themselves at the head of the disturbed masses.

Active as the extreme political left was, it was the USP which, in the Ruhr, constituted the real source of concern to the government throughout the war. Although the local members of the Reichstag voted in favour of the war credits at the SPD caucus meeting on 3 August 1914, most of the party establishment of the Lower Rhine branch did not feel at ease with the *Burgfrieden* right from the beginning of the war. In Düsseldorf the first police report written soon after the outbreak of the war stressed a great deal of discontent with the new course of the party. Dittmann writes in his memoirs about an anti-war *Flugblatt* being printed in Solingen in the first week of the war, which however, was not distributed.[88] The newspapers also give the impression of obvious shock. Otto Niebuhr's article in the *Freie Presse* illustrates the pain and confusion in the minds of many.

Followers, friends of social-democracy. We ask you with all the seriousness of this very bitter hour to follow the law and to obey those who are in charge of it. Any offence would be punished terribly severely. Beware of provocations. Keep out of arguments in public. Stay out of the bars and refrain from drinking alcohol. . . . We refer especially to those who are liable to military duties. Should mobilisation be declared, and this is most likely, nobody must try to evade his obligation . . . as the military laws punish this very harshly.[89]

Although von Gayl had asked for a generous approach towards the SPD press—seeing that the socialists too had now become supporters of the *Vaterland*—most of the regional party newspapers had run into trouble before the first months of the war were over. The *Volkszeitung* in Düsseldorf was the first to be placed under preventive censorship. On 24 August the editorial in the *VZD* objected to the massacre of Belgian civilians by German troops in retaliation for the alleged murder of German civilians by Belgians. The paper objected to the outburst of the chauvinist press urging bloody revenge, especially as the original accusations did not stand up to close scrutiny.[90] Like the *Niederrheinische Volksstimme* and the Düsseldorf *Volkszeitung*, by the end of 1914 the *Freie Presse* in Elberfeld, the *Bergische Arbeiterstimme*, the *Remscheider Volksstimme* and the *Arbeiterzeitung* in Essen, had all had their first term of preventive censorship.[91] Dittmann is certainly right when he writes in his memoirs that the 'kritisch abwartende Stimmung' of the first months of war soon gave way to open opposition.[92]

By the end of the year the party branches began to speak up against caucus policy. Scheidemann's heavily patriotic New Year message to his fellow workers in Solingen was received with dismay by party officials.[93] When in early May 1915 Scheidemann visited his electorate for the first time since the outbreak of war he encountered open hostility from party members, although a big gathering the next day proved more enthusiastic towards him. The 1915 annual convention of the metalworkers' union saw strongly worded resolutions from the Remscheid and Düsseldorf delegates:

The convention expects that the metal-workers' newspaper will pay more respect to the international character of the workers' movement and will pursue a course in line with it. The convention expects also that the newspaper will take up a more cautious stand concerning differences of opinion within the movement and will cease to cause conflicts through its indiscreet writings.[94]

No vote was taken on this motion, and the convention agreed to a milder formula which asked the editors of the *Metallarbeiterzeitung* for restraint.[95] In 1915 the Lower Rhine branch of the party issued a *Memorandum to the party leadership* which demanded an end to the *Burgfrieden*.[96] At a further conference in January 1916 the branch accepted a resolution in favour of the 'enlarged minority' who had voted in caucus against the war credits.[97]

The motions and resolutions were carried with the support of the delegates from Hagen, Solingen, Remscheid and Düsseldorf. They were opposed by the branches from the western bank of the Rhine—Mönchen-Gladbach, Krefeld, Moers and Kleve-Geldern—and by some of the delegates from Essen, Duisburg and Barmen-Elberfeld. The socialists in Düsseldorf, Hagen and the Berg district also welcomed the formation of the *Sozialistische Arbeitsgemeinschaft* in March 1916 and the union leaders from these cities made up the backbone to the opposition within the Metal Workers' Union. These branches, however, did not work towards the split. When the division of the party seemed inevitable they still passed a resolution in support of unity. But once the break had occurred at Easter time 1917 the majority of the Lower Rhine branches went immediately over to the USP.[98] The Essen branch decided not to join the USP but stay in opposition within the SPD.

The Independent Socialists encountered much stronger obstacles in the Westphalian parts of the coal region. The centre of the opposition here was the electorate of Dortmund where a vote taken among party members in 1916 on the policies of the caucus showed a creditable 73 out of 175 votes in favour of the opposition.[99] In Dortmund the USP was founded by Adolf Meinberg at the end of 1917 and was credited with having a 'very strong' following.[1] There were also several USP branches in the electorate of Bochum-Gelsenkirchen. In Werne, a mining community in the far north of the region, a full SPD branch went over to the USP.[2] By spring 1918 the Independent Socialists had set themselves up in all major mining communities in the north.[3] Small as their membership was, they proved to be very active.

Given the tight restrictions of martial law, how did the opposition function? First there was the press. The local AK applied a most rigid standard of censorship, which made it very difficult to use the newspapers for anti-war articles or for treatises on political dissent.[4] The local police, too, acted as guardians of strict censorship. Most active in this field was the police chief in Düsseldorf, Robert Lehr. Lehr was then at the starting point of a long and successful administrative and political career which was marked by application to the task of hunting down the political left. He was placed at the head of the Düsseldorf police department in January 1915. It was an office which—as the lord mayor of the city, Oehler, told him at his installation—'had the pleasant duty of becoming a protector and a supporter of the poor and the weak, of putting those who erred back on to the right path . . . but also . . . , where evil intention shows itself, of safeguarding the well-being of the community'. Lehr set out immediately to put 'those who erred'[5] back on the proper path. His censorship of the *VZD* surpassed that of all the other censors in the region.[6] Indeed it reached such a stage that von Gayl had to interfere on behalf of the newspaper.[7] Extensive reporting on the deterioration of living conditions from 1916 onward caused great concern to the administration. Control could not be exercised so easily in this field as the writings were non-political. 'We know that the workers in our municipality are poorly off', writes an exasperated town clerk to the government president, ' . . . but this is not overcome by these insidious articles in the *Volkszeitung*'.[8]

The only way to get political messages across was by publishing Reichstag's speeches. Normally they were not subject to censorship and could be reprinted in the newspapers. The AK, however, rarely shrank from prohibiting the printing of the more controversial speeches of minority socialist dissenters.[9] After the signing of the peace of Brest-Litovsk the only USP papers left in the region, the *Bergische Arbeiterstimme* and the *Bergische Volksstimme*,[10] published regularly news from and reports about progress in Russia. Printed without comment as official news items these extracts constituted a skilful piece of propaganda for socialism and the Russian Revolution.

For more outspoken criticism of the war and of German politics the dissenters had to rely on pamphlets. *Flugblätter* were distributed on a large scale in the Rhenish-Westphalian Industrial Region. The denunciation of the havoc and the devastation of the war assured the success of the pamphlets, some of which were said to have had a circulation of 50,000.[11] The pamphlets concentrated upon 'daily bread-and-butter issues' and the fostering of anti-war sentiments until the final stages of the war. The last weeks saw an increasing number of *Flugblätter* inciting revolution distributed throughout the region.[12] The police claimed to have found 300,000 copies of the pamphlet *Arbeiter Aufgepasst.*[13] The strength of the wording in the pamphlet suggested Spartacist origins yet its widespread distribution depended on the co-operation of the Independent Socialists.

It is difficult to estimate the extent of USP agitation in bringing about strikes before January 1918. Most documents on strikes during the war stress that it was the lack of food and rising prices which were the cause and make no mention of agitation.[14] However, there were exceptions. Besides Wolfstein and Seidel from the extreme left, some of the names associated with the Barmen food riots were those of later USP members.[15] The Düsseldorf Police Chief, Lehr, reports that, according to his *Spitzels* in mid 1916, the socialist left was urging workers to strike.[16] Lehr writes to the government president a few months later: 'the real source of all these disturbances is the strong radical left-wing tendency of [Düsseldorf's] Social-Democrats, whose persistent subversive activities attempt to bring about strikes.'[17] Lehr is consistent in putting the bulk of the blame for the strikes in Düsseldorf upon the opposition socialists. The government president of Münster too, in a report on a wave of strikes in July 1917, refers to the 'radikale Verhetzung',[18] and the government president in Arnsberg claims to have evidence that the Social Democratic left was behind the April strikes of the coal-miners in Dortmund.[19]

From January 1918 onward the agitation of the USP for industrial action revealed itself more clearly. As elsewhere in Germany the wave of strikes in late January/early February was predominantly political. Demands for peace and constitutional reform as well as the common complaints about deteriorating living conditions and low wages were raised at a number of meetings throughout the whole of the region from the steel factories in Hagen in the south-east to the mining town of Bottrop in the north-west. The important role of the USP and to a lesser degree of minor SPD officials behind the action is well documented.[20] The strike has been covered extensively[21] and there is no need for this book to go into the details again. It was eventually crushed very severely. As a result 520 workers were drafted into the army, half of whom came from the colliery Viktoria in Lünen where the strike had lasted the longest. There is also no doubt that the USP agitation was behind the rolling strikes in the metal industry which throughout 1918 attempted and partly achieved the shortening of working hours.[22]

Not surprisingly then, the USP now bore the full brunt of the government's persecution. From the earliest times of wartime industrial unrest the police had the 'ringleaders' at mines or factories called up to the front. They seemed to have hesitated to act against the leaders of the minority, however, thinking perhaps that the arrest of a popular local political figure would do more damage than would be done by controlling his activities. Of the dissident minority socialists, only Berton and Dittmann were drafted into the army by 1917. But with the growing unrest among the workforce the authorities must have changed their attitude. During the first months of 1918 the USP leaders Merchel in Solingen,[23] Lore Agnes and Hans Pfeiffer in Düsseldorf,[24] Banko, Strassek, Gonsior and Granek in the region Bottrop/Gladbeck/Osterfeld and Gross in Bochum[25] were arrested mainly on charges of having distributed literature detrimental to Germany's war effort. In a secret report of the political police issued in June 1918 it was maintained that these arrests had ensured that

> there can be no talk at present of the USP being able to work for unrest or strikes. . . . The few persons who are left in some kind of leadership position show themselves frightened and reserved . . . [thus] at present the agitation of the USP in the Lower Rhine lacks any leadership.[26]

The report admits that the workers were 'to the highest degree embittered' but, it continues 'there is no way to improve their situation'.[27]

The arrests would have hampered the activities of the USP but certainly did not crush them. Indeed, the political police did not even get at the core of the movement in the region. By mid 1918 the socialist agitators Otto Brass in Remscheid, the baker Ulrich Rogg in Duisburg, and the gardener Woczek in Bochum were still at large. The editor of the *Volkstimme* in Remscheid, Brass, who was to become the leading figure of the revolution in the Lower Rhine, does not even receive a mention in any of the police reports. The activities of Rogg and Woczek were known but they must not have been regarded as dangerous enough to warrant arrest.[28] The pressure behind the strikes for the reduction of working time shows that the USP was far from being silenced, as does a series of 'disruptions' of Pan-German pro-war meetings which can be traced back to the USP. The most spectacular of these 'disruptions' occurred at Solingen when Scheidemann on his second visit to his electorate during the war was shouted off the stage.[29]

By way of conclusion it can be said that the SPD had nothing to do with bringing about the November Revolution. The extreme left, the Spartacists and syndicalists worked hard but were either too beleaguered or too small to be regarded as a significant cause of the revolution. The USP did not make the revolution. Their own belief was that a revolution can not be 'made' but had to come from the people. The function of the political party was, first, to act as a contributing agent or catalyst to create a 'ripe situation' and, secondly, to give the revolution its proper socialist direction.[30] The Independent Socialists in the Rhenish-Westphalian Industrial Region had fulfilled the first requirement. They tenaciously exploited the effect of the war on imperial Germany and by mid autumn 1918 they were to prepare to deal the empire its death blow. 'The revolution must come', said a speaker at a USP meeting in Düsseldorf on 13 October 1918, 'but it will not come from above, that's what we don't want, but from below. The revolution will come with certainty and we have to prepare for it, so we can say proudly one day, that we too were ready for it'.[31]

The USP was expecting the uprisings. The police and the government authorities,[32] the industrialists and the right wing of the socialists knew that they were ready for it. Eschewing any illusions the two latter were already preparing counter measures.[33] It is not very important whether the USP was physically on the spot when the demonstrations of mutinous soldiers and workers signalled the advent of the revolution.[34] What was important was that within hours of the outbreak they were ready to place themselves at the head of the events.

III

Revolutionary upsurge, November 1918–January 1919

News about the mutiny of the marines at Kiel first reached the newspapers of the region on 5 November 1918. Initially it did not figure prominently, since it was overshadowed by discussions about the Kaiser's resignation, Wilson's fourteen points and the October reforms. Before the full importance of the German admirals' fatal decision to save their honour was recognised the revolution had already occurred in the Ruhr. After having swept through Hamburg and Bremen on 6 November and through Brunswick and Hanover on 7 November it reached the Rhenish-Westphalian Industrial Region the next day. In the night of 7 November Kiel marines, who had got through to Köln, and soldiers of a regiment which was stationed there stormed the gaol and freed the political prisoners. Next morning a Workers' and Soldiers' Council was established at Köln. From here troops and marines left for the industrial centres to the north. They reached Düsseldorf and the Berg district by the afternoon and by the early evening the revolution had spread to the eastern outskirts of the Ruhr.[1]

The pattern of events was the same everywhere. A small number, at some places not more than a handful, of soldiers arrived at the local railway station where they were joined by demonstrating workers. They combined, disarmed the local police and—where there were gaols—freed the political prisoners. By night-time the local USP had placed themselves at the head of the revolution in most cities. The local authorities were considering counter action but they found themselves replaced before they could make up their mind.[2]

On 9 November, encouraged by the news from Berlin, the local SPD joined the action and Workers' and Soldiers' Councils were formed throughout. The 10th, a Sunday, was celebration day when the revolution was consolidated at a series of mass meetings, some of which were claimed to have had a crowd of 100,000.[3] It is difficult for the historian today to recreate the spirit of the 10 November. Even the *WAVZ* was excited:

> If someone wanted to find out about the feeling of the people, he had the chance to do so at the *Fredenbaum* in Dortmund. Never before were there so many people. How many? It was estimated that there were 50,000–60,000 visitors. Never-ending streams of people advanced in huge columns with banners and music from all sides. Speeches were given from four rostrums. The speakers dealt again with the bankrupt autocratic regime, which had completely collapsed. Class rule, they declared, had never received a weightier popular condemnation than it had in this revolution. The people [now] had reason for joy, because the gates of freedom were wide open.[4]

It does not do justice to the revolutionary spirit of these days to dismiss it with the claims that 'They [the mass of the workers] wanted peace and freedom but they did not want to achieve this through force, insurrection or civil war but through parliamentary democracy'.[5] The men and women who were singing the socialist *Internationale* in the streets of Düsseldorf,

Essen or Dortmund were celebrating the end of the hopelessness and suffering which had been caused by the war. But they were also celebrating the dawn of a new age. Of course they wanted freedom and democracy but there was more to it. Hopes were high that the future would lead the people to their appropriate place in society—not only institutionally but also economically and socially. They were pinning their aspirations on the socialist Republic which the speakers at the platform were announcing.

In retrospect, to what extent does a study of the Ruhr help to elucidate the causes of the November Revolution in Germany? Here we find the same reasons which have been analysed for the general outbreak of the revolution in Germany although with different emphasis. The deterioration of living conditions was of prime importance. The Ruhr was the most densely populated area within the empire, so the impact of the continuous shortage of food and other basic commodities had undermined the morale of the workforce to an extent that 'no word was too strong for the masses and their temper, which was expressed in a continuous storm of applause, was downright revolutionary'.[6]

The unfavourable outcome of the war, vital as it was for the bringing about of the November Revolution in Germany as a whole, was less dominant here. Although the newspapers carried reports that the German army was retreating, the troops were still in enemy territory and, according to bulletins issued in the very last days of the war, still fighting successfully.[7] The widespread realisation among government officials that the war had been lost was, however, important as it thwarted counter-revolutionary actions.

Since a large part of the region was a centre of the USP's left wing the Rhenish-Westphalian industrial region had more than its share of leaflets and other forms of political propaganda and agitation. A study of the Ruhr confirms the truth of de Tocqeville's observation that a regime is never in greater peril than when it sets out to reform itself. The release of imprisoned political leaders, the relaxation of the laws of assembly *(Versammlungsgesetze)* and the easing of the restrictions on free speech led to a series of political meetings at which an increasingly radical atmosphere prevailed.[8] The news from Berlin that parliamentary democracy had been established failed to make an impact upon the workers, despite great efforts by the local unionists and SPD leaders.

Monday 11 November was declared a public holiday and hence became another day of rejoicing. By now, too, a Supreme Soldiers' Council *(Generalsoldatenrat)* had displaced von Gayl at the AK in Münster. The political and military power was completely in the hands of revolutionaries. From 12 November onward it was back to normal. Though the first days of the revolution had been the same throughout the region, differences now became apparent.

Chapter 5

Limited revolution: The Eastern Ruhr

Nowhere in the Ruhr was the strength of the SPD in the early days of the revolution so unchallenged as in the former Reichstag constituencies of Bochum-Gelsenkirchen and Dortmund.[1] Moderate socialists had been in full control of the party and the unions before the war[2] and their position was strengthened further during the war when the opposition was ousted from the party.[3] By October 1918 the co-operation of the Majority Socialists with imperial Germany at last bore fruit. The *Bergarbeiter-Zeitung*, the *Volksblatt* in Bochum and the *WAVZ* were jubilant about the establishment of the government of Prince Max of Baden. The *WAVZ* selected an article by the leading party member Cunow to illustrate the success. 'The revolution has arrived', stated the article,

> not a bloody revolution [*Keine Revolution mit wallenden Flammenhaar*] . . . but a peaceful revolution, which nevertheless might perhaps be one day as important for the fortunes of the German working class as the Russian revolution is for that of the Russian workers.[4]

The 'malicious' pamphlets of the USP which incited further uprisings could, on the other hand, only help the counter-revolution. 'The Independent Socialists', wrote the *WAVZ* on 29 October 1918,

> have distributed during the last few days a large number of leaflets which aim to establish bolshevism. . . . They want to misuse the workforce for a dangerous, criminal game [and] some who follow these Independent anarchists do not seem to have realised this as yet.[5]

But this message did not get through any more. Feelings had become too radical to be calmed by the vague news of constitutional reform which was coming from Berlin. Government officials agreed that there was something in the air 'which was making further developments inevitable'.[6] The spokesman for this explosive atmosphere became the *General-Anzeiger* in Dortmund.[7] To the anguish of the *WAVZ* this paper embarked upon a radical course in the weeks immediately preceding the revolution. It presented extensive coverage of the speeches of the USP[8] and demanded 'a further revolution in the German system of government'.[9]

In its last issue before the revolution the *Bergarbeiter-Zeitung* had this to say about the pamphlets which were circulating: 'They are the products of a morbid mental disturbance. In fact, their content must be described as insane'.[10] On the day the newspaper went on sale, 9 November, the writers found themselves at the head of the revolution in the eastern Ruhr.

The troops that set out on the morning of 8 November from the southern parts of the Rhenish-Westphalian Industrial Region reached the eastern Ruhr at around 8 P.M. on that day. In Bochum they disarmed the local police and, after having been joined by about five hundred people, freed the political prisoners who were held in the city.[11] According to the *Volksblatt* the whole procedure took place in a most orderly way, which was largely due to the presence of the union secretary and local SPD leader Husemann and the *VBB* editor Steinisch who both kept a watchful eye upon events.

In Gelsenkirchen, following rumours that the local USP was preparing a coup, the lord mayor, with the support of local SPD party officials, had called for a meeting at the central station to exhort the workers to maintain law and order. But during the meeting groups of workers and soldiers disarmed the authorities and freed prisoners. At the same time Woczek and Noysters, the city's USP leaders, distributed leaflets calling for a public meeting on the next morning to consolidate the revolution.[12]

On paper Dortmund was prepared for uprisings. As early as July 1917 von Gayl had thought it necessary to arrange for security precautions. Troops stationed in the neighbouring countryside were detailed to occupy key points in the city. Fodder for their horses was arranged and even the places where military courts were to be set up were selected.[13] On the afternoon of 8 November police inspector Richard instructed the police force on the action to be taken against the insurgents and distributed carbines and ammunition. The Lord Mayor, Dr Eichhoff, nevertheless preferred to leave the city. At ten o'clock the marines arrived and were joined again by several hundred locals. They split up, with one group deciding to march upon the police headquarters and the other upon the local gaol. At the police headquarters Richard, feeling that the odds were too unfavourable, surrendered and handed over the arms. His colleagues at the gaol did likewise and at 11 P.M. Dortmund too was in the hands of the revolutionaries.[14] By midnight Mehlich and the local SPD leadership thought they had better act and decided to join the revolution. In the late hours of the night a Workers' and Soldiers' Council was formed.

The Dortmund Workers' and Soldiers' Council was headed by Ernst Mehlich, editor of the *WAVZ*. His assistant editor, Schröder, was elected deputy chairman and Klupsch and Bartels were selected as secretaries. Below these top positions was the executive council of fifteen members. This number was enlarged later to include Linke and seven other USP men but the power remained in the hands of the SPD.[15] There was also a clear SPD majority in the Bochum Workers' and Soldiers' Council which was set up on Saturday 9th.[16] Throughout this day Workers' and Soldiers' Councils sprung up in the region and were normally headed by the SPD. If there was a USP branch the socialist parties formed a joint Workers' and Soldiers' Council, although, as in Dortmund and Bochum, the power was normally with the SPD.[17] Of the larger cities, only in Gelsenkirchen did the USP succeed in gaining the leadership in the Workers' and Soldiers' Council. Here about ten thousand people followed the summons of the USP to come to 'the lawns', the public meeting place, on Saturday morning. Speakers of both parties addressed the meeting. The USP suggested a Workers' and Soldiers' Council of seven members. They claimed that a majority for the USP was justified as they had been the driving force behind the revolution. Despite the protests of the SPD they carried the day. On 11 November at another large public rally on 'the lawns' the Council was enlarged although the executive power remained with the smaller body.[18] Outside Gelsenkirchen the USP could establish parity with the SPD only in the small town of Lünen,[19] north of Dortmund, and in the colony of Ickern, north-east of Bochum. But as the composition of the first district Workers' and Soldiers' Councils' meeting showed these were exceptions.[20] The last decade of party history had exerted its effect. Control of the newspapers and of the key party and union offices had ensured that the power would be in the hands of the moderates. The limited scope of the revolution in the eastern Ruhr which resulted from this soon became evident. It stood out in the dealings with the administrative officers, in the formation of the security guards, in the emphasis on early parliamentary elections and, above all, in their determination not to let the revolution slip any further to the left.

The executive council of Great Berlin and the Council of Peoples Delegates had issued warnings to the local Workers' and Soldiers' Councils not to dismiss public servants or to interfere unduly in the administration. This reminder illustrates how little credit the leaders in Berlin must have given to the general ability of the rank and file. It was an unwise move, as the local Workers' and Soldiers' Council leaders were very conscious of the precariousness of the situation and of the need for co-operation between themselves and the administration. It also hampered the dismissal of the few public servants who were obstructive and refused to adapt to the new situation. During the first weeks of the revolution there were virtually no problems between Workers' and Soldiers' Councils and the public service in the eastern Ruhr. The files list the dismissal of two police officers in Dortmund,[21] of one police inspector in Wanne[22] and of one high-ranking public servant in both Wattenscheid and Eickel.[23]

To work with the administration the Workers' and Soldiers' Councils in the cities and larger towns either formed boards to assist in various fields, as in Dortmund,[24] or they elected deputies *(Beigeordnete)* to assist or confer with the authorities, as was the case in Bochum and Gelsenkirchen.[25] At the smaller places no division of functions was necessary as the Workers' and Soldiers' Council here could deal with the whole administration. The *Volksblatt* and the *WAVZ* became the official newspapers where the daily decrees and announcements were published. These were normally signed by the chief administrator and by the chairman of the Workers' and Soldiers' Council. Finally, as a tribute to the revolution, the Red Flag was hoisted from all public buildings.

There were four basic problems which faced the Workers' and Soldiers' Councils in the Rhenish-Westphalian industrial region as elsewhere in Germany; to maintain law and order, to secure an uninterrupted supply of food, to assist in the demobilisation of the troops and to deal with the employment situation.

One of the first steps all Workers' and Soldiers' Councils took was to fill the vacuum which was created by the collapse of the military and to a lesser degree of the local police forces. Immediately after the overthrow they started recruiting security guards by offering a daily wage of about ten marks with a further food allowance of three marks.[26] The offer was lucrative enough to attract many young men. The size of the guards varied with the size of the cities and towns. Smaller towns like Lünen or Hamm for example recruited about fifty men.[27] Larger towns like Herne had a guard of about three hundred.[28] The cities of Gelsenkirchen and Bochum had over four hundred men enlisted[29] and Dortmund's guard, which was the largest, was almost two thousand strong.[30] It is interesting to note that in Dortmund the guard was not formed primarily to safeguard the revolution but, as Mehlich pointed out when justifying the expenditure,[31] because the Dortmund middle class feared that the lower classes might get out of control and start rioting and looting. The security guards were led by army officers who were responsible to the Workers' and Soldiers' Councils. The personal details of some of the rank and file have survived. In general they were from an SPD background. The profession listed most frequently was either worker or craftsman, although a few were soldiers. There was only a small number of students. Thus, unlike the *Freikorps,* the guards were not right-wing in outlook. On the whole nothing happened during the first weeks of the revolution which could not have been dealt with by a revitalised police force. It is possible, however, that the mere presence of large security forces prevented any major crime. The guards did not become active until January 1919 and then they were used for different purposes.

The procurement of the necessities of life continued to be a major operation. For a short time the food situation improved. The end of the war had raised hopes of an end to the blockade and there was a slight increase in the weekly food rations. The abandonment of the meatless weeks and the hand out of 500 grams more bread and a few more potatoes were especially welcome. The release of large numbers of draught-horses from the army led to a temporary abundance of horse meat. Finally, at least some of the Workers' and Soldiers' Councils were willing to make a serious effort to combat the black market and eradicate the inequalities in food distribution. The Workers' and Soldiers' Councils in Gelsenkirchen, Dortmund, Wanne and some of the smaller places empowered the security guards and the police force to investigate black market food dealings. Raids were made upon private houses, small companies and shops and if unlawful quantities of food were found the goods were confiscated.[32] As they concentrated upon the small offenders the overall effect of these actions was limited. Most black market food was held by the big companies,[33] and the SPD chiefs shrank from raiding their premises.

The Workers' and Soldiers' Councils faced a series of tasks which they had either inherited from the war or which arose with the armistice. The transport situation grew worse under the terms of the armistice and demanded special attention.[34] The concern of the authorities about crime in general and juvenile delinquency in particular was shown in a series of decrees which curbed the liquor-trade closing hours, restricted the sale of liquor and directed parents to keep their youngsters off the streets after dark. The return of enemy prisoners of war caused additional work. The prisoners had to be properly clothed and were to be provided with food and a small amount of money for their return home. Some of the Workers' and Soldiers' Councils were also concerned about the degree of sexual intercourse of German women with prisoners and issued appeals to uphold decency and honour.[35]

The demobilisation of the armed forces proved a further massive task. Luckily for the authorities in the region the eastern Ruhr was not on the main route of the returning troops. The cities and towns were spared the ugly scenes of scuffles between returning soldiers and local workers which occurred in Düsseldorf and the Berg district. In the eastern Ruhr a few soldiers who were passing through had to be accommodated privately but most came from the neighbouring region and could return to their homes. Still, a certain amount of hostility towards the new situation was reported from among the soldiers and had to be calmed by the new leaders.[36]

The soldiers were given a tumultuous 'welcome home'. The lord mayors, mayors and other prominent local personalities, including the chairman of the Dortmund Workers' and Soldiers' Council, Mehlich, made many speeches in which they praised the returning men for their bravery and wished for their satisfactory reintegration into civilian life. Then the soldiers were taken to the public washing facilities where they were bathed, and deloused. Finally they were given new clothes and—most important—were put back into employment.

As the war was drawing to its close the government had become increasingly concerned about the importance of a smooth demobilisation. Especially in defeat the immediate return of the soldiers to their jobs was vital. Plans to arrange for this were distributed in the last weeks of the war[37] and when the collapse finally came the government was ready to act. In charge of the operation was Koeth at the Economic Demobilisation Office *(Wirtschaftliche Demobilmachungsamt).*[38] He was assisted regionally by the *Demobilmachungskommissare* who were attached to the government president. Below the latter, at the local level, were the demobilisation boards on which employers and employees were equally represented. Their main work was to ensure employment for the returning soldiers. By late November/early December 1918 the traditional employment agents, the city employment office *(Städtischer Arbeitsnachweis)* and the staff offices of the major companies, together with the local chambers of industry and commerce, were also concentrating upon the same problems. This is certainly indicative of a widespread fear that the revolution might move still further to the left. A confidential letter of the German Industry Council to the *Zentralverband Deutscher Industrieller* and the *Bundes der Industriellen* firmly warns its members to put reason before profit,

> The end of the war places difficult tasks ahead of us. . . . If we do not succeed in maintaining law and order during the demobilisation, [we will not be able] . . . to carry out the restoration of Germany's economic life. . . . To maintain law and order it is necessary to ensure that the returning workers and soldiers are not idle but are employed, even if this is not economically sound for a company.[39]

This view was shared by the local authorities.[40] Although the fear that unemployment would lead to further social instability was certainly justified, the demand for labour by the coal industry soon ensured that there was no significant job shortage in the eastern Ruhr. The coal industry had been understaffed throughout the war and it had lost about one-fifth of its workforce with the repatriation of enemy prisoners. Thus throughout the coal region unfilled vacancies soon outnumbered employment seekers by a wide margin. In Gelsenkirchen, for example, there were 70 per cent more vacancies than job seekers. In Bochum the relation was two to one.[41] Judged from the evidence available this favourable employment situation made the demobilisation boards here virtually superfluous. The local boards had little influence upon other factors of importance during the economic demobilisation such as transport and the procurement of

V A ‘Kolonie’, Bergmannsglück, Hassel

Aufruf!

Bürger und Kameraden!

Der Einwohnerschaft der Stadt- und Landgemeinde Dorsten wird hierdurch zur Kenntnis gegeben, daß sich am Sonntag, den 10. November ein Arbeiter- und Soldatenrat gebildet hat. Er wird im gesamten Stadtgebiet die öffentliche Ruhe, Sicherheit und Ordnung in vollem Umfange aufrechterhalten.

Ihren Weisungen, die zur Aufrechterhaltung der öffentlichen Ruhe, Sicherheit und Ordnung ergehen, ist unverzüglich Folge zu leisten.

Wir sind gewillt, mit den gesamten bisherigen Verwaltungen weiter zu arbeiten, sofern sie sich den Anordnungen des Arbeiter- und Soldatenrats fügen.

Jegliche Ausschreitungen oder Plünderungen werden mit den schwersten Strafen geahndet. Jeder muß unverzüglich seinen Geschäften nachgehen. Arbeitseinstellungen ohne Zustimmung des Arbeiter- und Soldatenrats sind zu vermeiden. Keine Ansammlung darf den Verkehr stören oder hindern.

Jugendliche bis zu 17 Jahren haben von 7 Uhr abends an die Straße zu verlassen.

Dorsten, den 10. November 1918.

Stadtverwaltung:

Lappe, Bürgermeister.

Arbeiter- und Soldatenrat:

Weidemann, Witte, Berger, Clahsen, Winkelhäuser, Arnoldt, Bettin, Kaiser, Fattroth.

VI Poster proclaiming the revolution in Dorsten

raw materials, as these were dealt with on a subregional and national scale.[42]

With the return of the soldiers into industry by mid-December 1918 the rule of the Workers' and Soldiers' Councils came practically to an end in the eastern Ruhr. For a number of Workers' and Soldiers' Councils this is a flattering remark. There is evidence that the Herne Council, for example, existed only on paper. Except for being responsible for the security guard it did not participate in the running of the town at all.[43] The documents suggest the same conclusion about the Bochum Council. A letter of the city's war board proudly refers to the absence of food raids in Bochum and proclaims that such activities will not occur in the future either.[44] Nor do the local columns in the Bochum *Volksblatt* hint at any major involvement of the Workers' and Soldiers' Council in the daily affairs of the city. Of course the mere presence of a Workers' and Soldiers' Council was important. Since it was composed of workers and since it gave the impression that revolution was occurring it calmed discontent about various problems, especially occasional lapses in the food distribution, which otherwise might have led to unrest. Most useful was the fact that the Workers' and Soldiers' Council headed the security guards, the law and order force in the region. Had this function been undertaken by troops—not to mention *Freikorps*—it would not have been sanctioned by the majority of the workers. The absence of documents suggests that the Workers' and Soldiers' Council was a mere façade in a considerable number of places in the eastern Ruhr. Since the administrative files have generally been well preserved, it seems unlikely that relevant documents have subsequently been destroyed or lost.

Notwithstanding this, there is evidence that there was, for a time at least, genuine government by Workers' and Soldiers' Councils elsewhere. In Dortmund, Wanne, Lünen and the small mining settlement of Sodingen,[45] for example, the Councils were in command and participated in the administration to overcome the difficulties of the early post-war weeks. Most active was the Gelsenkirchen Workers' and Soldiers' Council which extended its influence beyond maintaining law and order, distributing food and organising demobilisation by interfering in the city's education system. The Council attempted to remove one of the inequalities of the German education system by cancelling all afternoon classes and thus set the same school hours for lower and higher schools.[46] It also dismissed some priests from their teaching posts, a step which was in line with the long-standing party policy of curbing the influence of the churches upon education.

Both decisions had to be reversed on instruction of Konrad Hänisch who had joined the Majority Socialists during the war and who had accepted the complaints of the city's lord mayor and the government president in Arnsberg.[47] Another unusual step—to judge from the political climate in the eastern Ruhr—was the dismissal of the Gelsenkirchen lord mayor by the Workers' and Soldiers' Council because 'his views did not accord with the new times and because he failed to give in to certain acts'.[48] But Gelsenkirchen was an exception. By mid December 1918 the traditional representative assemblies had met everywhere, encouraged by the new Prussian ministers, Hirsch and Ströbel,[49] and had approved the extra expenditure for the Workers' and Soldiers' Councils and the security guards. The fact that *Stadtverordneten*, elected under the old Prussian three class franchise system, sanctioned the activities of the Councils by approving this expenditure was an indication of the limited range of the revolution under the leadership of the SPD. By the end of December the Workers' and Soldiers' Councils were left with only one real function which was to maintain 'law and order', or more precisely to guard the nation against the challenge which was starting to come from the left. By this time too, little more than a month after the collapse of the old order, the emphasis in the eastern Ruhr had shifted from revolution to political electioneering.

The co-operation between the two socialist parties was fragile from the very beginning. It lasted whilst the USP in Dortmund, the centre of the two electorates, was led by Linke and Jakobi. Linke had been in the forefront of the party for a long time. Records of annual party conventions show him slightly to the left of the local party establishment. The documents do not indicate when he joined the opposition during the war but his association with the USP was short lived. When the situation became more turbulent in January 1919, he was among the first to return to the SPD.[50] About Jakobi very little is known. A bank clerk by profession, he was a relative of one of the city's banking families. From the few references in newspapers it seemed to have been his anti-war sentiments which led him to join the USP. He left Dortmund for Berlin early in 1919 and there is no trace of him from then on. Both men were USP moderates. They did little to influence the course of events after 9 November but followed in the wake of Mehlich and the SPD. The situation changed with the return from the front of a young man who was to lead the extreme political left in the eastern Ruhr for the next turbulent years. His name was Adolf Meinberg. He was born in Wickede near Dortmund on 3 October 1893. His parents must have been comfortably off as he went to a training college from which he was dismissed on the grounds of insubordination. He became a travelling salesman of religious pictures and, later, a crane operator. He joined the SPD before the war, was drafted into the army in 1915 and released shortly afterwards because of his bad eye-sight. On his return to Dortmund he started to agitate against the policies of the SPD caucus and was expelled from the party in late autumn 1917. Shortly afterwards he founded a USP branch in Dortmund and 'in the interest of public safety' he was drafted again into the army where he stayed until the end of the war.[51]

When Meinberg returned in late November he was not impressed by the revolution in Dortmund. König, SPD chief of the region, had just given a speech to the electorate's Workers' and Soldiers' Councils which over the next few weeks was to be repeated by himself and other SPD leaders at countless election rally meetings throughout the country. Entitled 'Where are we heading?' this speech claimed that the people wanted 'release from servitude, hunger and despair . . . but a new dictatorship was not the remedy . . . the people want peace, the bolshevists on the other hand want to continue the war with the Allies.'[52] He then proposed a resolution which supported freedom and democracy but condemned bolshevism and stressed that socialism could only be achieved through the 'constitutional . . . German National Assembly'.[53] The resolution was passed by a large majority.

This was a questionable speech. By virtually equating everything to the left of the right wing of the USP with 'bolshevist anarchy' he helped to set the scene for the hysteria of the strife ridden months of early 1919. The fact that there had not been a clash between the opposing forces on the left and right by late November 1918 makes König's speech the more unfortunate as it added to the already tense atmosphere. Yet it made good election material.

The SPD party ticket in Western Westphalia was headed by Max König, who had come to Dortmund from Saxony. König had learned the smith's trade and in 1891 was one of the founders of the Metalworkers Union. Between 1898 and 1901 he edited the Bochum *Volksblatt* and in 1901 he established a Workers' Secretariat in Dortmund which was headed by him until 1906. He then was elevated to the position of party secretary of Western Westphalia which he still held at the time of the revolution. By this time too he was member of the Reichstag and town councillor at the Dortmund *Stadtverordnetenversammlung*. In 1920 he climaxed his career when he became government president in Arnsberg. The second man in the district, Ernst Mehlich, was at an earlier stage of his political career. He had been the successor of Hänisch as editor of the *WAVZ*. By the end of the war he headed the party in Dortmund and during the revolution he was the chief of the Workers' and Soldiers' Council. He was soon to become town councillor, leader of the SPD in the city assembly and a little later deputy to Severing, who was to hold the newly created office of *Reichskommissar* for the Rhenish-Westphalian Industrial Region. Between these men and the rank and file there was now a social discrepancy, and the same can be said of the Bochum leaders Hue, Husemann and Sachse. The years of climbing the ladder of the party bureaucracy and the powerful position given to them by the plurality of their offices had made these men rather inflexible in their judgment. Rarely did they waver. They knew what was best for the people and they were not to be deterred by fickle hotheads. And they were willing to use any means, including force, to save Germany from irresponsible elements.

König's speech had marked the start of the election campaign both for the National Congress of Workers' and Soldiers' Councils,[54] and for the National Assembly. Electioneering was the strength of the SPD, acquired in many battles for Reichstag seats. The goal they had set themselves was to reach a vote of more than 50 per cent so they could implement their policies. For a full month the leaders in Bochum and Dortmund staged a massive campaign. Every weekend and on many nights during the week they travelled up and down the countryside and addressed countless meetings. Their wives and female supporters made special efforts to win over the women to whom the revolution had just given the vote.

Against this powerful campaign the USP could do little. As it had during the war, the lack of a newspaper deprived them of the main channel of communication. The party also lacked able speakers. Only Meinberg, and to a lesser extent Jakobi, spoke consistently at SPD election meetings where they warned the audience to beware of a premature gathering of a National Assembly. Such a body, they warned, would absorb the power which the revolution had given to the workers and would jeopardise the introduction of socialism.[55] But their arguments were soon dismissed. How could they dare to suggest that the SPD was not heading towards socialism? Hadn't the working day been reduced to eight hours? And the unions recognised? And pay for the miners and other workers increased? Had the Council of People's Delegates not set up a socialisation committee? And more was to come. Of course this had to happen in an orderly fashion and work had to be still carried out industriously but the future was theirs. The German Revolution was an orderly revolution and was not to be carried away by bolshevist disorder. These were convincing arguments and carried the day at one election meeting after another. The SPD leaders were well known and widely respected and what they had to say made sense. The fact that Jakobi was a bank clerk and related to one of the city's banking families led to further ridicule of the USP. So did the ill-famed Thyssen affair in which a USP member of the Dortmund Workers' and Soldiers' Council was involved.[56]

What sealed the fate of the USP for the immediate future was what has become known as the 'Dortmund Spartacus Putsch' of 7 January 1919. The events on that day occurred at the time of the *Vorwärts* occupation and renewed fighting between workers and government troops in Berlin.

The local newspapers vied with each other in their reporting of Spartacist atrocities. Ill founded as these reports were, they made the atmosphere explosive and the *Vorwärts* occupation had some influence upon the general unrest and the occupation of newspaper offices which occurred in the week from 7–14 January. But, as an analysis of the individual events will show, the incidents in the region of this study stemmed largely from local developments.

According to the official report, on the night of 7 January Spartacists and other unruly elements implemented a plan to overthrow the lawful authorities in Dortmund. The usurpers attacked three key points. These were the Reichsbank, the SPD newspaper office and the *Klosterschule*, headquarters of the security guard. Thanks to the decisive opposition of the Dortmund security guard, however, all their attempts were completely foiled. So claimed the official report.[57] It was compiled by Workers' and Soldiers' Council officials and administrators under the leadership of Ernst Mehlich. Mehlich wanted to leave no doubt that his was the true version of the night's incidents, and he instructed the press to print no other account of the events.[58] The testimony of the USP, which questioned the official reports, failed to be printed[59] and there are reasons to suggest that whatever happened on the night of the 7th bore little resemblance to Mehlich's official report.

First there was no substance in the term 'Spartacus Putsch'. There were no Spartacists in the electorate of Dortmund. Mehlich had ensured that a representative of the Düsseldorf Communist Party, who was on a lecture tour of the region, was captured and released only on condition that he did not return.[60] Nor is there any evidence which suggests that the *Putsch* was pre-planned. The leaders of the left in Dortmund, Meinberg and Jakobi, were arrested and, because it was feared that to keep them in Dortmund would cause further outrage, they were sent to Münster. Here they were interrogated by the city's attorney and released because of lack of evidence. Indeed, the attorney was convinced from the hearing that far from causing the disturbances they helped to pacify the angry crowd.[61]

It can be conceded that a temporary or token occupation of the *WAVZ* was planned. This sort of thing occurred throughout Germany in the wake of the *Vorwärts* occupation. Admittedly too there was a meeting of returned soldiers and disabled war veterans on the evening of 7 January which was attended by soldiers from throughout the region, including a group from Essen. It was claimed that this group came to assist the coup in Dortmund but evidence again fell far short of substantiating the claim. There was nothing unusual in the holding of such a meeting. The SPD paper in Essen complained that the members of the city's security guard had become the victims of a gross error.[62] It seems unlikely indeed that these few men, who came to Dortmund virtually unarmed, were part of a plan to take over the city with the largest and best equipped security guard. According to a report of the *Oberstaatsanwalt* Essen the meeting came to an end when news arrived that some of the sailors who were to attend the meeting were arrested by the security guard. It was then that they decided to stage a demonstration march to release the prisoners.[63] It was almost certainly this demonstration which was fired upon when the marchers reached the centre of the city outside the Reichsbank. The official account maintained that a group of marchers, several hundred strong, advanced upon the Reichsbank with the intention of storming it, since, according to Mehlich, the proper way to make revolution was by taking over the press, the Reichsbank and the police.[64] When the group approached and guns were just about to be distributed a small cordon of security guards opened fire whereupon the crowd fled in all directions. Two people were killed and nine soldiers seriously injured.

It is doubtful that a hold-up or an occupation of the bank could have been so casually planned. A police report written shortly afterwards stated that a group of people approached the bank probably with the intention of plundering there, which has a very different connotation. It also stated that the lights in that part of the city needed to be improved at night.[65] What appears to have happened was that those who had attended the soldiers' meeting were marching, probably shouting angrily, towards the security guard headquarters when the soldiers at the bank panicked and shot into the crowd. Thus the bloodshed was the product of the tense atmosphere which Mehlich had greatly helped to bring about. The confrontation later that night at the *Klosterschule* and the *WAVZ* are also likely to have been the sequel to the Reichsbank shooting, rather than part of a plan to take over the city. Fortunately, the people in charge there remained more cool-headed and no further blood was shed. The night of 7 January was to go into history as the Spartacus Putsch in Dortmund. The USP was never able to give their version of the incident. They were furious and denounced the whole affair as an SPD election stunt.[66] This may be unjust to Mehlich and his friends but as far as the immediate future of the USP was concerned the affair was disastrous. The event was reported throughout the region and beyond as a further bloody Spartacus uprising with USP backing. No decent worker could associate himself with such people. The USP in Dortmund broke up. Linke and the moderates went back to the SPD. Meinberg had seen the light too, and he founded the KPD in Dortmund.

With the left muted, the SPD in Bochum and Dortmund could concentrate all their election efforts upon the right. The main opponents of the socialists in Kaiser's times, the National-Liberals, running now under the more fashionable name of *Deutsche Volkspartei*, had ceased to be a major political force in the region even before the Great War. The DVP drew its support from the Protestant middle-class groups whose overall percentage of the population had steadily diminished. The main opponent on the right of the SPD was the Catholic Centre Party *(Zentrum)* which still had a good following among workers throughout the northern part of the region. In the six weeks before the election the Catholics mounted a massive campaign against the socialists. In their newspapers, from the pulpits and in public meetings they fiercely attacked the policies which were coming out of Berlin.[67] There was a considerable amount of talk about seceding from the Reich. The main target of this crusade was Adolf Hoffmann's education policy. Hoffmann, the new USP Minister for Culture in Prussia, had issued five decrees designed to remove the basis for the inequalities of the German education system. One of these was aimed at weakening the hold of the churches upon the schools by making religion an optional subject. Hoffmann's policies were in line with the long-standing party principle of fighting for equal educational opportunities in order to achieve a more just society. From the SPD's point of view there could not have been anything objectionable about Hoffman's step, but it was election time and these were often times when votes came before principle. They were most relieved when the USP, and with it Hoffmann, left the Prussian government in late December 1918 and press articles upon his departure were loaded with scorn.[68] Hoffmann's successor, Hänisch, modifed the impact of the planned education policies by deciding to postpone their implementation.

The SPD made considerable electoral capital out of the anti-national secessionist tendencies of the local *Zentrum.* They also attacked the Catholic candidates for their pro-war stand[69] although, coming from the SPD, this was a two-edged sword. Finally, they used political chicanery. An article published the day before the election on how large quantities of illegal food were stored at the house of an opposition candidate almost certainly made an impact. In return, the *Zentrum* relied on equally emotional issues.[70]

The election to the National Assembly on 18 January showed that the efforts of the SPD leaders bore fruit. In both electorates the socialists improved their votes to over 50 per cent of the total. In Dortmund their share rose from 44 per cent at the last Reichstag election in 1912 to 53 per cent. In Gelsenkirchen they scored almost 60 per cent, in Wanne the total socialist vote rose from 31.4 to 57.6 per cent. In Bochum the result was slightly less favourable, amounting to only 45 per cent.[71] The proportion of USP to SPD votes was shattering to the former. The SPD outscored them by 15 to 1 in Dortmund and by more than 10 to 1 in Bochum-Gelsenkirchen.

In the whole electorate of Western Westphalia there were three election results which did not follow this trend. One of the three places, the steel city of Hagen and its neighbouring townships, had until 1918 belonged to the Niederrhein branch to which the book will turn in the next chapter. The other two places warrant a brief analysis.

First there was the mining town of Lünen to the north of Dortmund where the USP scored about a third of the votes given to the socialists.[72] Coal production in Lünen did not begin until the turn of the century and by 1914 its miners numbered about 10,000 living in a series of colonies around the colliery Viktoria. The mine was the centre of attention during the January/February strike of 1918 when—probably because wages here were below average[73]—it was the scene of the largest stoppage.[74] The government's response of drafting 260 miners into the army caused a great deal of bitterness. Not surprisingly, when the revolution offered the chance, the miners demanded the dismissal of company director Walkhoff, who was held responsible for the discrimination against the workforce. As the management of the colliery took no action to comply with the demands of the miners they resorted to self-help. They occupied the administration, dismissed Walkhoff and elected their own Works Council which was headed by the pit foreman *(Steiger)* Schürken. These steps were not as drastic as they seemed. The Works Council did not interfere in the administration of the mine, Schürken insisted on his willingness to step down once a cordial solution to the problem about Walkhoff had been found and production continued very effectively.[75] The situation in Lünen did not come to a head until the first general strike which followed the socialisation attempt of the Essen Workers' and Soldiers' Council in February but the bitterness which was carried over from the war explains the strong early following of the USP here and its comparatively good showing at the January election.

Most unusual was the result in Ickern where the USP matched the result of the SPD.[76] Ickern is a large mining colony built around a colliery of the same name, situated in the north-east of the *Landkreis* Dortmund. The first conflict arose in the wake of the Essen model. The miners here too formed a Works Council which on 14 January claimed to be in charge of the mine. In response the mine administration turned to the neighbouring Workers' and Soldiers' Councils for help.[77] On 15 January, led by a deputation from Dortmund, the security guards of Castrop, Bladenhorst, Rauxel, Mengede and Sodingen met at Rauxel and marched upon Ickern to deal with the 'Spartacists'. The miners in Ickern decided to give in to the demands—to withdraw from the mines and hand over all arms and ammunition—thus no blood was shed.[78] Still, the affair caused bitterness with the local population and explained the good showing of the USP at the 19 January election.

On the whole the results of Lünen and Ickern were too insignificant to concern the SPD leaders in Dortmund and Bochum. The overall election result in the eastern Ruhr gave them good reason to be satisfied. As far as Germany as a whole was concerned the SPD failed to gain an absolute majority. It is doubtful whether the disappointment about this, which was stressed in newspaper comments on the election, was altogether genuine. They probably were too experienced as politicians to believe that they could have improved their share of the votes from little over one-third to over 50 per cent. In any case they had a ready-made scapegoat in the destructive policies of the USP, which turned potential voters away. What was more alarming, or at least should have been, was the fact that even in the Rhenish-Westphalian Industrial Region the result of the eastern Ruhr was nowhere repeated. This was partly because the social and political history of other areas in the Ruhr ensured that the party machinery would not be completely controlled by the Majority Socialists. There was also growing uncertainty about whether the improvements which were advocated by the SPD revolutionaries would materialise.

Chapter 6

Radical revolution: In and around Düsseldorf

The Workers' and Soldiers' Councils in the steel and metal industry cities to the south of the Ruhr were led by the USP. In their dealings with the bureaucracy, their handling of day-to-day problems and in their approach towards the socialist goal of the revolution, the Independent Socialists took a very different stand from that of the Majority Socialists in the Eastern Ruhr.

The war had caused a pronounced swing to the left in the Berg district. The leaders and party members in Düsseldorf, Solingen and Remscheid, and, to a lesser degree Elberfeld and Barmen, became increasingly hostile to the policies of the party caucus. Deteriorating living conditions ensured that their stand would be supported by the bulk of the workforce and by autumn 1918 the USP had the upper hand in the region. They had survived determined attempts by the SPD to destroy their organisation as well as large-scale arrests and call-ups on the part of the government. If anything, persecution seems to have strengthened the USP's position. The turmoil of the last weeks of war, which has been noted in the eastern Ruhr, occurred here too. A secret conference of USP delegates in Elberfeld agreed that the collapse of the empire was imminent and decided to foster a revolutionary spirit among the masses.[1] After the easing of the *Versammlungsgesetze* a series of mass meetings was held throughout the Berg district. The meetings at which Dittmann spoke were especially popular. The halls were reported to have been unable to accommodate the thousands who turned up.[2] The *Volksstimme* in Remscheid and the *Bergische Arbeiterzeitung* published longer and longer articles on the great Russian Revolution and its successes, on its program of socialisation and on the nationalisation of the banks. 'To be prepared is the command of the hour' was the headline of the two newspapers on 31 October. The news from Kiel was greeted enthusiastically: 'Haltet Euch Zum Eingreifen bereit', read the headline on 6 November. At this stage the spirit among the workers was so radical that the leaders at a further mass meeting on the eve of the revolution had to admonish their followers to be patient and stand by.[3]

On the afternoon of 8 November the soldiers from Köln reached Elberfeld and Barmen. The process of the insurrection followed the normal pattern. On their arrival at the Döppenberg Railway station in Elberfeld the marines were joined by a few hundred workers.[4] By night the marines had gone on to Solingen where, together with a large crowd of workers, they marched upon the Town Hall and demanded the release of political prisoners and the disarming of the police. The local lord mayor gave in to the demands whereupon the demonstration went on to the union headquarters to form a provisional Workers' and Soldiers' Council.[5] The revolution did not reach Remscheid until the morning of 9 November but by noon of that day this region too was in the hands of Workers' and Soldiers' Councils.

Nowhere in the Rhenish-Westphalian Industrial Region did the rule of the Workers' and Soldiers' Council commence with such fervour as in Remscheid, Solingen and their neighbouring towns. In Remscheid the revolution brought for the first time into the centre of attention a man who was to lead the extreme political left in the Lower Rhine for several years. His name was Otto Brass, who had been born in Remscheid and had learned the trade of a file cutter. Young Brass, a local, had worked himself up the party ladder, and by 1918 he had become the business executive of the *Volksstimme.* Together with four other USP leaders (Schliestedt, Otto Schmidt, Willy Grütz and Paul Schliessmann) Brass sat on the executive of the Remscheid Workers' and Soldiers' Council. The Council members in Remscheid numbered forty-five; and its executive established eleven *Kommissariate* which controlled the administration and presided over all aspects of daily life ranging from security to food, traffic and commerce.[6]

There was no doubt that the views of Otto Brass and his colleagues about what constituted a revolution differed substantially from those of the SPD leaders in the eastern Ruhr. In his first article after the collapse of the old order Brass lists the most urgent steps the revolution had to take before attacking the more complex issues of the new socialist society. These were the confiscation of the property of the higher nobility, the abolition of all parliaments and, as far as the situation allowed, immediate reform of the legal and administrative system. Brass was sceptical of the policies of the Council of Peoples' Delegates and refused even to consider the possibility of a National Assembly. Remscheid protested very strongly when the AK, encouraged by Hirsch's and Ströbel's decrees, reminded the regional Workers' and Soldiers' Councils that they were not to dismiss police officers. The leaders of the revolution in Remscheid certainly did not hesitate to dismiss the town's higher police officers.[7]

A few days after 9 November Brass wrote a very strong letter to Dittmann, which is a good illustration of the revolutionary spirit in the Berg district.

> We now see the fatal consequences of the policies [pursued by the USP leadership] in Berlin. At a number of places the government socialists . . . attempted,

unfortunately with success, to challenge our strong position. Should everything we have been fighting for over the last years now be forgotten . . . ?

Since yesterday even in Düsseldorf, where we were in complete control, they [the USP] shared the power with the people around Gerlach [the SPD]. The disastrous effects of such policies is shown in a compromise which allows for the *Freie Presse* [the local SPD newspaper] to be printed at our press. . . . But we will fight rigorously against you, if you join the half-hearted policies of the government socialists. . . .

For the time being we assume that your entering the government was a tactical manoeuvre. We certainly expect that you will take the consequences and quit the government if the government socialists do not comply with your conditions completely.[8]

To keep the revolution alive the *BAZ* and the *BVS* printed extracts from the Spartacist *Rote Fahne* rather than the USP *Freiheit*. Speeches or essays of such radical left-wingers as Liebknecht and Merges were quoted regularly.[9]

With few exceptions a left-wing USP ran the towns and smaller industrial settlements around Solingen and Remscheid.[10] As far as revolutionary élan was concerned Solingen was not far behind Remscheid. As in Remscheid there was an executive council here which headed a large Workers' and Soldiers' Council and a series of *Ausschüsse.* The most influential men in revolutionary Solingen were the two USP chiefs Merchel and Christmann. The Workers' and Soldiers' Council in Solingen laid claim to the legislative as well as the executive and judicial power[11] and it went well beyond the boundary of municipal affairs when it compelled the local industrialists to give employees two weeks' notice before dismissal and four weeks' full pay.[12]

However, the vigorous course the revolution took in the Berg district came to an abrupt end within a month of the collapse of the old order. The armistice agreement had established that Allied troops would occupy the left bank of the Rhine and establish a few bridgeheads across the river. One of these bridgeheads was to be set up opposite Köln and was to extend as far north-east as the Remscheid suburb of Vieringhausen. It thus included the whole of Solingen and its neighbouring towns. The imminent occupation of Solingen and its hinterland was announced on 6 December but it took another week before the troops actually arrived.[13]

The British would have none of the Workers' and Soldiers' Councils. One of their first actions was to restore the power of the traditional authorities. The Councils did not have to be abolished but were stripped of their power. Provided that they did not indulge in any activities such as the spreading of propaganda leaflets, they could still call themselves Workers' and Soldiers' Councils.[14] As might be expected the Workers' and Soldiers' Councils in and around Solingen were not interested in adopting such a humiliating role, and resigned.

In subsequent months the Majority Socialists in Solingen could rely upon the British troops in their struggle against the left. In January, for example, the British commander supported the efforts of the local SPD to gain control of the two left-wing newspapers which were both printed in Solingen. On 18 January the *Bergische Arbeiterstimme* and *Volksstimme* called for a one-day strike in protest against the murder of Liebknecht and Luxemburg. Although the strike notice did exclude the occupied territories, 'advisers' to the British military leaders succeeded in closing down the press. The newspapers were outlawed for a fortnight and then reopened under a moderate team of editors, who, as they claimed, were given permission to continue the socialist newspapers on more acceptable lines.[15]

Although parts of its eastern suburbs were occupied, Remscheid remained just outside the bridgehead. Still, the proximity of the British troops and the threat that the occupation might be extended had its effect upon the Remscheid Workers' and Soldiers' Council. Unlike its Solingen counterpart, it remained in office but its activities quietened. It abstained from undertaking any controversial action, avoided a clash with the town's administration and restricted its polemics to the occasional newspaper article. The local mayor and the leading administrators also preferred to keep things calm. They must have thought that allied, or, at a later stage *Freikorps* intervention would be more harmful than beneficial. They might also have feared unrest in the town and so avoided any showdown with the Council. Thus the two bodies, the traditional administration and the *Volksrat* as the Council was called in 1919, continued their activities in mutual agreement. As the Workers' and Soldiers' Councils withered away elsewhere in Germany real power in Remscheid, too, soon returned into the hands of the town assembly and the administration. Yet the *Volksrat* was not ineffective. For example it prevented the recruiting of volunteers for the *Freikorps*[16] and succeeded in excluding SPD representatives from the Second Workers' and Soldiers' Congress in Berlin.[17] Remscheid also became a refuge for persecuted left wingers and remained for a short period the headquarters for the regional council of the Lower Rhine Workers' and Soldiers' Council.

The Remscheid *Volksrat* survived until the summer of 1919, longer than all other left-wing Workers' and Soldiers' Councils. After having defeated uprisings throughout Germany the right wing troops finally decided to mop up the remnants of the left. Two *Freikorps* units, Bergmann and Gerstenberg, were assigned to deal with Remscheid. The way they did this came to be cited as a model by Nazi and other right-wing historians. The Bergmann unit decided not to launch an all out attack upon Remscheid first, as this might have warned the persons they wished to arrest and given them time to escape, but to precede the occupation by a massive kidnapping. Thus on the night before the planned attack a column of *Freikorps* soldiers drove into Remscheid in private cars, and raided the houses of prominent left-wing politicians. The men were bundled into the cars and driven to Essen where they were put on trial on various charges of insubordination. Then Remscheid was occupied.[18] The effective rule of the *Volksrat* in Remscheid, however, had ended with the occupation of the bridgehead by British troops in December 1918. The leaders of the USP in Remscheid, and Brass especially, now transferred a great deal of their efforts to the cause of the revolution in the Lower Rhine. They stood behind the establishment of a district Workers' and Soldiers' Council which was decided upon at a regional conference of all the Lower Rhine Workers' and Soldiers' Councils held in Barmen on 25 November 1918. The radical tone of the meeting is reflected in the decisions made there which bear the stamp of the Remscheid radicals.

> Starting from the facts that the revolution has only just begun and that the proletariat has to fight for the introduction of socialisation . . . [and] that those who are attempting to gain central power, in part already with success, are pursuing a counter revolutionary policy, the Workers' and Soldiers' Councils of the Lower Rhine branch declare:
>
> All power is in the hands of the Workers' and Soldiers' Councils . . .
>
> The goal of the revolution . . . is the transfer of the means of production from the hands of a few into the possession of all . . .
>
> The Workers' and Soldiers' Councils of the Lower Rhine branch will not tolerate policies or measures directed at hampering the course of the revolution . . . [19]

The Lower Rhine Workers' and Soldiers' Council's district conference also issued a set of guidelines designed to help the local Councils in their efforts to achieve the specified goals. The radical policies were passed with the votes of the delegates from Düsseldorf, Solingen, Remscheid and Hagen. Opposition came mainly from Elberfeld, from some of the Duisburg and Essen delegates and from the left-Rhenish representatives.[20] During the first month of the revolution Brass remained the most outspoken critic of the National Assembly elections at many meetings throughout the Ruhr. But his speeches and the radical resolutions of the Lower Rhine left had little effect on the course of the German revolution. Faced with the fact that a *Nationalversammlung* was to be elected, Brass concentrated his efforts upon luring support from the SPD to the USP.[21]

To the east of Remscheid, in the steel city of Hagen and its neighbouring towns, the revolution was led by the USP too and started with as much vigour as in Remscheid and Solingen. Hagen was well outside the bridgehead and the British occupation had no effect there. The USP stayed in power until the city was occupied by the *Freikorps* in the spring of 1919.

The socialists in Hagen concentrated their efforts upon the western Westphalian region as the city was geographically closer to Dortmund and Bochum than to the Lower Rhine cities, and Hagen was to become the centre of opposition to Mehlich and the Eastern Ruhr SPD.

In Elberfeld and Barmen the USP did not follow the radical course they had embarked upon in the later stages of the war. There the USP leadership proved much more moderate than in Solingen or Remscheid and joined forces with the SPD. Their united Workers' and Soldiers' Council in both cities functioned cordially for the first two months but they were too close to the centres of unrest to escape the January turmoil when the situation in the Wuppertal, too, became greatly polarised. As both Hagen and Wuppertal have been the subject of major studies, they will not be dealt with in detail.[22]

In Düsseldorf,[23] too, the socialists had moved further to the left during the war. The wave of police repression embittered the workforce and increased support for the USP. The food riots of June 1916 and the heavy gaol sentences which were imposed by the court had added fuel to the flames. Still fresh, too, was the memory of the ill-famed takeover of the *Volkszeitung* after which 10,000 workers cancelled their subscriptions.[24] With this background the stage was set in Düsseldorf for anything but a peaceful train of events when the troops arrived on the afternoon of 8 November at about 5 p.m. The police were disarmed within an hour, the prison was stormed and a provisional Workers' and Soldiers' Council was formed. For the next few hours the provisional Workers' and Soldiers' Council and the local authorities discussed the maintenance of law and order. Their negotiations came to an abrupt end at about 10 p.m. when the local USP leaders arrived on the scene, some straight from prison, and took over the leadership of the Council. They refused to have any dealings with Lehr, and demanded his resignation. When this was not forthcoming they dismissed him on their own authority in the early hours of the morning. Just before he was forced out of his office Lehr managed to destroy part of the files on his political opponents, although some of them fell into the hands of the workers. Lehr's first enforced absence from office lasted for only 24 hours. He was temporarily reinstated when the Lord Mayor, Oehler, persuaded the Workers' and Soldiers' Council that his dismissal would be detrimental to Düsseldorf's security.[25]

On the next day, USP led Workers' and Soldiers' Councils took control throughout the Düsseldorf *Landkreis*. For a short time it seemed that the enthusiasm of the revolution would overshadow the old feuds between the socialists. The USP agreed to the SPD joining the first Düsseldorf Workers' and Soldiers' Council, which was made up of one-third USP, one-third SPD and one-third soldiers of the local 31st Reserve Infantry

Regiment. It met twice a week and was chaired by the USP chief Wilhelm Schmitt.[26] As in the eastern Ruhr, the Düsseldorf Workers' and Soldiers' Council set up a series of departments, although the total number of these (25) was much higher than in the east. All twenty-five were headed by either SPD or USP members of the Workers' and Soldiers' Council.[27]

A week after 8 November the middle classes too made their bid to participate. After having recovered from the shock of the revolution, Kruse invited representatives from the whole government district to the *Tonhallen* theatre in Düsseldorf: Kruse gave the opening speech:

> I wish to state clearly that no political discussion will take place . . . [We are only concerned] with very simple questions, which will have to be answered in the near future . . . we will have to work together with the new rulers . . . the Workers' and Soldiers' Council, and help them with our experience, knowledge and institutions.[28]

In the subsequent series of talks representatives of the middle class offered assistance. The spokesman for the Catholic workers demanded the inclusion of Catholic union representatives in the Workers' and Soldiers' Council, a step which had been taken already at several places in the Ruhr.[29] But the *Niederrhein* socialists rejected this. Schmitt declared that the meeting was illegal, yet, allowing for their good intentions and providing that no element of counter-revolution emerged, he permitted it to continue.[30] For Brass, Schmitt's permissiveness went too far. He declared:

> It seems that the gentlemen from the middle classes here have not quite realised that the full economic and political power is in the hands of the Workers' and Soldiers' Council . . . and I would like to draw your attention to the fact that we are not willing to give away one iota of this power. Just as our former rulers have used the most brutal force [against us] we too will fully use our power against them. If they say that they support the new regime, then we can take this with a grain of salt. We do not need them to maintain law and order. The Workers' and Soldiers' Council will take care of this, now, and in the immediate future and they [the gentlemen from the middle class] will have to obey. . . .[31]

The 'Brotherhood' with the SPD did not last for too long. Although the USP did permit the printing of the *Freie Presse* on their premises the fact that the USP had taken possession of the *Volkszeitung* again caused a lot of ill feeling with the SPD. To make matters worse, the USP moderates, who in the turmoil of the first revolutionary days had made peace with the SPD, were being subjected to increasing criticism and there was a growing demand to reverse the decision. Before the end of November the SPD decided to quit because the 'consistent insults and attacks made any fruitful co-operation impossible'.[32] The leadership of the Workers' and Soldiers'

Council was now in the hands of an executive council of five: Schmitt, Schmittgen, Agnes, Obuch and Vossmeier.[33]

The Düsseldorf Workers' and Soldiers' Council, or as it was called from December 1918 onward, the Düsseldorf Workers' Council,[34] faced basically the same problems as those specified in the chapter on the eastern Ruhr, although, as the large number of departments indicated, the Düsseldorf Workers' Council had a different concept of its role. There was a close working relationship between the Council and the administration. The former controlled all key administrative positions including the government presidency where its representative Obuch, a lawyer, kept a check upon procedures.[35] The city's assembly met only once, on 26 November. At the meeting a few speeches complained that the revolution was financially extremely expensive but on the whole, an atmosphere of futility prevailed and the new leaders refused to take notice of the meeting.[36] The city's old assembly did not meet again until after the liberation of Düsseldorf in March 1919.

In Düsseldorf, too, one of the first steps was to form a security guard. The Düsseldorf revolutionary Workers Detachments, which had a membership of between 750 and 1,500, became famous for a series of spectacular raids upon company premises. Immediately after seizing power the Workers' and Soldiers' Council had issued instructions to all factories and works canteens to register their food stocks.[37] When this proved unproductive it authorised investigation squads to search the plants. These squads were not intimidated by famous names or big companies and their discoveries were startling.[38] For the workers at the Rheinische Metallwarenfabriken and other plants which were raided over the next few weeks this meant loss of their extra rations; still it is indicative of the spirit of fraternity which prevailed in revolutionary Düsseldorf that they all agreed not to impede the hand-over of the food to the public.[39]

The seizure of large quantities of food was helpful and stabilised the food situation for a short period. But, unfortunately for the people in Düsseldorf, what they gained on the swings they lost on the round-abouts. The Allied troops on the western bank of the Rhine had cut off the Düsseldorf milk supplies from the regions across the Rhine. As might be expected this had a disastrous impact upon the diet of children and infants.[40] Düsseldorf is noted for its extremely high child mortality in early post-war Europe.[41]

The Düsseldorf Workers' Council did not hesitate to seize administrative records. They were thus able to read their own personal police dossiers as compiled by Lehr and Gauer. But they also discovered that a number of city fathers, who had been critical of those who lacked stamina to carry on with the war, had themselves obtained special food deliveries.[42] The Workers' Council censored the middle-class newspapers when it was felt that an article was hostile towards the revolution or designed to spread unrest among the population.[43] It arranged for extra accommodation to overcome the pressing shortage of housing by making it compulsory for landlords to register vacant rooms,[44] established an auxiliary hospital[45] and drew up plans for Middle Schools for working-class pupils.[46]

The return of the soldiers proved a difficult task in Düsseldorf as the city was on the main route of the retreating armies. Many of the returning soldiers were already hostile to the new situation at home and a strongly worded proclamation by the Düsseldorf Council which stated that the old military regime had dishonoured itself and that no imperial flags were to welcome the soldiers, increased their anger. The middle-class citizens further heightened the tension by circulating slogans which called for 'liberation from the red mob'.[47] Not surprisingly then there were a series of clashes not only in Düsseldorf but also in the Berg district. A nasty scuffle between officers and workers occurred at the Hotel Breidenbacher Hof in Düsseldorf.[48] In Vohwinkel returning soldiers arrested the Workers' and Soldiers' Council and very rowdy scenes were reported from Lennep and Ohligs too.[49] It was to the credit of the Workers' and Soldiers' Councils that the situation was calmed within a short time.

For the first two months of the revolution Düsseldorf became a centre for the political left. There were meetings almost every night of the week and political rallies at the weekends which were arranged by the USP, the Spartacists or the syndicalists. Brass and his colleagues from Remscheid, together with local leaders, spoke at numerous USP meetings. Minster, who had returned from Holland and was now editing the Spartacist *Freiheit* in Mülheim, and Karl Hammer from Essen drew large audiences to their speeches on bolshevism and communism. Windhoff spread the syndicalist gospel again. He was supported by Fritz Kater, the head of the syndicalists in Germany, who travelled from Berlin to give lectures in the red centre of the Rhineland.

Numerically the strongest section on the left was the USP. At their gatherings it was demanded that 'the goal of the revolution must be the socialist future'. Resolutions were passed condemning the convening of the National Assembly and demanding that revolutionary goals be secured first. Berton had come back from the front by the end of November and his articles in the *Volkszeitung* warned against co-operation with the SPD and the middle-class parties and his paper published numerous treatises on the socialisation of German industry.[50] Berton attacked the point of view taken by the USP moderates. At the national congress of Workers' and Soldiers' Councils held in December in Berlin he criticised Hilferding's argument that, in the light of Germany's precarious economic situation, a slow approach towards socialisation was called for. 'I don't know', Berton exclaimed, 'whether the capitalists who own the factories today, will shoulder the burden of the transition to a peace-time economy, and put their factories into good order again, and then say to the People's Delegates: Please, help yourself'.[51] Although the USP left was in a majority in Düsseldorf the reports of meetings show that some members were more in line with the moderate Berlin leadership of the party. But when the congress of Workers' and Soldiers' Councils finally decided to opt for an early meeting of the National Assembly the moderates were as disappointed as was the bulk of the Düsseldorf USP branch.

The USP in Düsseldorf also refused to be drawn into the Bolshevist witch-hunt which was pursued in the right-wing socialist and middle-class press. The *Volkszeitung* gave some space to the publication of Spartacist news and announcements and, in general, it stressed that the USP was closer to the Spartacists than to the SPD. 'Our goals are the same but our tactics differ' was the approach taken by the *Volkszeitung*. In December the Spartacists replaced the Majority Socialists as the second power in the executive council of the Workers' Council. The Spartacist organisation in Düsseldorf was led by Ochel, a sculptor, who had returned from Holland at the end of the war and who, supported by Schmittgen, Rosi Wolfstein, Melcher and other radicals, was building a steadily expanding party group in Düsseldorf.[52]

Karl Windhoff and his syndicalists too found growing support for their movement in the first weeks after the war. In early January they staged a spectacular strike at the Rheinische Metallwarenfabriken in the Düsseldorf suburb of Derendorf during which thousands of workers occupied the administrative building and forced the administration to accept their demands on wages and working conditions. The management soon withdrew the concessions as it could justifiably claim that they were made under duress and the overall result of the syndicalists' strike was negligible.[53]

By January 1919 the relatively good natured atmosphere of the revolution in Düsseldorf had changed. There were several reasons for this. First there was the problem with the Düsseldorf middle classes. The difficulty was not, as Lucas claims, that the 'bourgoisie here was distinguished by its pronounced militancy . . . '[54] but that there were so many of them. As Düsseldorf was a centre of administration, finance and industry, the social cleavage between the well-to-do suburbs and the working-class areas was more pronounced than in the other cities of the Ruhr which lacked a larger middle class. The hostility between the opposing social factions was imminent from the time of the collapse of the old order. It had emerged in newspaper articles[55] and was emphasized by quarrels during the time of the return of the soldiers. And there is perhaps no better illustration of the disdain felt by a large section of the middle classes towards the *Pöbel* which had usurped power than in these lines of the *Oberregierungsrat* Glaubach. The essay was written many years later at a much happier time for the author, but it recalls the feelings entertained at the time of the revolution.

> For the professional public servants the revolution was a terrible blow. It seemed as though the ground, upon which they had stood securely for so long suddenly gave way. . . . How much beautiful old Prussian tradition, held in high esteem for generations, was lost for ever. . . .
>
> It was for the members of the [Düsseldorf] government a disgraceful humiliation, when, during a speech of the right-honourable president Dr Kruse . . . the Spartacist chief [Obuch] in his fantastic cowboy suit interfered . . . completely ignorant . . . with an important look on his stupid face.[56]

A further important factor in the precarious situation during early January 1919 was the number of unemployed. The industrialists were warned by the demobilisation board to put reason ahead of profit and prevent at any cost an increase in unemployment. Although this warning was generally heeded there were limits to the sacrifices some of the industrialists were willing to undertake and to many the importance of dividends to the shareholders could not be completely obliterated. By the time of the armistice war industry in Düsseldorf employed a workforce of 100,000, 50,000 of whom worked at the Rheinische Metalwarenfabriken. In the first weeks after the war, by Koeth's direction, weapons and ammunition continued to be manufactured to prevent lay-offs. By the middle of December the managements must have felt that this was a rather aimless procedure and started to dismiss employees. By Christmas the number of unemployed had reached 14,000.[57] The Workers' Council was embarrassed by the rising unemployment and blamed Düsseldorf industry for trying to boycott its work.[58] They also demanded, in agreement with a report by the local trade inspectors,[59] the introduction of planned industrial policies aimed at rebuilding Germany's greatly reduced industrial stocks.[60] But the authorities in Berlin had no interest in moving Germany's industry towards socialism. Koeth, in particular, was only concerned to tide the economy over the troublesome weeks of demobilisation[61] and the answers from the capital were vague letters which relied heavily upon the assumed economic ignorance of the Düsseldorf socialists.[62]

A small part of the unemployed could be absorbed through relief work, but this was only a drop in the ocean. The coal industry in the north was badly in need of workers but the severe housing shortage did not allow for families or even single men to move there.[63] Nor was commuting possible, owing to the poor state of the railways. There were rumours that the countryside needed additional workers but these had little substance.[64] By December the situation in Düsseldorf was becoming desperate. There was a great deal of bitterness among the unemployed and it was among them that the Spartacists found their early strong following in Düsseldorf. Speeches at their meetings grew more and more radical. There was a growing demand for the replacement of the Workers' Council, which was denigrated for being too weak and ineffective. When, finally, the news about the *Vorwärts* fighting in Berlin arrived the Düsseldorf communist leaders felt compelled to act.

On 7 January the newly founded Communist Party declared that the executive council of the Workers' Council was removed from office and announced a new executive. The chairman of the old council, Schmitt, was dismissed and at the news of this Obuch resigned too. In his place Berton agreed to join the new executive.[65] Two days later, following the escape of the Lord Mayor Oehler to the western bank of the Rhine, the KPD member Schmittgen was appointed as acting lord mayor. Thus, in contrast to Dortmund, the term 'Spartacus Putsch' was not altogether incorrect for Düsseldorf. Still, the term here too does not stand up to closer analysis. First, the new executive was still made up of USP and KPD members, although the balance might have swung towards the communists. Moreover, the new Executive Council submitted its decision to displace the old Council, as well as all major steps it was to take in the future, to the greater Workers' Council where the USP had a clear majority.[66] This body, after a thorough discussion, did sanction the new policies. In terms of membership the USP far outweighed the communists who also depended heavily upon the favourable press which Berton provided in the *VZD*. The fact that Schmittgen was acting lord mayor is not to be overrated either, as that position had been vacated. Schmittgen too never left any doubt that he was holding office on a temporary basis only. Thus the term 'Spartacus Putsch' is flattering for Ochel and his friends. A much more accurate description would be to say that on 7 January the Workers' Council in Düsseldorf moved further to the left.

The communists' rule in Düsseldorf proved to be an ill based and ill fated affair. From the records available Ochel, for example, was little more than a lout who created an atmosphere of social tension. An attentive observer who had shared Ochel's company during the war in Holland had described him as fanatical,[67] which, to judge from the course of events in Düsseldorf, seemed accurate. The communists' first step was to occupy the premises of the right-wing *Düsseldorfer Nachrichten* on 8 January and to publish the paper under the name of *Rote Fahne vom Niederrhein*. The first page listed the policies of the KPD as passed by the party's foundation congress, the rest of the newspaper remained untouched and printed its normal items.[68] If this was a doubtful venture, the consequences of their next step were tragic. On 9 January a few leading Düsseldorf personalities were arrested and charged with having planned to occupy the city with British troops.[69] The arrests were caused by the fear of counter-revolution and by frequent reports of separatism which were circulating among the Catholics in the Rhineland. For the persons concerned these arrests were not pleasant; still they were fairly treated and, as the charges could not be substantiated, they were never kept for long.[70] Hence the stories of the murder and bloodshed which the Spartacist dictators were blamed for having planned to let loose on 9 January were not true.[71] One of the men arrested, Paul Siebel, for example, still received his normal lunch (wine, bread, eggs and sausages) brought to him from an hotel, had his wife visit him with afternoon *Kaffee und Kuchen* and was released after less than 24 hours.[72] However, Oehler and Lehr, who had also been arrested, decided that there were limits to what they could endure and fled to the western bank of the Rhine. Whether Kruse was on the arrest list too is not clear. He decided to leave Düsseldorf—as he first put it—to escape the Spartacist terror. He later qualified his early statement by saying that he left because he was not able to continue his administration properly in Düsseldorf.[73]

For the democratically minded citizens these arrests were the last straw. The liberals called for a huge protest march against the oppressors on 10 January. The SPD did not want to lag behind and arranged for its own protest march to be held simultaneously. Company managements gave their employees paid leave to join the demonstration and tens of thousands of citizens marched through the city towards the railway square. At the central station the Workers' Council had established a small outpost to guard against a possible storming. As the protest marchers filled the railway square staff members of the Hotel Bristol, opposite the railway station, opened fire upon the guards. The latter returned the fire and shot into the crowd. Fourteen people were killed and twenty-five injured. The middle-class newspapers claimed that the guards shot without provocation yet there is a great deal of evidence to support the claim that the guards were shot at first. The records of the court cases have been lost but as the court procedures were covered extensively by the local newspapers an account of what happened is still possible.[74]

It was one of those trials, not uncommon for Weimar Germany, which made a mockery of any justice or legal ethics. The chief judge, Wenkenbach, dismissed all witnesses, among them many middle-class citizens, who saw the shots being fired from the hotel by telling them that their eyes must have betrayed them. When Obuch, the defender of the accused, was about to present a witness who admitted to have been shooting, the latter was dismissed as mentally ill. Imprints of shots on the clothes of the guards were discounted too.[75]

Thus, tragic as the event was it was not the one-sided murder which historians have depicted.[76] The great bulk of the workers in Düsseldorf did not blame their leaders for the tragedy and remained faithful to the USP as the election of the National Assembly on 19 January showed. Of the 90,000 votes given to the socialists in Düsseldorf, 58,000 went to the USP.[77] The other Niederrhein left-wing centres, too, had a good USP vote. In Remscheid the USP outdid the SPD by a margin of three to one.[78] In Solingen the result was closer but still favoured the USP.[79] The branches of the party in Düsseldorf, Solingen and Remscheid had put considerable efforts into the election campaign for the National Assembly, which shows that the Independent Socialists here had realised that the November Revolution had reached its limit. They had hoped for, and worked hard towards more substantial gains than were being achieved. But the Allies' occupation had silenced part of the most radical region and the cities were economically dependent upon the nation. A growing number of left-wing Independent Socialists were realising that they could not carry on with the revolution on their own.

Notwithstanding the tragedy of 10 January it was not in the USP strongholds, Düsseldorf and the Berg district, where the revolution took a violent course. This happened a few miles to the north.

Chapter 7

Revolution from below: Hamborn and the Western Ruhr

On 24 December 1918 a huge crowd marched across the river Emscher towards the mining town of Sterkrade in the west of the Ruhr. It was a grey day and although the temperature was milder than normal for Christmas the worn clothing of the marchers provided no real protection against the gusty winds which were blowing from the west. Still, the marching men, women and children, many of whom were carrying red flags, were in good spirits. The exercise and the stirring songs played by the band which led them helped to keep them warm. Shortly before noon the marchers reached the Sterkrade mine. They disarmed the guards which the local Workers' and Soldiers' Council had established at the gates, occupied the machine rooms and forced the shift to ascend. After the miners of Sterkrade had agreed to join the strike the march went on to the Hugo colliery where, in anticipation of the demonstration, the afternoon shift had already decided not to work. Finally the marchers went to the Osterfeld mine where they arrived just in time to prevent the afternoon's shift from descending. Satisfied with the result of their actions they then decided to return to their homes. They came from the Deutscher Kaiser colliery (GDK) in Hamborn and their deeds on 24 December were a result of the development of syndicalism, a new force on the German industrial scene.

By the end of 1918 few Germans outside the region would have heard of the city of Hamborn, which had become a town through the amalgamation of several parishes in 1900, and had been elevated to the status of a *Grosstadt* little more than a decade later. Between 1900 and 1914 the population of Hamborn had quadrupled to 120,000. The pace of this growth was set by the industrialist August Thyssen. The latter had bought the Deutscher Kaiser colliery in the 1880's to provide coal for his expanding steel-works at Styrum near Mülheim. In 1889 Thyssen decided to build a further steel-works, next to the coal-mines in Hamborn, which started to operate in 1891. By 1913 the seven coal-mining shafts of the Thyssen works, together with its steel-works and harbour facilities, employed close to 30,000 people. The result of such rapid industrialisation was that in terms of overcrowding, housing costs, lodging, employment instability and percentage of foreign and eastern workers, Hamborn's statistics were the worst in the Ruhr.[1] Whereas the second mining company in the city, Neumühl, is noted for having provided decent standards of housing[2]—91 per cent of its employees lived in 1–1½ storey houses with gardens and facilities for small animals—this is how a contemporary saw the Thyssen colonies:

Really, one should only see this suburb when the weather is foggy or rainy, when at least part of the most sombre impression of doleful grey is softened. This massive block of stone seems to be a city of death in which the sun's rays only serve to illuminate misery.[3]

The radical potential created by such conditions was already evident when Hamborn was the scene of some of the fiercest clashes between strikers, scabs and police during the 1912 strike.[4]

In 1912 Hamborn also became the first city in the Rhenish part of the coal region in which the syndicalists gained a footing. Among the founders of the *Freie Vereinigung der Bergarbeiter* was Heinrich Heiling, who was to lead the syndicalists during the revolution.[5] For most of the war the activities of the syndicalists quietened, but in the final weeks they were noted for their agitation[6] and their real chance came with the collapse of the old order.

The background to the history of the revolution in Hamborn and its neighbouring towns in the western Ruhr were two agreements made between the four miners' unions and the coal producers. Imminent defeat in the war belatedly softened the *Herr im Haus* standpoint of the Ruhr industrialists. A meeting of the mine owners' association held in Essen on 14 October 1918 decided to reply favourably to a letter from the unions asking for discussion between industrialists and representatives of labour.[7] The meeting took place on 18 October[8] at the building of the mine owners' association. It was attended by the leaders of coal-miners' unions (three from the *Alte Verband*, three Christians, three Poles and one representative of the Hirsch-Duncker union) and by ten representatives of the coal producers.[9] The dominance of the industrialists was shown by the fact that Hugenberg was appointed chairman without the unionists making any attempt to have one of their delegates appointed as co-chairman. The negotiations reveal that the leaders of the four unions were contented with the mine owners' recognition of their organisation and that they had decided to pursue a mild line. The industrialists agreed to implement immediately wage increases promised to the miners after the August rise in coal prices.[10] The unionists also succeeded in having the 'yellows' excluded from future meetings. But on all their other demands, for a minimum wage, for extra pay for Sunday and overtime work, and for the abolition of black lists, no progress was made.[11] Less than a month later, on 14 November, a few days after the revolution had begun, the representatives of the coal-miners' union and the mine owners met again. The latter then agreed to a reduction of working time by half an hour to eight hours, 25 per cent overtime pay on weekdays and 50 per cent on Sundays, and the introduction of a minimum wage for miners.

Again the unionists were jubilant. They claimed to have at last achieved their long-standing objectives and advised the miners to be responsible and disciplined and to work industriously so that the fatherland would not fall into disorder.[12] The mine owners too were contented. Admittedly they had been forced to make concessions, but the agreements with the unions left them in a very strong position to hold off the threats and unreasonable demands which were sure to be forthcoming from radical elements among the workforce.

It soon became evident that the satisfaction of the union leaders with their achievements was not fully shared by the miners. The claim of the Minister for Trade and Commerce to have information that the miners were expecting the introduction of a six-hour shift, a minimum wage of 15 marks and a bonus payment of three months' wages and urged the unions to curb such excessive demands.[13] Discontent with the unions' achievement showed itself soon after the publication of the second agreement. The limited reduction of working hours was attacked at a mass meeting held by the staff of the Prosper and Arenberg mines in Bottrop on 17 November.[14] Speakers pointed out that since the introduction of the eight-hour day for all industries the miners had virtually lost the advantage of shorter working hours which had been conceded to them because of the extraordinary harshness of their profession. The fact that the agreement did not even include a wage rise was sharply criticised too. Similar criticism was also voiced at meetings at other mines,[15] and it was the Hamborn miners who assumed the leadership in this challenge to the unions' policies.

Although a considerable amount of radical agitation was evident in Hamborn during the last weeks of the war, the revolution in this city occurred without major incidents. News of the revolution reached Hamborn on Friday, 8 November. On the evening of that day the miner and USP member, Pütz, of the Hamborn suburb of Marxloh called a meeting which was attended by workers and soldiers, and which decided to seize control and establish a Workers' and Soldiers' Council on Sunday, 10 November. The arrival of marines and soldiers at the Hamborn railway station in the morning superseded these plans and a Workers' and Soldiers' Council was established early on Saturday evening. It consisted of seventeen representatives from the SPD, ten from the USP and ten soldiers.[16] Although the SPD was the strongest group, the Hamborn Workers' and Soldiers' Council was to prove more radical than the average council controlled by the Majority Socialists. This was to become evident when the Council, within hours of its foundation, issued five demands calling for the immediate conclusion of an armistice, the speedy introduction of democracy at all levels of government, the eight-hour day, a National Assembly and initial steps to prepare for the socialisation of the means of production. The Council also appointed *Beigeordnete* to control the local administration and a strong security guard was established.[17]

On 13 November the syndicalist Heiling moved resolutions at three GDK shafts which demanded a 7½ hour shift.[18] Next day the outcome of the conference of 14 November between the unions and mine owners was announced and the Hamborn miners, as did some of the mine managements in the region, interpreted the term eight-hour shift more liberally than was intended. They included the full travelling time of the whole shift in the eight hours which meant in practice a reduction of the actual working time to 7½ hours. The unions pointed out, on the other hand, that the eight-hour shift was from 'bank to bank', which meant the time between the descent and ascent of the individual worker. This more conservative interpretation by the unionists caused a great deal of anger among the miners in the collieries where the shorter shift was already in operation.[19]

On 20 November, again at the instigation of Heiling,[20] the staff at all GDK shafts elected representatives who met over the next few days and agreed on a list of demands. The two main points were the introduction of a minimum wage of 20 marks a shift and a lump sum compensation payment of 600 marks for married and of 500 marks for single miners. On 23 November the four unions and the mine owners' association met for the third time. At this meeting the wage situation was also discussed for the first time and the mine owners agreed to the moderate rise of one mark per shift. This increase was far too small to satisfy the Hamborn miners who, by the end of November, submitted their own list of demands to the administration of the GDK. The latter refused these demands, referring to the recent agreements between the two sides and claiming that any further dealings had to be at the central level.[21] In response, on 3 December the Hamborn Workers' Council issued again a statement that its interpretation of the eight-hour shift was valid. The Council also arranged for a summit meeting on 4 December which was attended by the lord mayor of Hamborn, leading administrators from the neighboring towns, members of the management of the two collieries and the head of the *Alte Verband,* Sachse. The latter, supported by the mine management, attacked the miners' position and demanded a return to the course set by the unions. The meeting achieved little and on Sunday, 8 December Sachse, at the *Altmarkt* in Hamborn, undertook the difficult task of persuading the Hamborn miners that he and his colleagues knew what was best for their future, and urged moderation. His speech aroused anger and he was constantly interrupted until the chairman of the gathering asked him not to continue. Instead the miners followed the advice of Heiling and joined the GDK shafts three and seven, which had already decided to strike for their demands.[22] By the next day all GDK shafts had gone on strike and organised protest meetings and demonstrations. At 7 P.M. three USP members of the Hamborn Workers' Council, Pütz, Sackritz, and Völker, went to the management of the GDK. They warned the latter that the miners were in such a frame of mind that unless the demands were accepted by 10 A.M. 10 December violence might break out. After having checked with the AK in Münster that no troops could be sent into Hamborn, the management decided—under protest and not until it had achieved some substantial amendments[23]—to give in to the demands.[24]

The news of the victory was announced on Tuesday amidst great cheers from a crowd of about 15,000. Völker gave the main speech. 'He called upon those present to return to work', reads the report,

> and asked them to leave the meeting in an orderly fashion, [So] nobody could say that workers were loafers but would have to talk of them with respect. It would thus be the responsibility of each worker, in view of all that had been achieved, to resume work. . . .[25]

Then Heiling spoke and reminded the audience that the *Freie Vereinigung* had greatly helped to bring about the success, and that they must leave the *Alte Verband* in order to strengthen the syndicalists.[26]

The joy of the GDK miners over their achievements was short-lived. The news from Hamborn had sparked off a series of strikes at neighbouring mines where similar concessions were demanded. Thus on 13 December the unions and the *Zechenverband* met again in Essen. This time the employers agreed to a 15 per cent wage rise as from 1 January 1919. In return the unions promised to support the coal producers' demands for an increase in coal prices.[27] On the next day, encouraged by this new agreement, the management of GDK withdrew their concessions in a statement which grossly misrepresented the events of Monday, 9 November by claiming that they had signed under duress.[28] The management also demanded a return to the full eight-hour shift before the benefits of the Essen agreement were to flow on. As might have been expected on 15 December, at a series of meetings which were also addressed by the Düsseldorf syndicalist leader, Windhoff, the Hamborn miners decided to go on strike again.

On the evening of that day Hue arrived and attended a meeting between the management of GDK and the representatives of the workers. The former agreed to maintain temporarily the shorter shifts and to accept the

Essen agreement without strings, provided the miners would abandon their original claims. Votes taken at all shafts the next morning showed that the great majority of the GDK miners refused to accept this compromise and were determined to continue the strike.[29] They now also began to use traditional syndicalist tactics to strengthen the impact of their action. Over the next few days Hamborn miners marched to neighbouring collieries, which they induced, either by persuasion or by force, to join their strike. These actions reached a climax on 24 December. After having struck at the three mines in the early part of the day[30] the miners attended a massive gathering at the *Altmarkt.* Here, in a series of speeches, they strengthened their determination to continue the struggle. The meeting then dispersed although part of the crowd went to the town hall to wait for the result of another conference which was to take place at 5 P.M.[31]

The settlement of the conflict depended on this conference which, beside the normal parties, was to be attended by chief administrators including the local government president. But to the disappointment of the workers the only higher official present was the lord mayor of Hamborn. The management of the mining companies also stayed away. The record of the conference provides interesting evidence on the state of living conditions in Hamborn.[32] Two members of the Barmen Workers' Council who had come because their city's gas supply was interrupted by the strike were deeply shocked by Hamborn's poverty. They did not hesitate to back the miners' demands for a bonus which would at least allow them to buy essential clothes and pay their food bills.[33] 'It is a fact', Pütz said, '. . . that the GDK has made immense profits and that it is capable of paying the compensation. Every typist and white-collar worker has received a Christmas bonus, why should the worker miss out . . . ?'[34] The conference then listened to the report of two delegates who had been sent to Berlin to discuss the miners' claims with the government. The men had talked to Haase and Barth and reported that both had responded favourably to a lump sum bonus of 300 marks for married and 200 marks for single miners. Barth was also quoted as having promised the early socialisation of the mining industry. Moreover it was announced that Ströbel, Prussian USP Minister for the Interior, was on his way to the Ruhr to settle the conflict. The Hamborn lord mayor, Schrecker, then suggested postponement of the negotiations until Ströbel's arrival and promised to put in a word for the compensation payment. Heiling was greatly disappointed. 'Is there no way at all so we can tell the people to resume work after the holidays?' His were the last words in the minutes. Workers had stormed the conference room and the meeting was abandoned.[35] That night, which was Christmas Eve, there was rioting and looting in the city leading to damage estimated at 30,000 marks. The tense atmosphere continued over Christmas and all hopes now rested upon the intervention of Ströbel, who arrived in Hamborn on 28 December.

For the last fortnight before Christmas 1918 the Hamborn miners were not alone in their fight against the shortcomings of the unions' policies. The news that the management of the GDK had given in to the Hamborn miners led over the next few days to strikes in support of similar demands at twenty-five mines, some of which were as far east as Gelsenkirchen.[36] The wage rise of 13 December pacified the region of Gelsenkirchen/Essen but the miners closer to Hamborn in Sterkrade, Oberhausen and Bottrop remained on strike until around 20 December when they returned to work because new negotiations were promised. Here too striking miners had adopted the syndicalist tactic of spreading the strike by force if necessary.

On the morning of 28 December Ströbel arrived in Hamborn and proceeded to Mülheim where the decisive conference took place at 5 P.M. the same day.[37] The meeting was well attended. Beside Ströbel and Giesberts *(Zentrum)* from Berlin there were representatives of the government president, the lord mayors of Hamborn, Duisburg, Oberhausen and Mülheim, several mayors, leading officials of the Department of Mines *(Oberbergamt),* Hue and Sachse, the mine administration of GDK and Neumühl and finally a delegation from the striking miners. Heiling was the first to address the conference with an emotional plea to help the men. He was followed by speakers from all sides and the bargaining between the miners, supported by Ströbel, and the rest of the meeting, went on for several hours. Finally a compromise was reached which guaranteed the GDK miners an extra payment of 200 marks for married and 100 marks for single miners. There was also a child bonus of 25 marks. To ensure that similar demands were not encouraged at other collieries terms like *einmalige Abfindung* or *Gratifikation* were avoided. Instead the payment was referred to as compensation for the distressed situation which had arisen in Hamborn because of the prolonged strike.[38] There was a final argument as to whether Sachse shall be allowed to put his signature to the agreement which lasted for 1½ hours and which showed how unpopular the *Alte Verband* was becoming. The argument was not resolved until the union leader eventually agreed to withdraw his name. The result of the conference was published the next day and the compromise soon proved to be unsatisfactory to both parties. The Hamborn miners were disappointed with the outcome but they decided, no doubt exhausted by their fortnight's strike, to resume work on the following Monday. On the other hand the hopes of the mine owners and unionists that the Mülheim agreement would at last bring peace to the industry proved illusory too.

Up to now the radicalism of the coal-miners had expressed itself only in industrial action and the political climate throughout most of the western

Ruhr remained moderate. The only exception was Mülheim which, although situated in the coal belt, was geographically, as well as industrially and socially, closer to Düsseldorf and the Berg district than to the coalfields in the north. In Mülheim the Workers' and Soldiers' Council from the outset of the revolution was headed by a left-wing alliance of USP, syndicalists and Spartacists.[39] A large contingent of left-wing troops was stationed in this city who supported the radicals in the western Ruhr in encounters with the forces of the right.[40] Mülheim made headlines throughout Germany when the leading industrialists Stinnes and Thyssen were arrested there on charges of high treason and sent to Berlin.[41]

The left in Mülheim was led by a well known radical in the region, Karl Minster. After his escape to Holland in 1916, Minster's life had taken a most dramatic course. Together with Wilhelm Pieck, later president of the GDR, and Hammer, he edited in Amsterdam the weekly *Der Kampf,* which was smuggled in small numbers into Germany. On 11 December 1917 Minster, after travelling by train to the Dutch border village of Kerkrade-Roldue, was overpowered by German security agents and abducted into Germany. The Dutch government registered a mild protest in Berlin, but this did not help Minster much, for he was tried on a charge of espionage and sentenced to death. Probably because of his American citizenship, however, the sentence was reduced to life imprisonment.[42] He was freed from prison after the revolution and returned to the Rhenish-Westphalian Industrial Region where on 1 December 1918 he established the Ruhr's first communist newspaper, *Freiheit,* in Mülheim. Through this medium and by giving a series of lectures on communism during ensuing weeks Minster, together with the Essen communists, helped to accelerate the pace of political radicalisation in the western Ruhr.

But it was neither Minster's radical newspaper nor the actions of the Mülheim Workers' and Soldiers' Council which caused the rapid political radicalisation of the coal-miners. The real reason was the approach taken and the policies pursued by the administration, by the unionists and Majority Socialists, and, above all, by the press. The strikers who marched upon neighbouring mines to make their comrades join their ranks were angered at being described as destructive vandals. They were not bent on destruction or violence, even if physical pressure was used sometimes to force a shift to ascend. The emphasis on non-violence was always illustrated by a band heading the marches and although a few people might have carried guns this does not detract from the basically peaceful character of the demonstrations. They felt they were honest and industrious citizens and had no doubt that their cause was just.[43] They had been working hard and suffering severely in recent years, but they had done their duty. Now they were exhausted, their own and their children's clothing were worn out, and they were longing for a decent meal. For the services they had rendered it seemed only proper that they should receive a bonus, especially after a revolution had occurred. Had the coal-miners' unions been farsighted enough to refrain from precipitate agreements with the mine owners, had there been more administrators like the lord mayor of Hamborn who at least tried to understand the problems of the miners in his city,[44] and finally had the industrialists been willing to part with some of their war profits the process of radicalisation among the coal-miners might have been arrested before it started. But the men in power did not act responsibly. They merely reiterated their appeals to the miners to be more industrious in order to stave off the complete collapse of the German economic system. When this did not bring the men back to work the newspapers, especially the SPD press, poured scorn and hate on the 'Spartacists criminals' who were out to ruin Germany completely and introduce bolshevist anarchy. No action, including military force, was too severe to deal with the vandals, and in the latter half of December 1918 the atmosphere was filled with such hysteria that it was only a question of time before the first blood would be shed.

The first fatalities occurred on 17 December when between 1,000 and 2,000 miners from the Bottrop colliery Rheinbaben marched upon the neighbouring Möller-Schächte in Gladbeck. The moderate Workers' and Soldiers' Council in this town had occupied the mine's premises with security guards who, without warning, shot into the approaching crowd. As a result one miner was killed and several others were injured.[45] In the next few days several mine administrations and the Düsseldorf Government President Kruse asked for a contingent of troops to be sent into the region. Although the army replied that no troops were available the *Landrat* of Recklinghausen West succeeded in having the *Freikorps* Heuck move into his district. On 27 December 1918 the management of the Gute Hoffnungshütte (Oberhausen), in expectation of a syndicalist march from Hamborn, asked Heuck to send armed guards to protect the Königsberg colliery in Oberhausen. Heuck agreed and when shortly after lunch several thousand miners, as always led by a band to stress their non-violent character, arrived at Königsberg the white troops fired into the crowd. Two miners and one bystander were killed and several people badly injured, including a ten year old boy. When news of the event reached Hamborn the security guard sent two truck loads of armed men into Oberhausen where the first encounter between workers and white troops took place. There were two deaths on each side. The *Freikorps* won the skirmish and arrested fourteen of their opponents.[46] The *Volksblatt* in Bochum was pleased with the drastic action of the *Freikorps*. 'All that is needed', wrote the newpaper, 'is a small volley directed at their feet and they won't return.

VII Gutehoffnungshütte in Oberhausen

VIII 'Hammer Fritz' Krupps, Essen

The miners [themselves] have sworn to show no more mercy when a few people come and audaciously and brutally give orders [in fields which] belong to the unions'.[47]

The editors of the *Volksblatt* could scarcely have evaluated the situation more wrongly. The miners in the west were outraged and demanded that the leaders account for their actions and be replaced. The moderates in the Hamborn Workers' Council were the first to go. A demonstration in front of the Hamborn Town Hall demanded the dismissal of the Council's chairman, Arnold, and of the SPD representative, Salzmann. Four days later the SPD faction left the Workers' Council, which was now led by Sackritz, Völker, and Pütz. Heiling took charge of the security council.[48]

On 30 December the miners of the GDK Lohberg colliery in Dinslaken, who lived in a colony of the same name, dismissed the SPD and middle-class representatives of the Dinslaken Workers' Council and replaced them with USP members.[49] On 3 January Oberhausen also swung to the left. Before the shooting at Königsberg the situation here had been remarkably peaceful. Unlike Hamborn, Oberhausen had few of the elements which made for radicalism. The growth rate of the city's coal and steel industry and of its population was moderate in comparison to Hamborn. Between 1880 and 1913 the population grew from about 17,000 to 97,000.[50] Oberhausen was also noted for its large percentage of Catholic *Nahwanderer* and small percentage of eastern *Fernwanderer*. It was not until the decade before 1914 that the number of Poles rose to 9.6 per cent of the total, which was still much less than in Hamborn and Gelsenkirchen. Housing too benefited from the gradual growth rate. There were only a few *Mietskasernen* in Oberhausen and even the Polish migrants did not live in segregated blocks.[51] Not surprisingly the socialists found it difficult to gain ground. In 1908 the membership of the Christian Unions in Oberhausen was still twice as high as that of the *Alte Verband* and a rigid administration thwarted the few attempts made by the socialists to establish themselves. As late as the Reichstag election of 1912 the SPD received only one-fifth of the vote.[52]

The revolution was a quiet affair in Oberhausen too. A Workers' Council was not established there until 17 November. Its chairman was a corporal who was sent from Köln for this purpose. The Workers' Council was made up of nineteen Majority Socialists, ten Christians, four Hirsch-Duncker unionists, five public servants, two middle-class citizens and ten representatives from the USP.[53] After a month had passed without major incidents the Hamborn strike wave spread to Oberhausen and the miners of the Concordia shafts especially came out in support of their comrades in Hamborn. But it was not until the shooting at Königsberg that the peace of Oberhausen gave way to unrest. In the afternoon after the incident there

IX Shamrock mine, Herne, 1916

X Workers' meeting, Hamborn Altmarkt [? 1918]

was an angry protest meeting at the market-place, and over the next few days a great number of miners went on strike.[54] On 3 January a large crowd, headed by a band and accompanied by some soldiers, occupied the Town Hall where they declared the old Council dissolved and established a new, predominantly USP, Workers' Council.[55]

Events in the two most northern mining settlements in the Ruhr, Holsterhausen and Hervest-Dorsten, took a similar course. These two colonies were built just before World War I around the Fürst Leopold and Baldur collieries, two of the few mines which were situated to the north of the river Lippe. The combined population of the two communities by the time of the revolution was about 12,000.[56] The revolution and its aftermath here had been completely uneventful with the Workers' and Soldiers' Councils controlled by representatives of the Catholic Union and middle-class citizens.[57] In late December the miners in both collieries joined the strikes for wage increases and bonus payments. Their action was fiercely attacked in the local newspaper, the Catholic *Volkszeitung* which was printed in Dorsten, a small town on the southern bank of the river Lippe. The *Volkszeitung* article, like so many others, denounced the strikes as Spartacist destruction. The miners and their families protested on Monday, 2 January at the newspaper's office in Dorsten and demanded the retraction of the report, in particular its allegation that the strike was political.[58] The strike continued over the next few days until on 6 January the mine management agreed to compromise on the miners' demands. But this did not ease the distrust between the majority of the workers and the middle-class citizens which reached its climax when the latter—obviously in expectation of Spartacist violence—formed a citizens' guard. The workers retaliated by disarming this *Bürgerwehr* and by replacing the Workers' Councils in Holsterhausen and Hervest-Dorsten with a left-wing Council.[59]

The Workers' Council in Bottrop, which was run by Free, Catholic, and Polish unionists, narrowly escaped an attempted overthrow. Bottrop was a town made up of an agglomeration of mining colonies built around six mines. It had a population of 80,000 at the end of World War I, 35 per cent of whom were of Polish descent.[60] Bottrop was situated in the government district of Münster, politically the most backward of the three local government districts,[61] and the socialists had the greatest difficulty in establishing themselves there before the war. During the later stages of the war a USP branch was formed in Bottrop, but its following and influence at the time of the revolution was insignificant. Still from mid-December 1918 Bottrop was to become a centre of unrest in the region second only to Hamborn. The shooting at the Möllerschachte on 17 December started a series of strikes and confrontations which were to reach their climax during the civil war in February 1919.[62] The Bottrop Workers' Council tried to ease the tension by admitting two Spartacists to the Council but this did not pacify the situation.[63] On 11 January a large crowd demanded the resignation of the Council. The latter survived the challenge mainly because of the arrival of troops on 13 January, but theirs was a Pyrrhic victory.[64]

Bottrop was fortunate to escape bloodshed during occupation by government troops but the neighbouring town of Buer, which was, like Bottrop, predominantly a mining settlement, was to witness the worst of the early white excesses. Miners in Buer too had demanded the admission of Spartacists to the Workers' Council and the dismissal of the Christian Union representatives. Two days after an angry demonstration on 10 January in front of the Buer Town Hall, the old Council resigned and a new USP and Spartacist body took control. On 14 January troops arrived. One of the town's leading public servants had called for the white troops, who immediately advanced upon the Town Hall believing that it was held by armed Spartacists. The Workers' Council had left the building a few hours earlier and, by the time the *Freikorps* arrived, it was occupied solely by administrative staff. On arrival the soldiers at once opened fire. Four people were killed and scores injured. The soldiers then hurriedly left the city, scarcely escaping being mobbed.[65]

By mid-January, the communists in Mülheim, Düsseldorf and Essen felt that they were gaining ground. Still, though a few Spartacists were admitted to some of the Workers' Councils the newly founded KPD was only just beginning to set itself up in the region. The outpourings of the middle-class and SPD newspapers, which blamed Spartacists not only for all strikes and demonstrations, but also for almost every kind of crime which was committed, were altogether distorted. Sackritz and Völker in Hamborn were still chairing the USP meetings in the Hamborn suburb of Marxloh as late as 8 January 1919.[66] The Oberhausen Workers' Council, which had taken control on 3 January, wrote a strongly worded letter to the Oberhausen *General-Anzeiger* protesting 'we would like to point out to you that not all steps taken by the Workers' Council should be described as Spartacist actions . . . as . . . the Workers' Council has nothing to do with the Spartacists'.[67] The Hervest-Dorsten miners' leader Fest, a USP member, was contributing news from the colony to the Bochum *Volksblatt* for many weeks after the revolution. The following extract from a report of a mission sent to the western coal region from Remscheid depicts the situation precisely:

As we were sceptical about the reports [about the striking miners] we visited the coal region . . . talked to the miners . . . and did everything to find out about the reasons for the strike. We noticed first that there was no connection between Spartacus and the strikes. When we visited the offices of the Spartacists we noticed that they knew little about the strikes . . . they were mainly busy with setting up their new political organisation. . . . On the contrary there was lack of confidence in the unions. . . . Sachse was especially unpopular.[68]

By mid January the KPD was rapidly making ground, and the fortunes of the party certainly received an immense impetus when on 17 January almost the complete USP establishment of the western Ruhr went over to the Communists.[69] But this growing support for the extreme left was the product of the incidents of late December/early January and not their cause.

In all this turmoil in the west there was one island of peace and this was the city of Duisburg. Led by the baker Ulrich Rogg, the USP with their small following staged the revolution on the evening of 8 November and established a provisional Workers' and Soldiers' Council. The Majority Socialists, who could claim the support of most of the workers, took control on the afternoon of the next day at a public meeting in the *Burgplatz*. The speakers of the local SPD authorities seemed to have been particularly worried by a few 'half-grown youngsters', who had been 'too rowdy in the streets at night' and who should not think 'that the rule of the Workers' and Soldiers' Council meant anarchy'.[70] The records of the meetings between the Duisburg lord mayor, Jarres, and the SPD-led executive council show that Jarres was very much in control of the sittings.[71] He made all the suggestions of how to deal with daily problems, and there was never an objection, rarely a discussion. Still, even Duisburg did not altogether escape from unrest. On 11 January 1919, angered by newspaper reports and encouraged by the wave of occupations throughout Germany, a demonstration of radical workers approached the building of the *NVS* to recapture the newspaper which they claimed had been stolen from them.[72] The authorities had placed armed guards at the building who repulsed the initial attack. Injuries were sustained both by the defending police and by the demonstrators who decided to ask for support from Mülheim. Troops from Mülheim arrived in the evening whereupon the defenders decided that the odds had become too unfavourable. The workers then occupied the building for several days.[73] The occupation achieved little but it again provided the press with rich material about 'Spartacist atrocities'. Although both sides suffered injuries, the occupation of the *NVS* detracts little from the fact that the revolution in this city took place in 'an orderly fashion' *(geordnete Verhältnisse)*.[74]

By the end of the first week in January it was obvious that the Mülheim conference had failed to pacify the situation in the western Ruhr. Now the price for the over rapid industrialisation in Hamborn, Bottrop, Buer and other mining settlements was being paid. Workers in the west had left the orthodox labour movements and were beginning to challenge the industrial *status quo*. Moreover the messages from this district were spreading. The attempt to cover up the special payments to the Hamborn workers by disguising them as strike compensation was a blunder. On 30 December miners in Oberhausen also demanded the 'Hamborn awards' and went on strike. On 2 January the management of the Gute Hoffnungshütte gave in.[75] Now there was no holding back. Within a week about twenty thousand miners in and around Essen went on strike in support of extra awards similar to those given at GDK. On 9 January the mine owners made an offer of 120 marks for a married and 60 marks for a single miner.[76] The unions agreed but the offer came too late and was well below the 'Hamborn awards'. On 11 January 15 percent of the miners, more than 60,000, struck in support of additional payments. By now the gas supply in Essen and the western part of the Ruhr had dwindled to such an extent that heating, lighting and gas-cooking were restricted to a few hours a day. Indeed a total collapse of the gas supply was imminent.[77] This was the situation when, completely unexpectedly, the news spread that the Essen Workers' and Soldiers' Council had occupied the premises of the mine owners' association and of the coal syndicate and had announced the socialisation of the coal industry.

IV

The struggle for socialisation

Chapter 8

The Essen model

Between mid January and mid February 1919 the attempt of the Essen Workers' and Soldiers' Council to socialise the coal-mining industry (referred to below as the Essen model) was the centre of attention in the Ruhr and elsewhere in Germany. It was the only time between November 1918 and spring 1919 that major steps were taken to push the revolution beyond the stage of mere constitutional change. Because of its unique character the Essen model has subsequently attracted the interest of historians. Peter von Oertzen in 'Die grossen Streiks der Ruhrbergarbeiterschaft im Frühjar 1919', presents the attempt to socialise the coal-mining industry as evidence for his argument that the German November Revolution offered a 'third way' between a 'red dictatorship' and a coalition with the conservative establishment.[1] His conclusions have repeatedly been challenged,[2] most recently by Erhard Lucas who depicts the Essen model as a means of forestalling an even more radical change in Hamborn and the western Ruhr.[3] A study of the background and course of the Essen model will enable us to decide whether in fact it was a *realisierbare Konzeption*[4] or a mere diversionary tactic.

The origins of the attempted socialisation of the coal industry, notwithstanding considerable research work undertaken on the topic, have remained obscure. Von Oertzen vaguely refers to pressure from below,[5] a concept which is also found in a more recent essay.[6] Lucas goes deeper into the causes, although his emphasis upon events in Hamborn does not explain why the impetus to socialise came from Essen. A short outline of the revolution in Essen may shed light on the background of the Essen model.

'It has been the fate of Essen', wrote Hans Luther, lord mayor of the city in 1918 and later *Reichskanzler* in Weimar Germany, 'to have always lived its own peculiar life in the region, and this accounts for the unorthodoxy of the revolution in Essen'.[7] His was certainly an accurate statement. While elsewhere guards of the right-wing socialists were shooting at the left and vice versa, in Essen the hostile factions, SPD, USP and KPD, sat together in, perhaps not amiable, but at least productive co-operation. The chief employer in Essen was the Krupp works but the city was also the centre of the coal producing area and by 1918 its population of about half a million made it the largest city in the region of this study. It stretched from the river Ruhr in the south over 30 km to the suburb of Karnap in the Emscher district. If Düsseldorf stood out because of the social cleavage between its well-to-do and working-class suburbs, Essen was noted for the diverse social background of its working population which was housed in the *Mietskasernen* of the Segeroth quarter on the one extreme and the highly praised Krupp 'village' of Margaretenhöhe on the other.[8] Discrepancies in social background were mirrored in the union membership of the workers and in their voting statistics. The Centre party and the Christian Miners' Union were powerful. The support of a vast section of the workforce ensured that the *Zentrum* was, in terms of votes, the strongest political party before the war. Even in the January 1919 National Assembly election the total of the two socialist parties only just surpassed the *Zentrum* vote.[9] In 1910 the *Alte Verband* had 12,000 members, and the Christian Union 16,500. The Hirsch-Duncker union was also doing well in Essen with a membership of 3,500.[10] The division of the Essen workforce into two large sections, coal-miners and metalworkers, provided a further contrast. In the coal-mining region the metalworkers, especially those in big plants, had a conservative image. Essen was to become the centre of the *wirtschaftsfriedliche Arbeiterbewegung,*[11] the yellow unions, and Krupp with its *nationale Arbeiterverein der Kruppwerke* was the only major company at which the yellows played more than a token part in employer-employee relations.[12]

This strong competition between workers' organisations may have explained the conciliatory nature of Essen's SPD. Whereas the war elsewhere soon led to intra-party polarisation, the Essen branch of the SPD played a peculiar role between the two warring factions. The Essen party leader and editor of the *Arbeiterzeitung,* Heinrich Limbertz, was suggested as press spokesman for the left opposition at the 1916 federal conference in Berlin. His nomination was not acceptable to the opposition and, on the objection of Ledebour, Stadthagen and Gottschalk, Limbertz withdrew in favour of Bock (Leipzig).[13] Still, Limbertz voted on all matters of importance with the enlarged minority. When the breach came Limbertz remained with the majority, although the Essen party branch decided to join the USP by a margin of 121:41. Even now the political atmosphere in Essen did not become as tense as in other parts of the region. Limbertz was on the left wing of the Majority Socialists and the paper he edited was proposed by the opposition's *Mitteilungsblatt* as an alternative to the two eastern party newspapers.[14] The Essen USP on the other hand was moderate in comparison to the radical branches of the Berg district and Düsseldorf. The quiescent nature of the city's party life is perhaps best illustrated by the fact that Scheidemann, after having been booed off the stage in Solingen, had no difficulty in addressing a workers' meeting in Essen.

The revolution, too, caused no great conflict among the Essen socialists. The marines arrived at the Essen central station in the early evening of 8 November, disarmed the police and local troops and freed political prisoners. After this the overthrow of the old order was proclaimed at the city's restaurants, coffee-houses, theatres and concert halls.[15] Next day the two socialist parties and soldiers formed a Workers' and Soldiers' Council of eleven members. Although the SPD and USP were equally represented the initiative in the early stages of the revolution was with the latter. They were led by Steinhauer, USP chairman in Essen since the split, and by Fritz Baade, a medical orderly and student of medicine.[16] With the other members of the Workers' and Soldiers' Council they were confirmed in office at a mass meeting of about 100,000 people held at the Bismarckstrasse Sportsgrounds on Sunday, 10 November.[17]

The local lord mayor, Luther, immediately adapted to the new situation and as the Essen socialists took a moderate stand, Workers' and Soldiers' Council and administration soon worked together effectively in dealing with daily problems. They were joined in their efforts by representatives of the Christian workers' movement, a concession to the strength of the Catholics in Essen. The socialists also, adhering to their slogan of *Kein Bruderkampf,*[18] admitted the Spartacists to the Council.[19]

For the first few weeks the administration and Workers' and Soldiers' Council met every day at 10 A.M. The records of these meetings show that Luther's claim to have called the tune in revolutionary Essen was an overstatement.[20] Methods of dealing with food, fuel and clothing shortages, and the maintenance of law and order were fully discussed and the Workers' and Soldiers' Council made considerable contributions on these problems. For the first two months of the revolution there were virtually no incidents which disturbed the peace.[21] An important reason for this was the smooth progress of demobilisation. A great number of Krupp workers were skilled or semi-skilled labourers on temporary leave from the army, who came from all over Germany and who were most eager to leave Essen. The fact that Essen was also a coal-mining city proved a further advantage as the latter industry was in great need of staff. The Krupp works were generous enough to pay every worker willing to leave a full fortnight's pay and fares, and this encouraged many Eastern European and other foreigners to return home.[22] A fortnight after the armistice Krupp had dismissed 40,000 employees and by the end of the year there was, if anything, a shortage of labour in Essen.[23]

The Workers' and Soldiers' Council was fully responsible for the maintenance of law and order. A peoples' guard was recruited during the early days of the revolution. It originally had a strength of close to two thousand men but it had dwindled to about one-third of this number by the time of its dissolution on 21 March 1919. The Essen peoples' guard fulfilled its tasks and not only kept the peace in its own city, but also, together with the Workers' and Soldiers' Council, became an important conciliator. Essen's central situation, geographically as well as economically, ensured that the guard and the Council were often called upon to mediate. The Essen Workers' and Soldiers' Council settled differences between the administration and the local councils in Wanne, Weddau and Kray-Nord.[24] Both Council and guard worked successfully to settle a series of strikes during December and January. Their main achievement during the first two months of the revolution was the prevention of what could have become a large-scale bloodbath in Bottrop during the mid-December strikes.[25]

But what was most unusual in Essen was the Workers' and Soldiers' Council which combined SPD, USP and KPD. Essen was fortunate to have had a comparatively left-wing SPD establishment and USP leaders who held that socialists ought to avoid faction fighting as well as a communist movement which was bent on co-operation. It was the only city in the Ruhr where a small organisation of Spartacists had survived the war. They participated in the action of 8 and 9 November, and one of their leaders, König, was, from the start, admitted to the Essen Workers' and Soldiers' Council. The *Arbeiterzeitung* wrote that he worked 'satisfactorily' in that body[26] which therefore saw no reason to refuse further Spartacist representation.

> Those members who were still doubtful [were won over] by the argument that it was preferable to have the Spartacists participating in the [daily] activity with all their difficulties . . . than to allow them to pursue their own course.[27]

The role of the communists in setting up the Essen model has never been fully evaluated. Later communist writers disassociated the KPD from the project.[28] Western historians, at best, imply that the KPD was forced to join the united front by the pressure from below.[29] This is surprising, as the evidence establishes not only that the KPD closely co-operated, but that they in fact initiated the model. To begin with, the object of the Essen model, namely workers' control through a system of works, factory or mines councils, resembles closely what had been at the centre of discussion in Russia since spring 1917.[30] The Spartacists were the only German socialists who watched the situation in Russia with interest and two prominent communist personalities, Leviné and Hammer, worked in the Ruhr and had their headquarters in Essen. On 1 February the *Bergarbeiter-Zeitung* gave a short and comparatively impartial account of the history of the Essen model. The article stated, that 'on 8 January we were told in a sitting of the Essen Workers' and Soldiers' Council by the Spartacist leaders Hammer and König that the Spartacists had decided to attempt the immediate socialisation of the mines. . . . '[31] This refutes the claim that it was not until later that the communists tried to make capital out of the Essen model.[32] In March 1919 the SPD leader in Western Westphalia, Max König, told the *Zentralrat* 'that the Independents and the Majority Socialists joined the Commission [of Nine] only to prevent the Spartacists from pressing ahead [with the socialisation of industry] on their own'.[33]

The wording of the first leaflet issued after the Essen Workers' and Soldiers' Council decided to work for the speedy socialisation of the coal industry shows its Spartacist background.

> Comrades.
> The perpetual conflict between miners and supervisory personell encouraged us to give you the following message.
>
> The socialisation of the coal industry is an accomplished fact for the miners and the overwhelming majority of the German workers. Socialisation means, especially, peaceful co-operation of all employed in the industry. . . . As long as capital ruled, the capitalists succeeded in inciting those employed in production against each other. The capitalists, greedy for profits, wanted the white collar worker to harass the miner and oppress him. To get everything out of the miner, notwithstanding life or health, was the job of the clerks. To curb wages and to grind people was what the capitalist demanded from them.
>
> We know: many supervisors supported this system only reluctantly; they had to follow the orders of the exploiters if they wanted bread. [Although] they [the white-collar workers] were relentlessly exploited themselves, they were still the tool of the exploiters under the capitalist system. This too is a reason why capitalism has to be abolished in the coal mining industry and socialism introduced. . . . [34]

This was not the language of SPD and USP moderates.

Finally, when the first stage of the Essen model was completed at a conference in Essen's *Städtische Saalbau* on 13 January, the meeting passed a resolution thanking the Essen Workers' and Soldiers' Councils, especially the Spartacists in the Council, for their efforts.[35]

The unusually co-operative approach of the Essen Workers' and Soldiers' Council ensured that the communists' attempt made at the 9 January sitting of the Council did get off the ground. The strikes of early January and the general tension helped to persuade the SPD and USP delegates in favour of the action; it also staved off immediate opposition from the *Alte Verband* and the orthodox SPD. On Sunday, 10 January, the day after the Council decided to proceed with socialisation, a 'Commission of Nine for the preparation of the socialisation of the coal mining industry' was set up which consisted of three Majority Socialists, three independents and three communists. A proclamation was issued appealing to the blue- and white-collar workers of the industry to unite so that socialism could be achieved.[36] On 11 January a 'peoples' commissioner for the socialisation of the coal industry' was appointed in the person of Dr Ruben, a member of the SPD and a *Landrichter* by profession. Ruben was assisted by two deputies, Graul from the communists and Heinzel from the USP. The Workers' and Soldiers' Council then occupied the building of the mine owners' association where Ruben and his assistants took up office on the same day. Their first decrees announced general wage and price controls, and, at the same time, they issued a strongly worded appeal to return to work.

Victory of Socialism

Today our people's commissars have occupied [the offices of] the coal syndicate and the coal miners' association. This is the first step towards socialisation. The centres of capitalist exploitation and the stronghold of the mine owners [*zechenherrliche Gewalt*] are in the hands of the people . . . now there is no more reason to strike. . . . [37]

On 12 January a group of two thousand people, led by Steinhauer, marched upon the Essen Town Hall and demanded a statement of support for socialisation from the Essen lord mayor Luther. Luther had no interest in socialism, indeed he was noted for his close relations with the leaders of German heavy industry.[38] Still, the crowd seem to have been content with his evasive speech.[39] On the next day a big conference was held at the *Städtische Saalbau* in Essen. It was attended by delegates of the regions' Workers' and Soldiers' Councils, by officials from all unions and by representatives of the government. Baade gave the opening speech in which he briefly outlined the recent events. Then Hue spoke on the topic of 'socialisation'. He defended the slow progress of the Berlin government in bringing about socialism and proposed that the conference should sanction the occupation of the mine owners' association's building as well as the other steps which were taken by the Essen Workers' and Soldiers' Council over the previous days. Rather than socialising the industry, they would merely establish a control organisation for the employees. He then referred again to the deteriorating industrial situation and warned of the consequences of further losses in coal production.[40]

After Hue a series of speakers discussed the pros and cons of immediate socialisation. Some attacked the policies of the Berlin government, others urged a compromise, whilst the moderates, including SPD speakers, warned of the consequences of over-hasty socialisation. The discussion was still going on and there was little evidence of the unanimity stressed by subsequent historians when some delegates, led by Steinhauer, entered the *Saalbau*. They brought a resolution from a crowd of several thousand people which had gathered outside the building to await the result of the conference. The resolution thanked the Essen Workers' and Soldiers' Council, especially the Spartacists, for their efforts and demanded 'the immediate socialisation of the coal mining industry most urgently'. It also warned the members of the *Alte Verband* to co-operate so that their followers would not lose faith in the organisation. In return the miners agreed to resume work.[41] Despite the preceding discussion, the conference unanimously adopted the resolution. Perhaps the presence of several thousand miners outside had intimidated the moderate delegates. Not even the representatives of the Christian Union spoke against the resolution.[42] On the other hand the motion was very vague and non-committal. The conference then elected a new 'Commission of Nine', which was now made up of members from throughout the Ruhr, and laid down rules for the election of a series of councils.[43] There was no reference to the functions of these councils. Two days later a poster was distributed throughout the Ruhr which was signed by Baade (USP), König (KPD) and Limbertz (SPD) and which was marked by its mild wording. The poster gave a short account of the recent events and cautioned the miners again not to strike as the election to all the councils would ensure 'that co-determination by workers in big as well as small matters was ensured'.[44] This was different language from that employed by the Spartacists a week earlier. Not unexpectedly, the latter were becoming disillusioned and the Essen branch of the KPD criticised the appearance of König's signature on the poster of 15 January.[45] They finally decided not to withdraw their support probably because Karski, who thought that the introduction of a system of councils would be a step in the right direction, arrived in Essen during the second half of January.[46] On 15 January Rubens issued the writs for the elections to the mine councils. His statement implied that the miners, from Christians to syndicalists and even the government representatives, were united in their stand.[47] This was an extremely optimistic interpretation of the decision which was taken on 13 January. Still, a start had been made.

On 16 January a delegation made up of the Essen lord mayor, representatives of the unions, the industrialists and the Commission of Nine went to Berlin. They found that the climate in the capital was not favourable. Since the USP had left the government the Majority Socialists no longer hid behind the Socialisation Commission but were outspoken in their resistance to immediate changes in the economic *status quo.*[48] The People's Commissar for Economic Affairs, Wissel, refused to recognise the Commission of Nine and to sanction the elections to the various councils which had been proposed by the conference of 13 January. But, so as not to appear completely unco-operative, he established a board of three *Sozialisierungskommissare* consisting of a representative of the workers, the mine owners and the government respectively. The government also called for the elections of 'committees' *(Ausschüsse)* which were based not on the Essen model but on the government's December decrees on workers representation.[49]

Opposition was not confined to the SPD leadership in Berlin. In the Ruhr the moderate socialists were divided in their approach. Some Social Democrats, especially in and around Essen, genuinely supported the Essen program. The SPD chief in Western Westphalia and member of the Central Council, König, also gave his backing, at least during the early stages, and deplored the 'lamentable attitude of the government to the question'.[50] As far as the *Alte Verband* was concerned there was little support. The *Bergarbeiter-Zeitung* made no reference to the Essen model until 1 February. It then stressed that the unions did not need the coaching of the Spartacists, since they had always fought for socialism, but that, in the present economic conditions, the time was not ripe for socialisation.[51] The attitude of the other SPD newspapers in the coal region was equally lukewarm. The *VBB* in Bochum at least printed the news from Essen in a front-page article. The paper commended the government for its constructive policy towards socialism since 9 November. But 'the reorganisation of private and communal property is of course no easy task . . . increasing efforts are needed to realise it . . . and a great deal of thought is necessary to avoid mistakes'. That was why the council of people's delegates set up the socialisation commission 'which in itself is indicative already of how difficult the realisation is. . . . Everyone will therefore be surprised, when we announce today that yesterday's conference decided upon immediate socialisation . . . '.[52] The paper still preferred not to make any detailed comment on the issue. It felt obliged, however, to point out that the decision was unanimous even if it observed that general acceptance of the resolution was facilitated by the fact that 'it guaranteed the immediate end of the strike'.[53] The *WAVZ* in Dortmund did not mention the events in Essen until 15 January. It then referred to a leaflet which was 'passed around in the streets of Dortmund' and which summed up the conference of 13 January and its decisions. The only comment made was well off the mark. It criticised the current high coal prices and demanded that something should be done about them.[54] The *Arbeiterzeitung* in Essen, in an otherwise non-committal account of the meeting, nevertheless stresses that 'some speakers *justifiably* stressed that the mines were generally in a bad condition and that immediate socialisation would by no means satisfy all the miners' wishes'.[55]

On 20 January a second miners' conference met in Essen. The conference refused to accept the policies of the government and decided to uphold their own program. They compromised on the question of the three

Sozialisierungskommissare by accepting the board but insisted that the latter would have to work in conjunction with the Commission of Nine. The meeting also decided that the election for the mines' councils should be speeded up and be finished by 1 February. Subsequently, the Commission of Nine and the *Sozialisierungskommissare* at last turned to the question of control function for the councils. The *Steigerrevierrat,* the lowest body in the planned system, was 'to ensure efficient mining in regard to safety standards as well as to successful production'.[56] The *Zechenräte* were to be given 'oversight of all managerial, economic and commercial dealings of the company [Einblick in alle betrieblichen wirtschaftlichen und kaufmännischen Vorgänge des Werkes]'.[57] This was scarcely what the Spartacists envisaged when they moved for the socialisation of the coal-mining industry on 9 January. There was still no comment on the function of the *Revierräte* or the *Zentralzechenrat.* To maintain peace and without committing itself to anything, the government now also sanctioned the elections to the councils and empowered the elected representatives, 'temporarily and until further notice, to represent the workers at negotiations with the owners, the administration and the *Sozialisierungskommissare'.*[58] Over the next ten days the elections were held. There were difficulties at many mines where the managements refused to hand out the staff lists. At several collieries, for example Lohberg,[59] Scharnhorst[60] in Brackel, Viktoria in Lünen[61] and Ickern,[62] the miners literally took over. At most of the mines the elections occurred without incident but then there seems to have been embarrassing indecision as to what to do next. This is illustrated by the following comment from the Arenberg colliery in Bottrop:

> Mine councils were elected at all shafts of the Arenberg colliery. During the short period of their existence they did not ask to participate in the management, although they did demand exemption from work. This the company refused.[63]

This comment could be applied to most of the other mines too. By early February there was still no indication of whether any genuine progress towards socialisation of the industry had been made. The government had not recognised the Commission of Nine and the miners were becoming restive again. There were new strikes. On 6 February the miners met for the third time. The proceedings of this conference,[64] which illustrate the shortcomings of the Essen model, are worthy of close analysis.

The opening speaker was the SPD member of the Commission of Nine, Schmidt. He referred to the difficulties the Commission experienced[65] with the elections and to the many problems with the mine management and white-collar workers[66] which involved lengthy negotiations. Yet it was not only the mine managements which caused trouble:

It is hardly believable what some shafts understood by the term socialisation. Deputations came every day or told us by phone: 'Today we have nationalised this or that mine'. When we asked how they did it we were told: 'Well, we elected a council and dismissed this or that supervisor whereupon we encountered opposition'. Comrades, these were not exceptions: this was the case at a whole series of mines.[67]

For Schmidt dismissal of obstructive high-ranking officials had as little to do with socialism as had the selling of coal by the miners or the printing of a mine's own currency, which he claimed took place at some collieries.[68] 'Wild Socialisation' of this type and the 'wild-cat strikes' which had become prevalent again had to stop before concrete results could be achieved.[69] Schmidt admitted, however, that the confusion would cease once a legal basis for socialism had been established.[70] And this, he claimed, would soon be hammered out in Berlin. There could be no retreat, he concluded, from progress towards socialism.[71]

Schmidt was followed by more radical spokesmen. They too admitted the great state of confusion but they were more decisive on who was at fault. In one of his last public appearances before his murder by white troops, the miner Fest from Hervest-Dorsten blamed the Berlin government. 'Had the government been serious about socialisation, it would not have caused so much confusion'.[72] He also questioned Schmidt's criticism of the dismissal of management staff and other white-collar workers,[73] which he claimed was not only just but essential for socialisation. Koering, KPD member of the Commission of Nine, took the attack still further:

As you can gather from the negotiations which we just had with the government all that is left of the council system is the name. But in reality these councils are no more than the previous set up we had before the revolution [the system of security men]. If all that is left from our demands is the term 'council' and if the gentlemen from the mines [the mine owners] can go on in their ruthless way, then we may as well forget about the whole thing.[74]

The climax of the conference was reached when Limbertz attacked the Essen model as unreasonable, claiming that most miners saw co-operation with the unions as the only productive way to escape the dilemma.[75] His stand was opposed by Baade, who emphasised the need for unity, but as the meeting went on it became clear that there was little agreement on vital points. Still, the conference decided to appoint Karski as economic adviser and adopted a series of demands culminating in a resolution which called for full legal status for the Commission of Nine until 15 February. Should the government not comply, the workers would feel compelled to enter into a general strike.[76]

The proceedings of the third conference reveal clearly the absence of any concrete goals or unity. Instead vagueness and confusion reigned throughout the short history of the Essen model. It was started on the initiative of the communists and, because of the unusually co-operative approach of the Essen Workers' and Soldiers' Council, it was supported by the two other socialist parties. The Essen model reached its high water mark on 13 January when a conference decided to 'urgently socialise' the coal industry and to elect a series of councils. But this meeting did not even touch upon the most vital questions of what was the power and the function of these councils and of who owned the mines. The alleged unity behind the model in the 13 January conference must not be explained by the strength of its program but by the absence of any specific proposals. The SPD government and the majority of the local party and union leadership thwarted all attempts over the next weeks to give the model some purpose. On the other hand whilst the discussion about the proposed socialisation of the coal industry was going on, an impression was given to the miners that something was being done. This kept them quiet at a time when further unrest could have greatly embarrassed the government, hence justifying Lucas's claim that the Essen model was window dressing *(Verschleierung)*.

By February Will and Stein, who presented the resolutions of the third conference to the government, found that the political wind had changed. They had difficulty in even obtaining an interview, and when they were at last admitted by Wissel in Weimar they were quickly dealt with.[77] They were told that the Commission of Nine would not be recognised and that councils based on the Essen model were illegal. All demands passed by the third conference were rejected outright. When the delegation referred to the threat of a general strike the ministers answered by pointing to the troops assembled in the region.[78] The initial reluctance to use troops, attributed to some of the Social Democratic leaders,[79] had obviously faded away, and by February 1919 they were in a very strong position to use force in the Rhenish-Westphalian Industrial Region. The rapidity with which the old forces of the imperial army were allowed to spread again within weeks of the collapse was indeed startling and illustrates the shallowness of the social change which had been achieved. Almost from the time of the overthrow the army establishment was able to employ an organisation of spies and con-men in the region, the Kölpin office in Münster.[80] Their activities were directed against the left-wing workers' movement and by late 1919 the spy ring was so well established that it could provide white troops with address lists for their murders of radical agitators during the aftermath of the March revolution of 1920.[81] By December 1918 eight regiments and three battalions of the old imperial army, which had to leave the Rhine region because of the Allied 10 km armistice clause, had moved into the Westphalian hinterland. According to the German Army Research Institute *(Forschungsanstalt des Deutschen Heeres)* these units were not trustworthy as the revolution had caused their decay.[82] More reliable were five *Freikorps* units comprising between two and three thousand troops which had formed around the Ruhr, partly in conjunction with the regular units. Although the formation of these corps was viewed with suspicion by most workers there were few attempts to stop their rapid growth. Some of the more radical Workers' and Soldiers' Councils, for example that of Düsseldorf, did prohibit recruiting for the *Freikorps* and tried to stop their formation. The most spectacular attempt to stop the counter-revolutionary white troops occurred in Hagen, where workers, following the decision of the *Generalsoldatenrat,* tried to disarm the *Freikorps* Lichtschlag.[83] But, except for this, the protest of the left achieved little. The Majority Socialists in the region supported the *Freikorps* because, in their view, they were needed to defend Germany's eastern border against Polish incursions.

In early February the government had moved more troops into the Rhenish-Westphalian Industrial Region and the 'clearing up of the Ruhr' began at Münster, the headquarters of the AK.[84] Here von Watter was appointed successor to von Gayl on 20 January and set out immediately to continue the policy of restoring the power of the army establishment which had been pursued so successfully in Berlin. The first obstacle to be removed was the Central Soldiers' Council of the AK. Since the November Revolution this had played an important part in the region, particularly through its outspoken support for the Hamburg points, passed at the December congress, calling for the reduction of the old army and its replacement by smaller military units of people's guards.[85] The Central Soldiers' Council was swiftly dealt with. Von Watter did not even bother to fabricate the usual excuses for military intervention. Supported by students from the local university several *Freikorps* occupied Münster on 12 February and arrested the members of the Council.[86]

The news from Münster was embarrassing to the local SPD and unionists. The leaders had always refuted as left-wing propaganda reports that troops were being assembled around the region to be used against the workers. The *WAVZ* referred to the obstructionist role of the *Generalsoldatenrat* in regard to the *Freikorps* and claimed that their stand was detrimental to Germany's potato output as the troops were needed to protect the eastern borders and hence the country's food supplies.[87] The *Alte Verband* adopted a more subtle approach. They urged that the negotiators in Weimar should at least appear to achieve something. On 14 February the government abandoned its hard line and officially recognised the Commission of Nine. But the functions of the various proposed councils were restricted so as to preserve nothing of worker codetermination, not to mention worker control of the industry.[88] The unions and the government had extracted a high price for the recognition of the Commission of Nine especially as the new agreement removed the basis for the threatened general strike. But, by February 1919, events had begun to overtake the negotiations. On receiving the news about the arrest of the Central Soldiers' Council the left wing in the central and western Ruhr had presented an ultimatum to the government that military action and a general strike would be called for if the Council were not released and if the activities of the *Freikorps* were not curbed.[89] Before the government could respond news reached the region that *Freikorps* regiments had occupied Dorsten on the Lippe and its northern mining settlements.

Notwithstanding the greatly distorted reports in the subsequent investigation of the Prussian parliament,[90] the political life in Hervest-Dorsten and Holsterhausen had been stable during the months before the arrival of the white troops. After the revolution's quiet start the events of early January had polarised the communities[91] and the distrust between the middle-class white-collar workers and moderate blue-collar workers on the one hand, and the great bulk of the miners on the other, did not ease after the dismissal of the original Workers' and Soldiers' Council. On 2 January, only a few days later, the new Council reinstated SPD representatives and members of the old Council. In general, business was run without incident in the two colonies during the rest of January and early February.[92] From the little evidence available the chairman of the Hervest-Dorsten Workers' and Soldiers' Council, Feist, emerges as an honest man and industrious agitator for the cause of socialism.[93] The Essen model, too, caused no great stir in Holsterhausen or Hervest-Dorsten. As at most other collieries the miners at Fürst Leopold and Baldur completed the elections for the *Steigerrevier-* and *Zechenräte* and seemed to be waiting for more specific details.

The event which started the first civil war and general strike in the Ruhr after the war occurred on 12 February. On this day the local administrator and president of the association of colliery clerks, Kohlmann, was shot dead on his way home. The murderers, Albrecht and Arnold, were members of the Hervest-Dorsten Communist Party and of the security guard.[94] Whatever might have been the motive for their deed, its consequences were fatal. Fest immediately resigned from his post as chairman of the Workers' and Soldiers' Council and declared that no obstacle would be put into the path of the police inquiry into the murder. However, the army command in Münster and the district administration had no intention of missing a perfect chance to clear up a trouble spot. In co-operation with the *Landrat* of Recklinghausen, Bürgers, the *Freikorps* Lichtschlag, strengthened by Münster university students, moved into Recklinghausen on 13 February and started to advance upon Hervest-Dorsten the next day.[95] The official excuse, that the Workers' and Soldiers' Council there sabotaged the investigation into the Kohlmann murder, was a fabrication but no middle-class or SPD newspaper would ever question the justification for their actions. On the contrary they gave their unqualified approval.

The troops first occupied the small mining settlement of Marl and then advanced upon Dorsten. Hearing of the approaching *Freikorps,* workers in Hervest-Dorsten and Holsterhausen had obtained a small contingent of armed support (60–100 men) brought up hurriedly from Hamborn and Mülheim. The first encounter at the Dorsten railway station ended quickly in favour of the *Freikorps* but the workers were able to stop Lichtschlag at the Lippe bridges to the north of the town. The white troops now used artillery to which the workers had no reply. Supported by local high school students Lichtschlag eventually stormed the bridges, the workers' resistance weakened and the two mining settlements were occupied.[96] Now the miners and their families were the first in the Ruhr to experience what was meant when the middle-class and SPD press wrote that government troops were sent 'to expedite the triumph of justice'.[97] There were countless atrocities. Fest was murdered in the Hervest-Dorsten church where he had hidden. His wife was molested when demanding his body. Zdunek, another prominent left-wing personality in the colonies, was 'shot whilst trying to escape'. The miners' death toll altogether was forty, that of the *Freikorps* two.[98]

The news from Hervest-Dorsten made it plain to the left-wing leaders and their followers that—if they were interested in saving the revolution—they had to act immediately. This they did. At a conference held in Mülheim on 16 February attended mainly by delegates from the western Ruhr, they decided to proclaim a general strike:

> Freebooters stand at the gates of the Ruhr. Only the general strike can now prevent bloodshed. The government of Ebert and Scheidemann is not capable any more of suppressing the dictatorship of the *Freikorps* officers . . . [who] try to frustrate the socialisation of the mines with armed force.[99]

Their action has been severely criticised. Karski in the brochure of the Commission of Nine described it as an 'ill conceived step'.

> A local conference should not have forestalled the decision of the whole proletariat. Moreover, their hurried decision ensured that workers were not at all informed. The strike was announced on Monday without the distribution of even one pamphlet to inform [the miners]. It was soon to become evident that this ill-advised step was to be exploited by the leaders of the Majority Socialists.[1]

This criticism has generally been upheld by later historians.[2] But recently, Kluge has questioned the condemnation of the Mülheim conference. He denies that the Mülheim conference consisted of utopians who disliked the

Essen program and claims that in the face of the military attacks their decision was the only answer. This is a valid conclusion especially if it is considered that the major left-wing parties, USP and KPD, did not take any decisive action. The USP in particular was hamstrung by the widely ranging political views of its members.[3] Now they were forced to make the decision, either to stay with the Majority Socialists and try to save the unity of the Essen model or to make a clean break. There was no time to be wasted any more and the Mülheim conference deserves credit for having initiated a last attempt to salvage the cause of the revolution in the Ruhr.

To the SPD—and Karski was correct here—the Mülheim decision resolved at last the dilemma of being caught between the policies of their Berlin leadership and the Essen model. Now they had the chance to leave this uncomfortable position without losing face as they could place all the blame upon the Mülheim Spartacists. On 18 February the representatives of the miners met for the fourth time. It was a rowdy meeting. From the start the KPD and USP argued against the SPD about the validity of many credentials. The SPD was accused of presenting more delegates than were permitted. The latter countered by pointing to the representatives from Hagen, Remscheid and Solingen, places outside the coal region. While the argument was still going on Limbertz demanded the opportunity to make a statement. He read a motion for the conference to pass before they continued with other business.

> The conference condemns most heartily the insidious convocation of the Mülheim conference which excluded most of the delegates of the Workers' and Soldiers' Councils, the parties and the unions. [The conference] denies that those who had gathered in Mülheim had the right to speak for . . . the workers. [The conference] regards the dangerous decision of the Mülheim conference with disgust and demands that the Workers' and Soldiers' Councils [take steps against] the armed bandits. . . .[4]

According to the minutes this was as far as Limbertz got. The word 'bandits' caused an immense uproar and the rest of his statement was drowned out. It took minutes before the tumult subsided and the SPD demanded that a vote be taken. When this was refused the Majority Socialists walked out of the *Saalbau.* The KPD and USP continued with the meeting and decided to call for a general strike.[5]

At last it had become clear how the majority of the SPD regarded the Essen model. The USP and communists were now free to remedy the model's main shortcoming, its indeterminate character, by developing a concrete program for the socialisation of the coal industry. In this they were to be aided by Karski. But as neither the USP nor the communists were represented in the government their efforts were to be seriously handicapped.

Chapter 9

General strike and civil war

The general strike of February 1919 was short and violent. It lasted from 18 February to 23 February and, at its height, is said to have involved 52 per cent of the miners. In the northern parts of the eastern and central Ruhr Majority Socialist led security guards descended upon the strike with such vehemence that they drove large numbers of miners into the arms of the extreme left. In the western Ruhr, where the workers had already been radicalised, the strike resulted in a full-scale civil war in which the forces of the left, after having started from a position of considerable strength, were soon defeated. There was no co-ordination or planning of their actions. On the contrary, some of the miners and their leaders were getting cold feet, and contradictory orders were given. Hence they proved no match for the much better organised *Freikorps,* who out-manoeuvred and defeated the radicals within a few days.

The violence in the February strike has been generally attributed to the Spartacists, even by historians who normally adopt a more careful approach.[1] Evidence does not support this claim. In the western Ruhr, where the radicals were in command, no incidents of violence were associated with the strike, which was fully supported in this part of the region. This support was not based on force. In Gladbeck, for example, the administrative authorities felt compelled to publish a statement which assured miners that the troops moving through the region were to be used against Bolshevist anarchists and not against striking miners.[2] The majority of the workers in Düsseldorf decided to join the strike immediately after the Mülheim conference and they did so in opposition to the USP leadership.[3] Of course Düsseldorf was not the coal region and—to use a common German phrase—Düsseldorf was always a *rotes Pflaster.* But in Duisburg where the radicals had no chance of using force the major mines and steelworks went on strike.[4] In Hamborn and Mülheim all workers went on strike. In the latter city there was even some participation from white-collar workers.[5] In Oberhausen and Sterkrade the striking miners were joined by tramway men, railway workers and steel-workers. The local SPD newspaper *NVS* attributed most of these supporting strikes to armed picketing,[6] a claim which is contradicted by the *Oberhausener Generalanzeiger* which reported that 'one did not notice much *Streikzwang* at all'.[7]

That the *Generalanzeiger's* would have been the more truthful observation is supported by Spethmann, who diligently compiled all incidents of 'Spartacist violence'. None of these occurred in the western Ruhr.

The real area of trouble during the February strike was the SPD controlled central and eastern Ruhr. Conditions in general had been more stable there until the February strike. This was explained by the press monopoly that the SPD newspapers enjoyed among the workforce and the strong position of the SPD led Workers' and Soldiers' Councils, which dampened the influence of the radical centres. By mid-February the majority of the miners would have still been in line with SPD policies and might have agreed with the latter's firm action against the 'Spartacist picketers' who, according to the newspapers, tried to prevent the honest worker from doing his job.

Spethmann claims that in eleven cases a small number of armed picketers prevented non-striking staff from working.[8] Judging from the percentage of workers involved in the strike this was not a significant figure and even with these cases, closer analysis might vitiate Spethmann's observations.

There was one incident where it could be established with some degree of certainty that fatalities were caused by striking miners. In a confrontation between strikers and blacklegs at the Engelsburg colliery south of Bochum a hand grenade was thrown which killed two blacklegs. Although witnesses' reports at the court hearings were contradictory,[9] the miner Utgenannt was found guilty of murder and sentenced to death. The sentence was later commuted. Whether Utgenannt was affiliated with any party is not known.

At the centre of clashes between striking workers and the forces of law and order was Gelsenkirchen and its neighbouring towns. The February general strike was well supported in and around Gelsenkirchen.[10] According to the official report on the strike there[11] the local security guard was instructed to protect, by force if necessary, miners willing to work but not to interfere at collieries where the staff had decided to stop work. At Graf Bismarck 1/4 the Gelsenkirchen security guard clashed with picketers of whom three were shot dead and several more injured. The guards, who suffered no casualties, claimed to have acted in self-defence.[12] On 20 February, in anticipation of an alleged left-wing putsch, the guards arrested a series of 'leading Spartacists' and brought them to Münster where they were tried before a drumhead court martial of the thirteenth division.[13] Steinicke, a leading USP personality who was taken into custody on charges of having planned to bombard a Gelsenkirchen main street with artillery, was shot 'whilst trying to escape'. Another leading Independent Socialist, Woczek, was alleged to have placed himself under protective custody. On the next day a huge demonstration approached the Gelsenkirchen police headquarters and sent in a delegation of three men who threatened violence unless the arrested men were released. According to the official report, on leaving the building the deputation's leader, Kalnischke, produced a hand grenade to throw at the police and security guard's office. A hidden machine gun, however, was said to have prevented this and to have killed him. The exploding grenade then was said to have killed the two other delegates.[14] There ensued skirmishes with the demonstrators of whom a further five were killed and many others injured, including women and children.[15]

The USP version of the story was different. It denied that Steinicke had entertained any of the plans alleged by the authorities, and claimed he was not shot whilst trying to escape but murdered by a guard. It also declared the Thursday demonstration to have been unarmed and denied that a hand grenade was used.[16] Woczek too in a letter to the lord mayor refuted that he had gone deliberately into 'protective custody' but said he had been arrested and manhandled.[17] The courts did not investigate the validity of the official version. The fact that there were no casualties among the security guards in any of the incidents undermines the repeated claim of the Gelsenkirchen authorities that they were faced by armed Spartacist insurrection. The workers in and around Gelsenkirchen were incensed. And as subsequent elections were soon to show they had no doubt that their version of the events was the truth.[18] Similar clashes between miners who were insisting on their right to strike and authorities who depicted their acts as Spartacist insurrections occurred in Ickern, Wanne, Sodingen and Lünen.[19] All these incidents resulted in fatalities and because of their severity in crushing the strike the Majority Socialists were becoming unpopular in the central and eastern Ruhr. The rigidity of the leaders' law and order stand and the readiness of the guards to fire on demonstrations disillusioned the miners. Left-wing extremism, as has been observed already in the western Ruhr, here too was the product and not the cause of the clashes between the miners and the forces of the right. A more immediate sign of disgust with the policies of the Majority Socialists was the increase in the number of strikers. But before the February strike could reach its full momentum it was suddenly called off on 23 February. Things in the west had gone too far.

On 19 February the forces of the left were at their strongest. They controlled the whole western region with the exception of Duisburg. In addition to Düsseldorf, Remscheid, Mülheim and Hamborn, radical Workers' and Soldiers' Councils controlled Oberhausen,[20] the Wupper cities[21] and Dinslaken,[22] which were taken over in January, and Sterkrade where a communist-led Workers' and Soldiers' Council was formed on 14

February.[23] Their military power was sufficient to halt the *Freikorps* troops at the river Boye between Gladbeck and Bottrop. In the eastern Ruhr the dominance of the Majority Socialists had begun to crumble. The USP stronghold in and around Hagen had become a counterpoise to 'the kingdom of Ernst the first'[24] and the course of the general strike further eroded the SPD's base. The commanding position of the radical workers in the Ruhr, the vigour with which workers in Berlin and parts of north Germany had fought the counter-revolution during the previous month, and the strength of the uprisings in Berlin, Saxony and Munich over the next two months, indicate widespread popular support for the extreme left. Had there been more co-ordination and central leadership the workers may well have kept the *Freikorps* in check. Yet nine days later their position in the Ruhr had completely disintegrated and radical Workers' and Soldiers' Councils were overthrown.

The battle of Bottrop marked the turning point of the revolution in the Rhenish-Westphalian Industrial Region.[25] Political life in Bottrop had never fully recovered from the confrontations of December and early January. The tension between the Workers' and Soldiers' Council and the majority of the mining population did not ease after the government troops had left the town and been replaced by the *Volkswehr* made up of local police and the security guard. The troubles in Bottrop started when this guard attacked workers who were returning from the Hervest-Dorsten encounter on 16 February. Although the February strike had the support of the vast majority of the miners, the *Volkswehr* decided to occupy Prosper I and arrest the pickets. One miner was killed in the process and several more injured.[26] This led to demonstrations and further clashes until on 19 February troops sent by the Workers' and Soldiers' Councils in the south arrived.

There are few documents on the organisation of the first Ruhr 'Red Army'. Spethmann's claim that it had 5,000 members is unrealistic.[27] The local newspaper report mentioned 1,000 men and artillery which also seems too high.[28] The men were recruited in the radical strongholds Hamborn, Mülheim and Düsseldorf and it was from this triangle that the operation was also directed.[29] Armed forces from these places had already supported the establishment of a left-wing council in Sterkrade on 14 February. The Bottrop administrators were informed of the advance of large numbers of troops about midday 19 February. They contacted the *Freikorps* Gerstenberg which had stationed itself only a few kilometres to the north-west of Bottrop in Gladbeck and were assured of assistance. The authorities then placed armed guards inside the Bottrop Town Hall with instructions to hold out until support arrived. But when the red troops approached later in the afternoon it soon became obvious that the odds were heavily against the defenders. After renewed phone conversations with Gladbeck the Town Hall decided to surrender at 5:30 P.M. Whether the news of the surrender did not reach all of the occupants or whether some of them thought that agreements made with Spartacists need not be adhered to remains unclear. The fact is that as the advancing troops proceeded to occupy the building they were again fired upon. The new shooting incensed the red troops, who now slaughtered several of their captives in renewed fighting.[30] They then took over the Town Hall. On the side of the authorities fourteen had died. The death toll amongst their opponents has been estimated as high as seventy-two.[31] Over the next three days the red troops occupied the city. They had stopped the advance of the *Freikorps,* who were waiting for reinforcements on the eastern bank of the river Boye. For the time being the two sides agreed on a truce to await the result of negotiations between representatives of the strikers and the government officials at Münster and Dortmund.

With the occupation of Bottrop by left-wing troops the February general strike had reached its peak. From this point the strike and the military action rapidly collapsed. The violence of the showdown with the counter-revolution had proved too much for some of the strike leaders. They may have used radical language but when suddenly faced with the reality of bloodshed, they lost heart. The violent turn the strike took was too much for Baade the pacifist and Essen USP leader. The distorted newspaper reports about the battle of Bottrop must have disheartened Wills (USP, Mülheim) too. The two men began to negotiate with the army authorities at Münster. An agreement was reached here that the strike would be called off, that the red troops would withdraw from Bottrop and that government troops would move into Bottrop as well as into Buer.[32] The workers in the Ruhr would then surrender all their arms whereupon the government troops would move north of the river Lippe on 25 February. The result of the negotiations was put to a hastily convened conference of striking miners, who agreed to the terms only after heated discussion. The bloody course events took seemed to have discouraged many of the striking miners but not all were willing to give up. The Hamborn miners,[33] for example, were critical of the strikes' sudden collapse. The terms of the agreement were published in the regional newspapers and the wording gave the impression of genuine compromise on both sides. Indeed they were even interpreted as a left-wing victory by some of the radical newspapers. The aim of the strikers' action, the withdrawal of the government troops, had seemingly been achieved. Yet the favourable wording blurred the reality of the situation which emerged from the records of the second conference between strike leaders and military authorities held on 22 February at Essen. The workers' representatives, Will and Baade, were joined by Brass (Remscheid), Köering (Essen) and Ochel (Düsseldorf). The army was represented by von Esebeck, von Leist, von Heeringen, von Ockermann and Tittel. The aristocratic character of the army's delegation was most noticeable. The records of the proceedings show that the army representatives called the tune by demanding the disbanding of the rebellious troops. Then 'provided all arms were handed over' they declared their willingness to withdraw from Bottrop.[34]

In reality they had no intention of leaving the region at all. The formula 'provided that all arms were handed over' was impracticable. 'The only good thing about the agreement', wrote one of the military chiefs, 'was that it was impossible to keep'.[35]

Bottrop was still 'legally' occupied. The red troops left according to the treaty and on 23 February the government troops moved in. This caused great hostility among the miners and the local USP and KPD made a final effort to keep them out.[36] They proved no match for the government troops but still their reaction showed how little consultation with the rank and file Baade, Brass, Will and the others had before they called off the strike. On 23 February the AK issued a statement which claimed that notwithstanding the agreements of the previous two conferences there were numerous offences, which forced the AK 'to establish order where the leaders of the workers fail to do so'.[37] Two days later the AK issued a further proclamation which described the announcements made in the press that the command had signed a treaty to withdraw troops behind the Lippe on 27 February as completely false.

> The Generalkommando on the contrary has stated most decisively that the government troops won't be withdrawn until all points of the armistice agreement have been fully complied with, until it has convinced itself that law and order has been secured and that the workforce is able to work freely and without interference.[38]

This statement was a direct response to the outcry which had come from the left over the occupation of Sterkrade. According to the official report a small contingent of troops arrived at the Sterkrade Town Hall in the early hours of the morning and arrested the members of the left-wing Workers' and Soldiers' Council. During the procedures the KPD member Fulneczek was shot 'whilst trying to escape'. The head of the Sterkrade KPD, Thiel, was, according to the report, manhandled by an angry mob on his way to prison. The soldiers also confiscated some arms. In the afternoon members of the Hamborn security guard arrived and occupied parts of the city. They had advanced already as far as the Sterkrade railway station when Baade interfered again and succeeded in persuading the men to return to Hamborn.[39]

From now on the liberation of the Ruhr proceeded with clockwork precision. Geographically closest to Sterkrade was Oberhausen, which was occupied on 26 February although the Workers' and Soldiers' Council had surrendered all their arms.[40] The occupation took place without incidents and there was no bloodshed.[41] Before its dissolution the left-wing Council there had handled the difficult situation satisfactorily. There had been only one major incident in early February when workers of the Concordia colliery discovered considerable quantities of food, sweets and tobacco. The mine management claimed that they were to be distributed among soldiers. The staff demanded to have the stores shared among them and when the administration refused, looting broke out which eventually spread to five shops in the city centre. For the next few days the Oberhausen Workers' and Soldiers' Council declared a state of siege and restored order.[42]

Hamborn, which was more noted than any other city in the coal producing area for left-wing dissent against SPD and union policies, did not give in to government troops so easily. The latter half of January and the first half of February 1919 were comparatively quiet in Hamborn. On 19 January the miners went on strike again, in protest against an ultimatum of the city's public servants which demanded restoration of the full function of the police and which called for a new Workers' Council. The ruling Council rejected their demands, which were withdrawn on the next day, and the workers returned to their jobs.[43] During the election to the National Assembly on 19 January several polling booths in and around Hamborn were dismantled. Although the left-wing authorities disassociated themselves from the event the affair provided new material for press allegations about Bolshevist anarchy. Völker actively participated in the work on the Essen model and members of the Hamborn workforce and the security guards had fought in the battles against the *Freikorps* at Hervest-Dorsten and Bottrop. The February general strike was supported by the majority of the workforce and the guards did their bit to ensure that there was a 'general strike' in the fullest sense of the term in Hamborn.[44]

The occupation of Hamborn was a massive and well planned operation which involved the city's secretly formed *Bürgerwehr* (citizens' guard), a regiment of regular government troops stationed in Wesel, the *Freikorps* Roden and the Duisburg security guard. The attack upon the city was officially explained by the failure of the Hamborn Council to surrender arms.[45]

The conquest of Hamborn began at 2 A.M. on 27 February with an attack of the *Bürgerwehr* upon the Town Hall and the major administrative buildings. The workers in Hamborn, who had received news of the planned attack the evening before, had fortified themselves in the police headquarters and the prison. They withstood the initial onslaught but when the government troops arrived and fired with 152 mm artillery the buildings were eventually taken over by the government's forces. Fierce street fighting continued for several hours until the numerical strength and the superiority of equipment produced a victory for law and order. There were three deaths on the government side, two on that of the workers, and there were scores of injured on both sides. After the fighting numerous 'Spartacist leaders' were arrested and brought for trial to Münster. Völker, Sackritz and Heiling at first escaped but were captured eventually and sentenced to long gaol terms by an *Ausserordentliche Kriegsgericht* at Wesel. The efforts of the Hamborn lord mayor, Schrecker, to maintain peace in the city were not appreciated. He was arrested during the night of the occupation by angry members of the *Bürgerwehr,* dismissed from his office and accused of co-operating with the Spartacists.[46]

The conquest of Hamborn was greeted with great relief by the Majority Socialists and middle classes and enthusiastically reported in the local newspapers.[47] A new executive Council was formed in Hamborn immediately, which was made up of eighteen members of the SPD, the Catholic workers' movement and their union, and middle-class representatives. The executive Council was to head the city until the new city assembly met.[48] The management of the GDK celebrated the liberation of Hamborn in its own way by announcing a reduction in wages and an increase in overtime, although they had to shelve their plans because of pressure from the Executive Council.

To the outside observer who was receiving his information and knowledge from reading the daily press everything seemed to be in order again in Hamborn. But the miners of the GDK answered the occupation with a full strike which lasted for over a fortnight. This strike was accompanied by large demonstrations for the release of their comrades and access of the left to the new executive Council. They also demanded the withdrawal of the white troops and the dismantling of the *Bürgerwehr*. At one of these demonstrations troops and guards fired on the crowd injuring several people and killing two children. The promised investigation by the public prosecutor into the tragedy never eventuated.[49] In two conferences, on 10 and 11 March, the mine management and the government agreed to admit five members of the KPD to the Hamborn Executive Council. They also agreed to dismiss the *Bürgerwehr* on the date the new city assembly met, to release the prisoners unless they were found guilty of crimes and to arrange for the removal of troops, provided law and order was permanently secured.[50] The miners now returned to work.

The election to the new Workers' Council was held on 4 April 1919. Over 17,000 people voted. Ten thousand gave their vote to the communist ticket, two thousand to the SPD and five thousand to a combined middle-class/*Zentrum* ticket. It was the first time in German history that a communist ticket gained an absolute majority. A few months later a minister of the Protestant church who had been working in Hamborn during the war wrote that 'when I left Hamborn in late summer 1918 the workers almost to a man were Majority Social Democrats. . . . When I was there recently the workers to a man were Communists'; and he continued

> From the many conversations which I had with the miners I can only affirm that I was deeply touched by the sincerity [*entschlossener Ernst*] of these people. There is something in these miners which is reminiscent of the spirit of early Christianity. The people feel that they are at a turning point in history, that they are fighting a holy war . . . against the inhumanity of capitalism . . . that they once and for all want to destroy capitalism with its complete disregard for human values and . . . its cold hearted exploitation.[51]

By the time Hamborn had fallen the second radical stronghold in the coal producing region, Mülheim, had already collapsed with much less resistance when the city was finally secured for the government with the occupation by the *Freikorps* Schulz on 8 March 1919.[52] By then the Wupper cities had also been brought under the control of government troops. They were occupied at the beginning of the general strike on 19 February after a series of bloody clashes between workers and white troops in which eleven people died and twenty-seven were badly injured.[53] The presence of British troops had silenced the radicals in Solingen and Remscheid, and so by the last day in February Düsseldorf was the only place left in the whole Rhenish-Westphalian Industrial Region which was still under the control of the left.

Things in Düsseldorf had gradually gone from bad to worse since the replacement of the original Workers' Council executive on 8 January 1919.[54] Recriminations over the shooting at the Düsseldorf central railway station on 9 January continued in a series of newspaper articles which culminated in an especially aggressive article in the *Zentrum* paper *Düsseldorfer Nachrichten*.[55] To avoid further clashes between the opposing factions the Workers' Council, by a vote of 19 to 12, decided to close down the middle-class newspapers for a week.[56] They were published again on 22 January after the editors had declared their willingness to abstain in future from their 'provocative way of writing'.[57] After the shooting at the central railway the executive Council also established martial law but there were no drumhead court cases.

The difficulties and clashes with the city administration and middle classes continued. On 19 January the former Düsseldorf lord mayor, Oehler, and his wife were arrested as they were trying to cast their vote in the National Assembly elections.[58]

XI Workers' meeting, Hamborn Altmarkt [? 1918]

XII Food queue in Düsseldorf, 1917

In February the staff of the telegraph office staged a successful strike against the employment of auxiliary staff.[59] On 4 February the majority of the city's public servants, supported by moderate blue-collar workers and the business community, staged their 'general strike' against the bolshevist terror. The strike was well supported and proved a great success for the middle-class community. A special problem was created at the *Stadthauptkasse* (City Treasury Office) where public servants had locked the safe before they went on strike. As unemployment payments were due on this day, Schmittgen, to forestall a further worsening of the situation, ordered that the safe be broken into and the necessary money taken out. The incident was again readily exploited by the press as a further act of Spartacist violence in Düsseldorf.[60]

There were other problems in Düsseldorf, in the face of which the executive Council was as powerless as any other local government would have been. As already mentioned milk distribution, because of Allied interference in the supply,[61] had fallen disastrously for children, whose mortality rate in the early months of 1919 was 70 per cent higher than its peak during the last stages of the war.[62] The food situation, after temporary improvement during the first weeks of the revolution, had started to deteriorate again. Unemployment continued to grow. By mid February 1919 the Workers' Council noted with disapproval that some of the Düsseldorf factories were still producing arms and ammunition. Yet, if they wanted to avoid a further rise in unemployment they had to comply with the companies' claim that this was the only way to bridge the time until the factories had been re-tooled for peacetime production.[63] The housing shortage became more pronounced despite the efforts of the Düsseldorf Workers' Council which were more strenuous than those of any other Council in the region.[64] The armistice terms and the general difficulties in the coal region put severe strains on the city's heating and gas supply. Here too Schmittgen could claim that he worked industriously and not altogether without success to combat the problem.[65]

By mid February for the national and international press Düsseldorf was the new centre of bolshevist violence. The French newspaper *Le petit Parisienne* writes:

> The Spartacists have taken over the government in Düsseldorf and have imposed a reign of terror. The workers have no jobs, there is no more economic activity. There is no bread and no food. The people . . . have barricaded themselves in their flats and don't dare to leave them. The lord mayor was thrown into prison and maltreated . . . and nobody knows what has happened to him since.[66]

On 20 February Scheidemann gave the following speech at the National Assembly:

The flourishing German city of Düsseldorf has become a beggar over the last six weeks. On 11 January it established a drumhead court, arrested many citizens and dissolved the city's assembly. Because of the Spartacists' mismanagement the city is almost bankrupt. . . . The lord mayor Schmittgen . . . had the forest of Count Spee completely cut down in the name of socialism (Hear, Hear). That is what the Spartacists in the Ruhr really look like (Interjection: They are Independents.) . . . They are not the innocent figures which have been represented here. They are common robbers, thieves and blackmailers.[67]

This account was distorted. The forest of Count von Spee was in Ratingen and not in Düsseldorf. Moreover it was not cut down but the Ratingen Workers' Council confiscated a handful of trees to help overcome the fuel shortage.[68] If Düsseldorf was close to bankruptcy, it was not the fault of the revolution. The debts and expenditures caused by the war amounted to ninety million marks, the bills for the revolution came to about one million.[69] This was the average amount for Councils and security guards in cities of Düsseldorf's size. Still the hopelessness of the situation for the ruling left in Düsseldorf was obvious by mid February 1919. The city could not be run along revolutionary lines when the old system was virtually re-established in the rest of Germany. The provision of funds for staff and guards was a problem for left-wing councils and how much it undermined the powers of the Düsseldorf Workers' Council was shown in the following letter of the Düsseldorf treasurer to Schmittgen and the Workers' Council.

Until very recently the city of Düsseldorf enjoyed excellent credit and had no difficulty in borrowing money. But because of the present situation all non-local banks have withdrawn their credit. There are hardly any new offers of money, the few which have been made have come from . . . crooks . . . at usurious interest rates. The local banks will soon be without money too. . . . The city will have to meet obligations worth seven million marks at the end of March, four million on 10 April and seven and a half million marks in May.

This money can be obtained only by means which are economically dangerous or illegal. There are some small amounts of cash available but the terms are so humiliating . . . that I will not consider [this alternative] without the agreement of the city assembly. But the city assembly cannot meet because the elections were disturbed and the returns were destroyed . . . I am sure that Düsseldorf will receive credit again once law and order has been restored. . . . Until then . . . I resign . . . and I am sure that you won't find anyone who will take over the treasury.[70]

Under the circumstances there was no way out of this dilemma. There was talk about the formation of an independent West German republic resting on the pillars of Brunswick in the east and the Ruhr in the west.[71] The Kölpin report even claims that the left-wing leaders contacted the Allies for support.[72] But there is no evidence that this plan was seriously contemplated. Nor would their military support have been strong enough to establish such an ambitious project.

By mid February the alliance of USP and KPD had begun to crumble in Düsseldorf. The rule of the executive Council steadily deteriorated. The number of incidents during food searches and other misdemeanours committed often under the cover of the security guard increased. At a sitting of the Workers' Council on 11 February the former head of the Workers' Council, the USP member Schmitt, questioned the purpose of the executive Council's policies.[73] The USP, even its left wing, seemed to have realised that the revolution had been lost and that a completely new start should be made. The Mülheim decision on the general strike caused the final break between the two left-wing parties.[74]

During its last days revolutionary Düsseldorf resembled, on a smaller scale, the Paris of the commune of 1871. While the counter-revolutionary troops were already approaching the revolutionaries quarrelled over trivia. On 24 February the executive Council was replaced by a new body of five which was still further to the left.[75] It lasted only twenty-four hours before it was ousted by the previous Council. The latter was now faced with the choice of preparing to resist the invasion of the government troops announced in big advertisements in newspapers or of capitulating. In a long sitting the Workers' Council decided in favour of the latter alternative and to provide the persons most likely to be victimised by the white troops with one hundred marks to get out of Düsseldorf. The conference closed at 3 A.M. 28 February, just in time for the leaders to quit.[76] At sunrise Lichtschlag, supported by several other units, arrived and found no resistance.[77]

The news of the fall of Düsseldorf, the final bastion of the left, caused great jubilation. The *RWZ* in a front page article under the title of 'In liberated Düsseldorf' noticed the 'happiness among young and old people' who 'all try to give something nice to the *Freikorps*'. The newspaper is also relieved at the sight of heavy armaments which should keep the Spartacists at bay.[78] What the *RWZ* or the other middle-class newspapers did not mention was that, if ever the term *Pöbelaktionen* was appropriate it was now. Irate sections of the population supported by *Freikorps* troops brutally manhandled scores of citizens, many of whom had had nothing to do with the revolution.[79]

On 1 March the Ruhr had been 'cleaned up'. The workers had not been able to consolidate their position, instead there was now a strong right-wing backlash from the middle classes. By March 1919 the counter-revolution was well on its way.

Chapter 10

Disillusionment and defeat

The collapse of the February general strike and the overthrow of the left-wing Workers' and Soldiers' Councils was greeted by the Majority Socialists and the *Alte Verband* with great jubilation. This was shown in a series of newspaper articles which revealed a serious misjudgment of the situation. The *WAVZ* analysed the strike after its breakdown and came to the conclusion that the Spartacists could only impose their strike in regions where the SPD and the unions had failed to gain a footing before the revolution, that is, where the 'industrialists and their yellows' had still been reigning.[1] The *Bergarbeiter-Zeitung* described the February strike as a struggle between autocracy and democracy and argued that for the majority of the German workers the 'will of the people is still the supreme law'. Only a small stubborn minority wanted the 'dictatorship of the proletariat' in the bolshevist fashion but 'of course no sensible worker can be won over to autocracy'.[2]

The most popular target for the region's Majority Socialists was the 'so-called Commission of Nine'. The *Bergarbeiter-Zeitung* referred to it as the 'triumvirate of a travelling salesman, a shop assistant and a saddler'.[3] The *WAVZ* depicted the commission's arguments as twaddle. 'One would have thought', wrote the paper,

> that after the miners had rejected the taste of their kind of socialism, a socialism which is based on machine guns and hand grenades, that these heroes would have departed from the field of their inglorious activities. . . .[4]

The emphasis upon the radicals' alleged lack of ability to run the mining industry was also evident in articles directed against Karski.

> With Mr. Karski the Commission of Nine has been stranded with a scientific bigwig. After all, such an important problem as the socialisation of the coal mining industry has to be scientifically investigated . . . so the common people show their due respect. And now Mr. Karski is to solve this big problem. Who is Karski? . . . [Together with] Rosa Luxemburg and Karl Radek he forms that triumvirate which has come to us as a present from Russia and which is the intellectual backbone of the Spartacist movement with its disastrous policies. Karski, like Radek, is also a member of the Soviet government.[5]

The passing of a socialisation bill by the federal government in Weimar in March facilitated their attacks against the left-wing dissenters. Now there was concrete evidence that the road to socialism need not pass through bolshevist anarchy and the government's statement 'Der Sozialismus ist da' was given great publicity. It must remain an open question whether the leading officials in the party and union did in fact believe in what they wrote or whether they tried to give an impression of firmness. In fact they had no reason for confidence. The overall situation had seriously deteriorated by March 1919. This was not solely because of the policies of the SPD and the unions. The hopes that with the armistice the food situation would improve proved illusory. The Allies had no intention of lifting their blockade until a peace agreement had been reached and the conference at Paris was advancing very slowly. A few shipments of food had arrived[6] from abroad but these were a mere drop in the ocean. Reports from throughout the region present a very gloomy picture. The lord mayor of Gelsenkirchen writes,

> there is a serious dearth of potatoes, we have distributed [our ration of the potatoes] until the end of March but these were partly rotten or frozen and the population has consumed much of the March ration. The city has no substitutes and is not able to get potatoes from anywhere.[7]

The report pointed out that milk consumption had decreased from 45,000 litres a day during peacetime to 9,000 in the last year of the war and was still falling.[8] The meat ration in March was 300 grams to which 60 grams of various fats was added.[9] The picture was the same throughout the Ruhr and led to pleading or angry newspaper articles about the inhumanity of the blockade and to food demonstrations. The communities of the south also were now experiencing the full impact of the food shortage which their comrades in the north had been familiar with for so long. The miners of the small settlement of Kirchhörde, for example, marched in a big demonstration, headed by a band, to the countryside and searched the surrounding farms for illegal food stores.

There was a sharp increase in food prices during the early months of 1919. In June 1918 the price for potatoes was 10 pfennig, by spring 1919 it was 20.[10] *Hamstern* was more prevalent than ever. Mehlich, at a conference of Workers' and Soldiers' Council deputies to the *Landratsämter*, referred to the connection between lack of food and political radicalism.

> Without coal there is no economic regeneration but the shortage of food paralyses the arms of the worker . . . . Many thousands of working hours are lost because people go out scrounging. Yet to clamp down on them would be dangerous as households would suddenly lose a considerable amount [of their daily food].[11]

There were also occasional administrative shortcomings. For example a load of fresh food which was destined for Duisburg was moved by various departments across the Ruhr for several days. When it finally reached its destination the goods had perished.[12] The SPD leadership in Western Westphalia, especially König, tried very hard to have the government's district food department moved from Arnsberg to Dortmund. This would have been a sensible step as the Ruhr was the problem area and Arnsberg was situated a long distance away in the Westphalian hinterland.[13] The administrators in Arnsberg put up a stiff resistance to the plan and eventually succeeded in having it rejected by the Prussian government.[14]

By March 1919 the demobilisation of the German armies was completed. The soldiers' return to their jobs and family life had laid bare the full severity of the housing shortage. There had been virtually no building of houses during the war and the industry was only slowly getting on its feet again. All cities in the Ruhr reported grave overcrowding.[15] What made the problem all the more regrettable was that housing facilities would have allowed more workers to enter the understaffed coal-mining industry, and thus have relieved the pressure in regions suffering from unemployment. To attract workers the project *Siedlungsverband Ruhrgebiet* was launched later in 1919 by the government and private enterprise which was to bring an additional 100,000 workers to the Ruhr.[16] The project took a long time to make itself felt, and when it finally did so, in the late 1920s, new problems had arisen which nullified the gains.

March 1919 also saw the old guard's return to its posts in the administration. Kruse, the government president of the Düsseldorf district, took up office again in Düsseldorf after the troops had occupied this city. He told a conference of high-ranking regional administrative officials that he had not left the Rhenish capital because of a direct threat by the Spartacists after all. Instead he felt compelled to leave Düsseldorf because he could not have pursued his business properly whilst the left was in command. His return led the *Arbeiterzeitung* in Essen to a bitter not altogether justified comment

> He is back again! Lucky us, he is still alive! Even past revolutionary days did not suffice to get rid of that fossilised bureaucrat. Dr Kruse must have known what he was up to when he took to the hills during the Spartacist revolution in Düsseldorf. We thought that he had run for obvious reasons into the protective arms of the Allied troops but now we hear that he left because of official obligations. Well, lucky us, we have him back. But he may as well have stayed in Oberkassel or have run to France or Belgium, nobody would have missed him.[17]

One of the pillars of the old Prussia was the *Provinziallandtage.* They were the regional parliaments made up of representatives of the nobility, middle-class dignitaries and leading administrators. When this body met for the first time the *WAVZ* too used the occasion to display its wit.

> The meeting of the Westphalian provincial parliament has the decadent smell of reaction. The dignitaries who speak here wait for the hour . . . of the counter-revolution. The people are made increasingly aware of the need for a thorough clean up. The revolution has not fulfilled its task as yet. . . . If the dignitaries have such a strong desire for Wilhelm they may as well follow him into Holland. The earlier they go the better it will be for our people.[18]

The *Volksblatt* in Bochum directed its attack against the 'lazy government in Arnsberg' which still worked in its bureaucratic traditions 'doing its daily show of work and leaving undone what can't be done even if the people in their suffering do not know anymore what to do'.[19]

The newspapers failed to report on the further strengthening of another conservative faction, namely, the military establishment. According to the army research institute the number of 'reliable units' had grown to twelve *Freikorps* of which some had the strength of a division. In addition to these there were several smaller units.[20] To leave no doubt about their ferocious character several of the *Freikorps* included the skull in their emblem. The headquarters of the government troops in Münster did not want the role of the troops to be confined to military action but wanted the struggle against the Bolshevists fought with 'spiritual weapons too'. A full campaign directed at 'the right places such as schools, churches or clubs' about communism and its impracticability and about Bolshevist atrocities would show people what really stood behind the Spartacists.[21] Hand in hand with the growth of army units went the strengthening of the numbers of spies and agents provocateur. In a bitter speech to the National Assembly Brass complained that the '*Freikorps* during recent weeks has spread a system of con-men throughout the empire which can only be described as shameless'.[22] Brass regarded it as interesting that this 'spy business' received its biggest support from the Social Democrats who until recently had been suffering the worst from the secret police. Brass demanded that Noske 'smoke out that gangster pub in Berlin, the Eden Hotel, where the murderers of Liebknecht and Luxemburg had their domicile'. It was 'a miserable state of affairs that this society travels throughout the country and arranges *Putsches* to show the public that its existence is essential'.[23] That his was not an exaggeration is shown by the documents at the Kölpin office in Münster and by the detection of several con-men in early 1919.[24]

Having been restored to full power some assemblies and city administrations were anxious to proceed with the task of disbanding the Workers' Council. Assembly members in Oberhausen[25] and Gelsenkirchen,[26] for example, decided to cut off the funds for these institutions at their March sittings. This was not a wise step and was to lead to angry clashes with workers. Most town fathers and administrators foresaw that the gains of such action were not worth the trouble which was bound to ensue. They decided to leave the Councils with a small control and advisory function on matters of employment and food distribution until they gradually withered away over the next two or three months. Some Workers' Councils decided not to continue as mere window dressing, benevolently supported by the town fathers, and resigned.[27] The dismantling of the institutions which had been created by the revolution caused anger among the SPD. A conference of Councils' delegates in Dortmund questioned the Western Westphalian SPD leaders about their future. But as always the party leadership knew how to console. In early March the region's SPD papers printed on the front page a statement headed 'against the tyranny' by the SPD federal leadership and the party's caucus.[28] It assured the workers that there was no chance that their councils would disappear, but that they

> must be changed into works councils which will have the most important functions of controlling and codetermining the economic process. It is just as impossible for the workers to sink into political servitude again as it is for them to sink into economic servitude.

Political and economic democracy was secured for the workers provided they 'remained united on the path of democracy and rejected the tyranny of irresponsible elements'.[29]

Not surprisingly, by March 1919 the faith of the workers in the SPD and its leadership of the revolution was rapidly waning. In the west, the inability of the Majority Socialists to bring about the desired social and economic changes and the occupation of the *Freikorps* had led to further disillusionment and hatred. The hostility towards the local SPD and union representative at the colony around the GDK mine Lohberg, for example, was so great that the latter felt forced to move out of the colony.[30] Here relatives even refused to allow their deceased to be buried alongside former SPD supporters.[31] Bitterness and discontent with SPD and union policies had now spread to the eastern and southern Ruhr too. On 13 March the *WAVZ* published a letter from a subscriber which summed up well the many grievances.

> I would like to reply to your article about 'revolutionary miners' by saying that there is more discontent than . . . you might be aware of . . . because most of us say that it can not go on like this. We are always told in nice terms to work. But our government does little to ensure a fair distribution of food. Usury and black marketing are still flourishing. In Hagen, for example, there is bacon in the windows [of the butcher shops] but the workers can not afford to buy it. It is there for the loafers and the free livers. . . . Everyday 800 people die of starvation . . . and

the children who die are not the children of the rich. For how long will such injustice be permitted to go on?

Under the former government injustice was normal [but] we have a revolutionary government. . . .

The time might not be too distant when a general strike will brush away this government too . . . when there is even discontent among the miners of the southern Ruhr [then a general strike] will not be stopped.[32]

The writer must have been a popular, long-standing member of the party and union rank and file as this letter was one of the few occasions that the editors of the regional SPD papers printed such strong criticism. Although the editor in his reply admitted knowing about the fall in support, he did not carry the soul searching too far but soon found scapegoats in the Spartacists and their 'senseless strikes'[33] and in the Allied blockade.

There were plenty of storm signals for the Majority Socialists. At the elections to the local assemblies in early March the party's vote in Essen, for example, dropped from 57,000 to 35,000. This still leaves a considerable decline even if the lower turn-out of voters is allowed for. The USP on the other hand improved its position slightly, and the *Zentrum* gained considerably.[34] In Dortmund where Mehlich had forbidden the USP to field candidates the SPD's share fell well below 50 per cent, from 62,500 to 39,500. This put an end to the party's high hopes of holding the absolute majority in the city assembly. The drop was even sharper in Bochum[35] and especially pronounced in the north where the strong Polish vote stood out. In Herne, for example, the SPD's share dropped by almost half from 11,892 to 6,311, the number of USP and KPD votes rose from 285 to 1,513 and 4,503 votes were given to the Polish ticket. In Gelsenkirchen the number of SPD votes was cut to one-third.[36] Where Poles did not stand their votes went straight to the communists. In Dinslaken, for example, the KPD caught up with the SPD, their votes being 1,394 and1,390 respectively. In the neighbouring industrial settlement of Walsum the communists outscored the SPD by almost three to one.[37] By the end of March the process of disillusionment with the SPD and union policies had gone further and some of the elections to the works councils and the second congress of Workers' Councils in Berlin were landslides against the SPD. The result in Hamborn where the extreme left achieved an overall majority was nowhere repeated,[38] but in Mülheim the ticket of syndicalist and KPD scored 6,000 votes to 2,000 for the SPD. The election in Hagen and Düsseldorf showed similar results. In Essen the Majority Socialists' share fell to just over 10,000, slightly less than the USP received.[39]

The swing away from the SPD at the elections was only one element in the turbulent situation which had developed by the end of March 1919. The people in the Ruhr were caught in a vicious circle. A huge coal output was needed to get the nation back on its feet again economically and to acquire food for the starving masses. But the lack of workers, the deterioration of equipment and strikes slowed down production, although there was more coal produced than could be transported by the railways. Lack of transport and poor housing kept additional workers away who could have been brought up from the unemployment stricken steel centres in the southern Ruhr. To close the circle, lack of food and poor working conditions weakened and radicalised the miners. The situation illustrated the need for centralised, non-profit oriented planning of the Ruhr industries and questioned recent favourable interpretations of the achievements of the Demobilisation office.[40] It is true that the work of the Demobilisation office in Berlin under Koeth served above all the vested interest of big business and organised labor. But the bulk of the workforce in the Rhenish-Westphalian Industrial Region did not benefit from the alliance between the industrialists and the union leaders either during the revolution or in subsequent years.

The SPD had not offered an escape from the circle and their failure to do so forced the workers to take the initiative. They could not improve the transport system or the housing, nor could they increase food production but they could cut down on the length of their shifts. The argument for the six-hour shift was put forward from the beginning of March.[41] It was logical and straightforward. The poor food rations did not enable the men to work for more than six hours. They could produce no more in eight hours because of physical exhaustion. The six-hour system, once things were back to normal, could lead to a fourth shift—hence to a considerable increase in production. The attractive working conditions created by the six-hour shift, and perhaps the good pay, would attract the unemployed in the steel cities. Had the government followed the advice and socialised the coal industry, the six-hour shift might have provided the chance of a way out of the vicious circle. But as they had failed to do so the regional SPD could do no more than defend the views of the industrialists who of course were strongly opposed to the shortening of working hours. On 18 March the miners in Hamborn and Sterkrade decided to call off their shift after six hours.[42] Over the next ten days thirty other mines thoughout the Ruhr followed their example.[43] Their spokesmen became the new Commission of Nine.

The February general strike left the Commission of Nine in a peculiar position. They had been recognised legally by the government just before the February strike but the defection of the SPD delegates and their replacement by USP and communists as well as their involvement in the strike had finished them as far as the government was concerned. The new commission was made up of five USP representatives, (Schneider,

Karl Wagner, Wiggeshoff, Teuber and Sperling) and four communists (Konieczny, Wagner, Koering, and Schürken). It met for the first time on 5 March at the Hotel Vereinshaus in Essen. The main speaker was Karski. He gave a low-keyed, moderate speech in which he argued again that the mere nationalisation of the mines would not suffice but that the industry had to pass into the hands of the workers. Noteworthy was his statement that this socialisation process did not have to follow the Bolshevist model in Russia.[44] The chairman of the *Alte Verband* Sachse was the next speaker but he was soon drowned out by a storm of protest. Eventually the following motion was passed:

The conference, which is attended by delegates from 68 mines decides that, first, it is the intention of the revolutionary miners that the socialisation of the mines based on the confiscation of private capital, the take over of natural resources and the means of production . . . shall be carried through . . . and that, secondly, the Commission of Nine shall continue with its work.[45]

In the following weeks the Commission of Nine made itself the champion of the demand for the six-hour shift which was incorporated in its political and economic goals. Its vocal stand gave the radical left an immense impetus and a further increase in support. The Majority Socialists and unionists treated the proceedings of the Commission of Nine with disdain but their attacks were losing their impact. Allegations of Spartacist-Bolshevist machinations did not become any more convincing because of their ceaseless repetition in the press. By the end of March the socialist right had no defence against attacks from the left. The government's announcement on the socialisation of the mining industry which followed in the wake of the March clashes between workers and troops in Berlin did little to strengthen its position.

The socialisation measures of the National Assembly consisted of two laws. The first confirmed that the *Die Arbeitskraft* (labour) was the highest economic asset, guaranteed the right to work for everyone and empowered the state in general to nationalise suitable economic enterprises. The second law dealt with the coal industry. It centred around the formation of a national coal council which was to be made up of representatives of the employers, the employees, government officials and representatives of the coal-consuming community. This body was to have an advisory function only and there was no reference to nationalisation or to limiting the power of the existing mine owners. The newspapers announced the passage of the laws at Weimar in big advertisements headed *Der Sozialismus ist da* but they failed to convince the workforce. The final act of revolution in the Ruhr began at the small town of Witten which was situated on the river Ruhr 30 km south of Bochum. Like the big neighbouring cities of the

Hellweg, Witten had a centuries old tradition. But the industrialisation of the nineteenth century barely affected the town, and its population was only 37,000 by 1919. The chief sources of employment were a few small coal-mines in and around Witten and some metal industries, especially the Witten Gusstahlwerk.[46] The prelude to the Witten tragedy which sparked off the April strike was an agreement reached early in March in Duisburg between the Metalworkers' Association and the employers granting skilled workers in the industry an hourly rate of 2.30 marks. The employers in Witten seemed to have been reluctant to pass the new awards on to their workers. There were several days of negotiations until on 19 March the workers decided to stage a protest demonstration. They marched to the Town Hall where representatives of labour and industry were still sitting and—after having waited for an hour—sent a delegation to the conference room. There were some noisy scenes, a company director even had ink spilt on his clothes, and the president of the Witten Employers' Association, Kuntze, whom the workers saw as the main obstacle to their pay increase, was forced to carry the red flag for a few blocks to a workers' meeting place.[47]

On the whole the affair up to that stage had been comparatively good natured and, as the employers had at last agreed to pay the 'Duisburg rates' the incident should have been finished. But, on the next day, 20 March 1919, the *Wittener Volkszeitung* published a report in which it claimed that a 'mob led by Spartacist agitators' manhandled Kuntze, demolished the conference room, and finally forced Kuntze to carry the red flag through the streets to the accompaniment of loud booing.[48] On reading this the Witten workforce reacted angrily. They had been quiet and orderly[49] and to be classed as a 'howling mob' was too much of an insult. Again a big demonstration was organised which this time marched to the building of the *Witten Volkszeitung* and demanded an apology and the name of the author. On Monday the paper printed the apology but did not disclose the origin of the articles. Again the workers gathered and marched upon the newspaper.

This time the situation at the newspaper office was different. The police chief, recklessly, had established in front of the building a police cordon armed to the teeth with cannons and carbines, and had issued guns to 'reliable citizens'.[50] As the demonstrators approached, the local SPD representative Beltzer did his best to persuade the police to disarm. This they refused and when the workers, angered by the sight of the heavily armed policemen, tried to wrestle their arms from them the shooting started. The picture of the Witten police firing into screaming women and children urged on by the shouts of their chief, Fettköter, of 'shoot, shoot, shoot' must have been one of the most tragic of the November Revolution in the Ruhr. Eleven demonstrators were killed, thirty-two seriously injured. On the side of the law one policeman was killed in the ensuing struggle.[51] During the later part of the afternoon guards from several neighbouring towns and cities arrived, summoned to supress the 'Spartacist' troublemakers but these guards left when confronted with the reality of the situation.

The bloodbath left the local population with an immense feeling of bitterness and on the next day a conference was held at the neighbouring settlement of Annen. Scores of witnesses laid the blame for the slaughter on the police force.[52] The records of the court case, which took place four months later, confirmed the findings of the conference although the judge dismissed any evidence which went against the police force and sentenced several demonstrators to short-term gaol sentences.[53] In a protest against the events at Witten which was followed by a similar fatal incident at Castrop where eight people were killed, the majority of coal-miners in the eastern Ruhr went on strike.[54]

By the time the conference of miners' representatives called for by the Commission of Nine met in Essen on 30 March, 37,000 miners had laid down their tools. The SPD and union leaders had tried to cut the ground from under the feet of the Commission of Nine. They were able to persuade the employers to introduce the 7½ hour shift from 1 April but neither this 'good news' nor the threat of expulsion used against anyone who attended the conference made any significant impact.[55] At ten o'clock on 30 March the conference opened at the Restaurant Alt-Essen near the Essen central railway station. It was attended by 475 delegates from 195 collieries.[56] The conference was determined to call for action. It agreed to establish a new union (the *Allgemeine-Arbeiter Union*) based on the council system and to start a general strike on 1 April. The strike was to last until all of the following demands were accepted: immediate introduction of the six-hour shift, 25 per cent increase in wages, settlement of problems about the health fund system,[57] recognition of the council system, enforcement of the Hamburg points, immediate release of all political prisoners, disbandment of the *Freikorps*, economic and political intercourse with the Russian soviet government, and disarmament of police in the region and in the nation.[58]

According to the strike figures issued by the mine managements on 1 April, 158,000 miners or 36.37 per cent of the total staff followed the call for strike action.[59] The main support of the strike during the first days was in the eastern Ruhr but it quickly spread to Essen and the western Ruhr. As early as 4 April two-thirds of all miners failed to report for work. On this day, too, the representatives of the striking miners met again and passed a resolution which stripped the *Alte Verband* of its right to represent the miners.[60] Over the next week the number of strikers continued to grow and, according to the mine owners' statistics, reached its peak on 10 April when three-quarters of all miners failed to turn up for their shifts. The figures issued by the strike leaders in Essen were considerably higher and would suggest that in its peak days more than 90 per cent of the miners were on strike.[61] Probably both sides exaggerated their claims and the real figure would have been somewhere between 75 and 90 per cent. If to this is added the number of supporting strikes[62] the claim of the Hagen *Volksstimme* that a total of 800,000 employees were at times on strike in the region it seems a reasonable estimate.[63] The strike of April 1919 was a general strike in the real sense of the word.

For the first time since the November Revolution the local SPD leadership was shaken. On 29 March the *Vorwärts* editor Kuttner attempted to give a speech at the Fredenbaum in Dortmund. He was shouted off the podium and Meinberg was called for instead. Two days later the Independent Socialists had invited Graupe from Halle, a leading party personality. In front of a large audience Graupe took issue with the policies of the SPD. There was an exasperated reply from the *WAVZ*.

All we hear are demagogues insulting the Majority Socialists . . . nothing else. . . . What did the revolution of 9 November achieve? A most liberal election system, freedom of the press, the right to assembly and the eight hour day. . . . Is all this [really] nothing?[64]

The Berlin government reacted to the news from the Rhenish-Westphalian Industrial Region with great hostility. The cabinet claimed that the strikers were trying to disrupt Germany's coal production and that this would sabotage food deliveries from abroad. The actions of the striking miners would also undermine the recent improvements introduced into the coal industry such as workers representation and the socialisation of the industry. In short the pillars upon which the nation stood were threatened by the miners. 'The government has to keep our people alive and it must not leave the republic prey to the deadly terror of one province or professional group'.[65] On 1 April the government declared a 'state of siege' *(Belagerungszustand)*. It derived the authority for this decision from a Prussian law dating back to 1851 which under a state of siege 'placed the executive power into the hands of the military and which increased the penalties for certain crimes'.[66] The military officials could now issue ordinances and orders which contradicted normal laws. In addition to this an 'extreme state of siege' cancelled citizens' basic rights *(Grundrechte)* and enabled the military to forbid meetings and gatherings of groups of people in the streets and to control the press.[67] This extreme state of siege was declared at most Ruhr cities at various stages during the April strike. Many troops were moved into the region, the *Freikorps* Schulz was stationed in Mülheim, Lichtschlag moved to Essen, Bergmann into Lünen, Brigade Fricke into Haltern and Kumichel into Herne.[68] To the local SPD leaders the steps of the government and the militia proved a further embarrassment. They did not object to swift and decisive action but the mass movement of troops into the cities went too far. This was especially the case in the Eastern Ruhr where the SPD newspapers had led their readers to believe that troops were only used to suppress the small group of Spartacists. Now troops under a 'socialist government' terrorised workers who had decided by a large majority that they wanted strike action.

The presence of the militia did little to curb the strike. The Berlin government also decided to create a new office. On 7 April the editor of the Bielefeld SPD newspaper Carl Severing was appointed by Noske as commissar for the Ruhr. There were no details about the length of appointment or the functions of his office. Initially it seems that Severing's was a temporary responsibility to last until the strike was settled. On 20 April the *Arbeiterzeitung* in Essen still wrote that Severing hoped to finish with his job within three or four weeks.[69] However, the office developed into a permanent one. It was supposed to give the region a kind of central leadership, hence overcome the disadvantages of being administered by three government districts. Right from the time of his appointment the Imperial commissar *(Reichskommissar)* was surrounded by controversy and an element of superfluousness. His geographical location caused a lot of criticism when he chose Dortmund as the place to set up his office. He might have appreciated the reliable assistance of Mehlich and König and the closeness to the union establishment in Bochum. Dortmund too had until April been a comparatively quiet place. On the other hand SPD officials, the lord mayor Luther and the police chief in Essen were surprised by Severing's preferring to work at the periphery of the region. They claimed that Essen would have been much more central geographically and politically. Reliable assistance would have been available in Essen too.[70]

On taking up office Severing issued two decrees. The first enabled the local authorities to call on all male citizens between 17 and 50 to carry out emergency measures at the mines. The second established that the penalty for refusal was up to 500 marks or a year's gaol. These steps were supposed to have placed the agitators in a difficult situation as they could either obey if called upon, in which case they would have to work and thus arouse the suspicion of their comrades, or they could refuse and be speedily arrested.[71] Yet the law merely provided more grounds upon which miners could be arrested and this was taking place on the largest scale already without Severing's decrees. The representative chairman of the *Alte Verband*, Husemann, complained about the indiscriminate arrests on the part of the government troops. Slander and denunciations had often led to the arrest of reliable rank and file members friendly to the government.[72] In Dortmund Mehlich kept a tight reign. There were restrictions on protest meetings and demonstrations even before the government announced the state of siege[73] and the *WAVZ* had to repudiate accusations that the Dortmund security was a 'white guard'.[74] There were arrests in this city during the strike. Miners were charged with having violated the laws of siege, with subversive talk or with picketing. The security guard in Gelsenkirchen too earned the praise of the city's police president:

> the guard's raids into Witten, Castrop, Sodingen Langendreer have given it a good name. [The guard] controls Gelsenkirchen and surroundings. It has undertaken the many arrests which were called for by the police without hesitation.[75]

To get rid of the strike leaders was most important. It was not until 21 April that Meinberg was arrested in Dortmund[76] but elsewhere law and order was more successful. Most of the Commission of Nine were arrested on 9 April in Essen. A few escaped, among them the Bochum USP leader Teuber and his arrest at the Essen central railway station was a particularly controversial affair. Teuber, a long-standing official of the *Alte Verband*, was recognised by the union president Sachse who informed the police. The latter immediately arrested Teuber who was held on remand for six months.[77]

By now the *Freikorps* troops had few hesitations to use their arms freely. On 5 April the *Freikorps* Schulz attacked a syndicalist meeting at a restaurant in Mülheim and arrested 150. Four people were killed. When, in response, the full workforce in Mülheim went on strike Schulz arrested the local workers' council and scores of the 'ring-leaders'.[78]

On 16 April, a commission of strike leaders met at Heiligenhaus 30 km south of Essen. Shortly after the start of the meeting Lichtschlag attacked by shooting without warning into the meeting. This caused panic among the 600 people in the conference room, who tried to escape through the windows. There were deaths and injuries and Lichtschlag marched 400 delegates off to Essen.[79]

In the coal region, the *Freikorps'* actions reached their peak in Essen, which had become the centre for the strike and which witnessed numerous atrocities[80] but by the middle of April the government was slowly getting on top. This was brought about not by force but by the miners being gradually starved into submission and by considerable concessions on the part of the government. On 9 April the federal SPD Minister for Labour, Bauer, came to Essen where he met representatives from the four moderate unions and the mine owners' association at the Town Hall. The unionists spoke in favour of the six-hour shift and stressed its necessity as the only means of curbing the Spartacists. Bauer refuted their argument and maintained that to give in fully would be judged as a sign of weakness which would only aid the Spartacists. Finally, as a compromise, the seven-hour shift was suggested. This roused the hostility of the mine owners who were perturbed by neither the threat of Spartacist anarchy nor the angry demonstrations of thousands of miners outside the building and insisted that the whole industry would collapse if any more concessions were made.[81] It was only after hours of heated discussion and after Bauer and the unions agreed to further increases in coal prices that the industrialists gave in. The seven-hour shift, extra food rations for miners willing to work,[82] and the fact that some miners had been without pay over a fortnight already, slowly brought a return to work. According to Spethmann's conservative strike figures the number of miners participating fell to 71.64 per cent on 12 April and to 58.93 on 15 April, only to rise again as a consequence of the Heiligenhaus massacre. On 22 April it was still as high as 211,565, 52 per cent of the total workforce.[83]

Again the strike was widely supported by other workers. Left-wing newspapers throughout Germany pleaded for understanding of the miners' actions. The *Volksrecht* in Frankfurt wrote that 'brutality does not help coal production' and warned its readers to be critical of the distorted middle-class newspaper reports about the miners' strike.[84] The USP Berlin *Freiheit* criticised the policy of white terror and blamed the government for knowing only one way to deal with the strike: brutal force.

> The government must have spoken its last word this time because a further escalation [of suppresive measures] is hardly possible. In the whole history of the workers movement one will not find a worse example of the way the Prussian and federal government treat striking workers.[85]

In the region itself the number of workers outside the coal industry who went on sympathy strikes outnumbered the miners. For several days the strike was almost total in Essen and Mülheim, involving all steel-works and public transport employees. There was considerable support for the miners in the steel region in and around Hagen[86] and sympathy strikes in the Berg district. Hamborn and its surroundings were also a strike centre,[87] but most attention again focused upon Düsseldorf where thirty-nine civilians (including four children) and four soldiers were killed in clashes during the April strike.[88]

During the last week in April the strike in the Ruhr finally collapsed. After the Heiligenhaus incident Severing, to avoid being seen by the workers as just another agent of government authority, permitted a conference of delegates from striking mines to be held in Dortmund on 17 April 1919. Stripped of all their leaders, the conference was still well attended. It decided almost unanimously to continue with the strike until the original demands were met and until the comrades arrested were released. But the workers could not go much longer than three weeks without pay and the food restrictions of the authorities helped to weaken their resistance. On 22 April the majority was still on strike. On 26 April 100,000 miners had not turned up for work,[89] but the end was now inevitable. The strike lasted longest in Essen, which was evidence of the white troops' oppression there. When the Essen miners returned on the last day of April the strike was finally over. By May all mines and other industry were at work. The SPD government and its local representatives had defeated the last attempt to improve the lot of the Ruhr workers during the revolution of 1918/1919.

Conclusions

This study of the November Revolution in the Ruhr has been based on an analysis of the economic and social background of the various parts of the region. A long urban tradition, early industrialisation and, stemming from it, social insecurity and frequent economic hardship, led to the growth of a comparatively radical labour movement in the country to the south of the Ruhr, particularly in the metal manufacturing region around Solingen and Remscheid and the Rhenish steel centre of Düsseldorf. In these areas the local SPD adhered to the Erfurt Program based on Kautsky's interpretation of Marx's dialectical unity of theory and practice. In cities here union and party branch life flourished, directing its efforts at the practical level towards relieving immediate hardship and improving the workers' position. But theoretical discussion was always important in these branches and the lower Rhine SPD enjoyed a radical image in the pre-war years. It was because of this radical background that from the start of the war the socialists in Düsseldorf and the Berg district were in disagreement with the *Burgfrieden* policies of the party's Reichstag caucus. As the war progressed they were among the most outspoken critics of official party and union policies and the majority of their members joined the USP immediately after the split. They were ready for the revolution in November 1918 and were willing to put theory into practice. The left-wing socialists in Solingen, Remscheid and Düsseldorf did not shrink from establishing a dictatorship of the proletariat and were ready to support the transformation of Germany into a socialist society. But less than a month after the revolution, the British occupation authorities had silenced the more radical parts of the Lower Rhine. In Düsseldorf the left wing remained in command and sharply criticised the course the revolution took under the SPD leadership. Gradually more and more Independent Socialists realised that the revolution had failed and that a new start had to be made. The revolution in Düsseldorf continued under the leadership of the left-wing USP and the communists until the city was occupied by government troops at the end of February.

The history of the origin and course of the revolution in the coal region to the north of the Ruhr was more complicated. The months between November 1918 and April 1919 witnessed a conflict between two developments which had been in evidence since the beginning of industrialisation. On the one hand there was large-scale proletarianisation brought about by excessively rapid industrial growth. On the other there was a burgeoning party and union bureaucracy which became increasingly alienated from the masses. Because of the conservative semi-rural background of the coal-miners, the SPD only gained ground in this region a generation after it had done so in the Berg district. The breakthrough came eventually in the 1890s in the south-east of the coal region. The miners in and around Dortmund and Bochum began to see the SPD as the only party willing to redress their grievances. The fact that the early party and union leadership emphasised *praktische Politik* but unlike the Lower Rhine branches, refrained from overt discussion of revolutionary theory, helped the party establish itself here. During the first decade of the twentieth century the revisionists consolidated their position by establishing a union and party bureaucracy and by ousting left-wing opposition. But by the time they had taken full control social conditions in the coal region had changed. The bulk of miners were now living close to subsistence level in a belt of slums which stretched from Kamen in the north-east to Hamborn in the north-west. The 1912 strike illustrated for the first time that for many miners moderate unionism was not the answer to their problems. The war widened even further the gap between the masses and the party and union leadership.

The revolution brought this development to a head. The SPD-controlled Workers' and Soldiers' Councils throughout the coal region concentrated their efforts on returning the Ruhr to what they considered to be normal. After a month the miners began to get restless when it became increasingly doubtful whether the revolution would achieve any major social change. Large-scale unrest and strikes then began in the western Ruhr, especially in Hamborn. During January and February the miners attempted to devise a plan for the socialisation of the coal industry but the government and most of the local party and union establishment strangled all attempts to give the Essen model direction and purpose. The region's SPD leadership together with the reconstituted old authorities saw no answer other than to send in their security guards and, later, the *Freikorps*.

The radicalisation of the Ruhr workforce was completed in the two big strikes of February and April 1919. During the February strike left-wing Workers' Councils established a red army to halt the advance of the *Freikorps*, whose brutality was dreaded in the Ruhr. Notwithstanding initial successes lack of leadership caused the first workers' army in the Ruhr to collapse within a few days, and enabled the government supported troops to occupy the region. There was a last desperate effort to stem the tide of counter-revolution in April 1919 when three-quarters of a million workers in the Rhenish-Westphalian Industrial Region staged a general strike. Although the government treated the workers with immense severity, this strike lasted for a full month. By May 1919 the counter-revolution had won, but for the SPD this was a Pyrrhic victory. Police and administrative reports agree that from this date there was a mass defection from the SPD to the USP.[1] At the Reichstag election of June 1920 the socialist left outscored the revisionists in some cities by 8 or 10 to 1. When the two parties eventually re-united the majority of Ruhr workers went over to the communists.[2]

To what extent does a study of the Rhenish-Westphalian Industrial Region help to clarify some of the questions raised by the recent discussions about the German November Revolution? Although it needs to be stressed that because of its high degree of industrialisation and its intense population density the Ruhr was not an average German region, we can nevertheless detect how a considerable section of the German working population viewed the events in 1918/19. There seems to be little doubt that the majority of the working population in the Ruhr were expecting and in fact were led to believe that the November Revolution would bring more social and economic change than was finally achieved. The claim that the 'prevailing political goals were predominately reformistic and radically democratic'[3] is not really supported. In the Ruhr the left-radical groups which attempted from the beginning to push the revolution on 'vehemently towards a complete change in the political and social order'[4] were not in a minority but had considerable support from the start.[5] Even most of those parts which did not turn to radicalism immediately failed to do so not because of their rejection of the dictatorship of the proletariat but because the local leadership gave the impression that parliamentary majority was the safest and speediest way to comprehensive social and economic change.[6] When this proved an illusion the full radical potential of the workforce was soon revealed. If to this is added the further strength of the workers as was shown in the spring uprisings of Berlin, central Germany and Munich we may well question whether the extreme left numerically was little more than insignificant splinter groups (true as this may have been for the KPD in its early stages). Although the radical left did not command the support of the majority of the German working population, had the uprising between January and May 1919 been co-ordinated by a united and competent leadership they could have seriously troubled the social-democratic conservative alliance. The German November Revolution was, then, perhaps more Marxist in character than it is recently given credit for. In a sense the traditional German historians were justified in claiming that modern scholarship underrated the strength of the revolutionary socialists although to list the numerous radical socialist groupings under the general heading of 'Bolshevism' oversimplifies the varying forces which were active during the revolution at the extreme left of the political spectrum. But even had there been the hypothetical situation of, for example, a properly led and widely supported Communist Party as mentioned by GDR historians, the Western powers would have acted against the establishment of socialism in Germany. This, in addition to the fact that recent works[7] on revolutions question the feasibility of a revolution occurring in advanced industrialised countries because of the complicated mechanism of modern society undermines any claim of a radical alternative.

Where does the material assembled in the book leave the possibility of a 'third way'? As far as the council movement is concerned there is no real evidence that the *Rätesystem* played such a vital part in the political thinking of the Ruhr workforce. It is true the recognition of the *Rätesystem* was part of the platform which was advocated by the new Commission of Nine in March 1919—among and less prominent than other factors such as the socialisation of natural resources and the coal industry, recognition of the Commission of Nine, introduction of the six-hour day—but as a study of the Essen model showed the concept of *Betriebsräte* was still very vague. The *Arbeiterräte* do show rank and file participation but the predominant positions were held by established party officials and leaders either from the SPD or from the USP. Consequently the character of the councils and the policies pursued stemmed mainly from local party tradition and did not show the burgeoning influence of the rank and file. The claim that the 'councils are the expression of a new social consciousness of the workers',[8] expressing the shaken confidence of the workers in the traditional organisations and leadership and that they have to rank as 'new instruments of the political class struggle'[9] sounds exceedingly optimistic.

In the Ruhr activities of the rank and file did not follow the reformist, radically democratic council system but were anarcho-syndicalist in character.[10]

Was there the chance for substantial reforms of the army of administration? The course of events in the Rhenish-Westphalian Industrial Region bears out Ulrich Kluge's recent findings.[11] In fact the only area where one could affirm this unequivocally would be the army. At the national congress of Germany's Workers' and Soldiers' Councils held in Berlin in December 1918 a large majority passed a resolution to replace the old army system with a new *Volswehr,* a citizens army. The Workers' and Soldiers' Councils were in a position to do this. The old army was in a shambles, some of the leaders had left the country, the military power was firmly in the hands of the soldiers council, there was no threat of foreign attack, in fact the Allies would probably have supported efforts which would have muted the Germany military complex. Had it not been for Ebert's early agreement with Groener the old army, one of the most reactionary and unpleasant of Germany's traditions, would not have survived. This no doubt would have saved Weimar democracy from one enemy.

A second area in which the old conservative establishment was well embedded was in the administration. As was shown in the Ruhr the leading civil servants were quite intimidated after the revolution and in almost all places there was instant co-operation between the Workers' Councils and the bureaucracy. In cities with radical Workers' Councils like Düsseldorf the administration was taken over by socialist deputies. But this co-operation between administration and Workers' Councils did not last long enough to show whether the administration could have been democratised in the long run. And given the high state of administrative centralisation in Germany, the professional civil servants could have made major changes in the administrative apparatus very difficult.

It was time which was needed for a gradual change of the old order and perhaps this time would have been gained by a more forthright approach on the question of socialisation. The process of growing unrest and increasing radicalisation might have been stopped if the government had acted on the earlier suggestions of the socialisation commission rather than treating the commission as window dressing.[12] Plans in December 1918 circulated by the socialisation commission[13] to nationalise the coal industry immediately and then gradually other sectors of the economy should have strengthened the government's economic and consequently its political position.

All in all these plans of the socialisation committee would have brought Germany to a stage comparable perhaps to that reached in Britain under the post World War II Labour government, that is still an essentially capitalist economy but where about 25 per cent of the nation's industries are state owned. Admittedly the modern welfare state, and that of England in particular, is the centre of a great deal of criticism today, but for Germany in 1919 it would have meant that the barons of the steel and heavy industries, Baron von Thyssen, Alfred Hugenberg and associates, the men who paid Hitler, or helped to destroy democracy in Weimar Germany, would have muted. It would not have brought the welfare state to Germany but it might have lessened the impact of the economic depression in the 1920s and 1930s.

Notes

Introduction

[1] For bibliographical summary: R. Rürup, 'Problems of Revolution,' *JCH,* 1968, vol. 3, no. 4, p. 109, and most comprehensive, E. Kolb (ed.), *Vom Kaiserreich zur Weimarer Republik* (Köln, 1972), pp. 405–25.

[2] Pp. 21–39. Note also the contribution by Oenken, pp. 5–20.

[3] A. Rosenberg, *The Birth of the German Republick* (Oxford, 1931); A. Rosenberg, *A History of the German Republic* (London, 1935).

[4] A. J. Berlau, *The German Social Democratic Party 1914–1921* (New York, 1949), and R. Coper, *Failure of a Revolution* (London, 1955).

[5] For bibliography: L. Winckler, 'Die Novemberrevolution in der Geschichtsschreibung der DDR', *Geschichte in Wissenschaft und Unterricht,* 1970, vol. 21, no. 4, pp. 213–34. Quoted in A. Decker, 'Die Novemberrevolution und die Geschichtswissenschaft in der DDR,' *IWK,* 1974, vol. 10, no. 3, p. 269.

[6] Originally W. Tormin, *Zwischen Rätediktatur und sozialer Demokratie* (Düsseldorf, 1954); W. Sauer, Das Bündnis Ebert-Groener (Diss. Freie Universität Berlin, 1957); H. Schieck, Der Kampf um die deutsche Wirtschaftspolitik nach dem Novemberumsturz 1918 (Diss. Heidelberg, 1958).

[7] E. Kolb, *Die Arbeiterräte in der deutschen Innenpolitik 1918–19* (Düsseldorf, 1962); P. von Oertzen, *Betriebsräte in der November Revolution* (Düsseldorf, 1963).

[8] See ch. 8.

[9] Kolb, *Kaiserreich,* pp. 24–5.

[10] Kluge, U. *Soldatenräte und Revolution* (Göttingen, 1975); Rürup, R. (ed.) *Arbeiter-und Soldatenräte im rheinisch-westfälischen Industriegebiet* (Wuppertal, 1975).

[11] Note, for example, A. Herzfeld's review of *Vom Kaiserreich zur Republik* in *IWK,* 1974, vol. 10, Heft, 1, pp. 109–10.

[12] *IWK,* vol. 11, Heft 4, p. 541.

[13] Quoted in A. Decker, p. 290.

[14] Note e.g. Jean-Claude Gillebaud, 'The Federal German Republic: The dwarf had grown up', *The Guardian,* 1976, September 30–October 1, October 17.

[15] The term Ruhr in this study refers to the core of the Rhenish-Westphalian Industrial Region, that is to the coal-mining and steel-producing area between the rivers Ruhr and Lippe and a belt of steel manufacturing cities to the south of the river Ruhr, from Hagen in the east through Solingen and Remscheid to Düsseldorf in the west.

[16] The first major work on the period was volume 1 of H. Spethmann's *Zwölf Jahre Ruhrbergbau* (Berlin, 1928, 5 vols.). Spethmann's work was commissioned by the Ruhr industrialists and was followed by three short articles by left-wing authors. Richard Müller, revolutionary shop steward and chairman of the executive of the Berlin Workers' and Soldiers' Council, published in the second volume of his *Vom Kaiserreich zur Republik* (Wien, 1925), a short account of the revolutionary events in the Ruhr. The *Illustrierte Geschichte der deutschen Revolution* (Berlin, 1970), the official history of the KPD, also devotes a richly documented section to the Ruhr miners. The third, P. von Oertzen's 'Die Grossen Streiks der Ruhrbergarbeiterschaft im Frühjahr 1919'. *Vierteljahreschefte für Zeitgeschichte,* 1958, vol. 6, pp. 231–62, is ranked today among the masterpieces of the literature on the revolution. A political scientist rather than an historian he stresses the possibility that socialisation

based on the mines and works councils as attempted by the Essen Workers' and Soldiers' Council would have provided the answer to the social problems of the Ruhr miners. His argument has been the subject of recent discussion. E. Lucas, 'Ursachen und Verlauf der Bergarbeiterbewegung in Hamborn und im westlichen Ruhrgebiet 1918/19' in *Duisburger Forschungen* Bd. 15, 1971; M. Kluge 'Essener Sozialisierungsbewegung und Volksbewegung im rheinisch-westfälischen Industriegebiet', *IWK*, 1972, vol. 16, pp. 55–65. For discussion of the recent controversy see chap. 8. Besides these articles there have been two studies of the Free Coal Miners' Union *(Verband der Bergarbeiter Deutschlands)* [M. Dörnemann, Die Politik des Verbandes der Bergarbeiter von der Novemberrevolution 1918 bis zum Osterputsch 1921 unter besonderer Berüchsichtigung der Verhältnisse im rheinisch-westfälischen Industriegebiet (Diss. Würzburg, 1966); C. Del Tedesco, Die Bergarbeiterbewegung im Ruhrgebiet im Schlussabschnitt des ersten Weltkrieges unter besonderer Berücksichtigung der Politik des Verbandes der Bergarbeiter Deutschlands (M.A. Thesis, Marburg, 1971)], an essay on the overthrow of the old regime in the Rhineland, H. Metzmacher, 'Novemberumsturz 1918 in der Rheinprovinz', *Annalen des Historischen Vereins für den Niederrhein,* 1967, vol. 168/69, pp. 135–265, and the East German dissertation by H. Walther and D. Engelmann on the development of left-wing extremism in the Ruhr during the war and the revolution. (H. Walther and D. Engelmann, Zur Linksentwicklung der Arbeiterbewegung im Rhein-Ruhrgebit unter besonderer Berücksichtigung der Herausbildung der USPD und der Entwicklung ihres linken Flügels vom Ausbruch des 1.Weltkrieges bis zum Heidelberger Parteitag der KPD und dem Leipziger Parteitag der USPD. 3 vol., Diss. Leipzig, 1965). This thesis is based exclusively on documents of the East German archives, of which extensive use is made. But with no access to the local archives (p. 15) the study is limited, especially as far as the period November 1918 to April 1919 is concerned.

[17] R. Rürup *Arbeiter und Soldatenräte;* J. Reulecke, *Arbeiterbewegung an Rhein und Ruhr* (Wuppertal 1975).

[18] E. Lucas, *Ursachen und Verlauf der Bergarbeiterbewegung*. E. Lucas, *Marzrevolution 1920* 2 vols., Frankfurt/Main 1973/74. E. Lucas and Claus Del Tedesco,: 'Zur Bergarbeiterbewegung in Hamborn 1918/19' in *Duisburger Forschungen,* Bd 22, 1975, S141–168. E. Lucas, *Arbeiterradikalismes; Zwei Formen von Radikalismus in der deutschen Arbeiterbewegung* (Frankfurt, 1976).

[19] A. Mitchell, *Revolution in Bavaria, 1918–1919: The Eisner Regime and the Soviet Republic* (Princeton, 1965); R. Comfort, *Revolutionary Hamburg: Labour Politics in the Early Weimar Republic* (Stanford, 1966).

[20] There is a short sub chapter on the German strike movement in David Morgan, *The Socialist Left and the German Revolution* (Cornell, 1975), pp. 222–29.

[21] Note for example R. Wheeler 'Zur sozialen Struktur der Arbeiterbewegung am Anfang der Weimarer Republik. Einige methodologische Bemerkungen' in H. Mommsen, D. Petzina, B. Weisbrod (eds.) *Industrielles System und politische Entwicklung in der Weimarer Republik* (Düsseldorf 1974) pp. 179–89. Also H. Poor, 'City versus country: Urban Change and Development in the Weimar Republic a Preliminary Report', pp. 111–27. For a recent regional study: Laurence Schofer, *The Formation of a Modern Labor Force. Upper Silesia 1865–1914* (Berkeley, 1975).

Chapter 1

[1] On the history of industrialisation: N. J. G. Pounds, *The Ruhr* (London, 1948); H. Spethmann, *Das Ruhrgebiet im Wechselspiel von Land und Leuten* (Berlin, 1933), vol. 2.

[2] W. Köllmann, 'Industrialisierung, Binnenwanderung und soziale Frage', *VfSW*, 1959, vol. 46, pp. 45–70.

[3] Name for the ancient road which, situated in a belt of open fertile country, crossed the Ruhr about halfway between the rivers Ruhr and Emscher.

[4] Pounds, pp. 61, 81.

[5] Pounds, pp. 100–2; Spethmann, *Ruhrgebiet,* p. 564; K. Hartl, *Die wirtschaftliche und soziale Entwicklung des Landkreises Recklinghausen* (München, 1909), pp. 152–3.

[6] Pounds, p. 107; Spethmann, pp. 464–76.

[7] R. Blum, 'Hamborn am Rhein' (Diss., Köln, 1933), pp. 17–18. Quoted in Pounds, p. 133.

[8] Pounds, pp. 117–20.

[9] Spethmann, *Ruhrgebiet*, p. 548.

[10] On migration: W. Brepohl, *Der Aufbau des Ruhrvolkes* (Recklinghausen, 1948) and *Industrievolk Ruhrgebiet* (Tübingen, 1957). Also W. Köllmann, 'Binnenwanderung und Bevölkerungsstruktur der Ruhrgebietsgrosstädte im Jahre 1907', *Soziale Welt*, 1958, parts 3–4, pp. 219–33.

[11] For 1850 figures: Pounds, p. 90; for 1875: *Statistik des Deutschen Reichs*, vol. 57 (old series); for 1910: ibid., vol. 240, I.

[12] V. Wedelstadt, *Die geschichtliche Entwicklung und wirtschaftliche Bedeutung der Stadt Gelsenkirchen* (Berlin, 1927), p. 24. Quoted in Köllmann, 'Industrialisierung', p. 46.

[13] Spethmann, *Ruhrgebiet*, p. 559.

[14] Köllmann, 'Grosstädte', pp. 229, 231.

[15] Figures taken from *Statistik des Deutschen Reichs*, vol. 217.

[16] E. Jüngst, *Festschrift zur Feier des 50 jährigen Bestehens des Vereins für die Bergbaulichen Interessen im Oberbergamtsbezirk Dortmund* (Essen, 1908), p. 109.

[17] On the following in addition to the works by Brepohl: H. G. Kirchhoff, *Die Staatliche Sozialpolitik im Ruhrbergbau 1871–1914* (Köln, 1958) and H. Koch, *Die Bergarbeiterbewegung im Ruhrgebiet in der Zeit Wilhelm des Zweiten* (Düsseldorf, 1954).

[18] Koch, pp. 13–14.

[19] These were abolished during Napoleon's occupation; Kirchhoff, p. 9.

[20] Brepohl, *Aufbau*, pp. 66–7.

[21] Individual contractual agreement.

[22] Kirchhoff, pp. 13–14.

[23] Koch, pp. 27–30.

[24] L. Pieper, *Die Lage der Bergarbeiter* (Berlin, 1903), p. 38.

[25] Of the numerous works on the miners' health: Verband der Bergarbeiter, *Bergarbeiterleiden, Massengräber, Radbod* (Bochum, 1909). Also the work of the Catholic unionist H. Imbusch, *Arbeitsverhältnis und Arbeiterorganisation im Deutschen Bergbau* (München, 1909) or his colleague from the Free Union O. Hue, *Die Bergarbeiter* (Stuttgart, 1910), 2 vols.

[26] H. Möller, 'Einige Argumente für die Verstaatlichung des Bergbaus', *Neue Zeit*, 1900/01, vol. 19(2), pp. 48–51. Also A. Brust, 'Der Bergarbeiterstreik im Ruhrrevier', *AfSS*, 1904/5, vol. 20, p. 496.

[27] O. Hue, 'Fünfzehn Jahre Bergarbeiterschutz in Deutschland', *Neue Zeit*, 1901/2, vol. 20(1), pp. 112–16.

[28] Imbusch, pp. 136–9.

[29] O. Hue, 'Ist die Wurmkrankheit ausgetilgt?', *Neue Zeit*, 1904/5, vol. 23(1), pp. 211–16.

[30] O. Hue, '15 Jahre Bergarbeiterschutz in Deutschland', *Neue Zeit*, 1901/2, vol. 20(1), p. 114. Also Imbusch, p. 135.

[31] Koch, p. 83.

[32] Vorstand des Verbandes der Bergarbeiter Deutschlands, *Bergarbeiterleiden in Deutschland* (Bochum, 1909), pp. 18–30.

[33] The two major mine disasters before the war occurred at the colliery Karolinenglück near Gelsenkirchen in 1898 when 116 people were killed and at Radbod close to Dortmund which took the lives of 344 people in 1908. Both catastrophes were followed—in vain—by a great public outcry for reform and more state control.

[34] O. Hue, 'Bergleute und der Preussische Landtag', *Neue Zeit*, 1905/6, vol. 24(1), p. 608.

[35] Ibid., p. 617. See also *Bergarbeiterleiden*, pp. 13–18; Pieper, p. 193. Of the many documents on primary material: File of the *Hörder-Berg-und Hüttenverein*, STAM, Reg. Arnsberg, I, 1525. For complaints: STAM, OBA, 249 or ZStA, M'burg, VII,3, Nr.6, Adh.2, vol. 2.

[36] O. Hue, 'Bergleute', p. 608.

[37] Ibid.

[38] Brust, 'Bergarbeiterstreik', p. 494.

[39] Imbusch, pp. 124–7; Pieper, chs. 4 and 5.

[40] Pieper, pp. 93–6.

[41] Kirchhoff, pp. 98–9.

[42] G. A. Ritter, *Die Arbeiterbewegung im Wilhelminischen Reich* (Berlin, 1959), pp. 34–6.

[43] Kirchhoff, p. 112.

[44] Ibid., pp. 154–9

[45] Ritter, pp. 22–3.

[46] *Jahr und Handbuch des Deutschen Metallarbeiterverbandes, 1913–1918,* p. 158.

[47] H. Croon and K. Utermann, *Zeche und Gemeinde* (Tübingen, 1958), pp. 111–14.

[48] On working conditions in the metal industry: *Jahrbuch DMV,* pp. 162–3; *Die Arbeitszeiten in der Metallindustrie* (Stuttgart, 1911); *Stenographische Berichte über die Verhandlungen des Deutschen Reichstages,* vol. 268, pp. 6476–513; W. Düwell, 'Aus dem Reiche der rheinisch-westfälischen Eisen und Stahlkönige', *Neue Zeit,* 1904/5, vol. 23(1), pp. 68–75.

[49] DMV, *Arbeitszeiten,* pp. 5, 7.

[50] *Stenographische Berichte,* p. 6488.

[51] Ibid.

[52] Ibid., p. 6490.

[53] Ibid., p. 6487.

[54] Düwell, 'Aus dem Reich', p. 75.

[55] Ibid.

[56] *Stenographische Berichte,* p. 6493.

[57] Ibid., p. 6490.

[58] Ibid., p. 6512.

[59] There were two major series of publication by middle-class reformers: *Schmoller's Jahrbuch* and the *AfSS.* See also the articles of F. Naumann, in vol. 3 of his *Werke,* edited by T. Schieder (Köln, 1966).

[60] For example Düwell, 'Aus dem Reiche', pp. 72–4.

[61] Koch, pp. 77–8; Kirchhoff, pp. 137–74.

[62] C. Booth, *Life and Labour of the People of London* (New York, 1902).

[63] The largest of these, Feig's 'Erhebung von Wirtschaftsberechnungen minderbemittelter Familien im Deutschen Reich', 2. Sonderheft zum *Reichsarbeitsblatt,* researched into 800 families. In more than half of the families annual income was below expenditure. H. Fürth's 'Mindesteinkommen, Lebensmittelpreise und Lebenshaltung in Frankfurt', *AfSS,* 1911, vol. 33, pp. 523–42, arrives at the same conclusions. Also: 'Inventarien in 87 Dresdener Arbeiterhaushalten', Statistisches Amt der Stadt Dresden. Summarised and reviewed in *Neue Zeit,* 1904/5, vol. 23(1), pp. 524–5.

[64] Fürth, p. 532.

[65] The only contemporary survey of living conditions which was undertaken in the Ruhr confirms this. See L. Fischer Ecker, *Die wirtschaftliche und soziale Lage der Frauen in dem modernen Industrieort Hamborn im Rheinland* (Diss. iur., Tübingen, printed Hagen 1913). Quoted and summarised in Lucas, *Ursachen,* pp. 16–23.

[66] The tables presented by Koch are, first, a list of the wages as published by the *Oberbergamt* Dortmund for a period of 24 years (pp. 148–9). The figures show a rise in the average income between 1889 and 1912 of 88 per cent. Not all of the increase would have been brought about by rising wages. Enlarged production, which greatly relied on overtime, would have added to the climbing curve. (See Pieper's objections, p. 176.) The figures show that the main growth had taken place by 1900, which confirms the proposition that the 1890s were a period of improvement. The statistical validity of the table, however, is questionable, as both the starting point in 1889 and the final figure in 1912 are well outside the average growth rate. The rise in 1889 is almost 40 per cent, as opposed to an average growth rate of 3.5 per cent annually. The rise in the last year, between the last quarter of 1911 and that of 1912, is again almost three times higher than the average. If these two years were omitted, which statistically should make no difference to the tendency Koch tries to prove with the aid of the table, the growth rate is reduced from 88 per cent to 29 per cent or to an annual growth rate of just over one per cent. Koch then contrasts the wages with a series of food prices. He takes the material from Jüngst's *Festschrift.* Jüngst was arguing for the

employers in their fight against the wage demands of the unions. A perilous base for the claim that real wages were rising. But even Jüngst's tables show that in the years 1889 to 1902 only the prices for potatoes and dark rye bread remained stable. Pork rose as much as 38 per cent in Dortmund, veal as much as 36 per cent in Essen, steak by 20 per cent in Bochum, bacon by 31 per cent in Essen to quote only the more substantial rises (pp. 79-80). It is even questionable whether there was an average price for the larger cities. The annual reports of the Chamber of Commerce in Dortmund for example published the prices for the region of Dortmund and its hinterland. The tables show for the various towns and parishes fluctuations for some of the food items of up to 50 per cent. More than likely similar differences prevailed in the larger cities which reduces even further the reliability of Jüngst's tables. (*Jahresbericht der Handelskammer Dortmund*, 1905, p. 61, 1908, p. 69.)

[67] R. Calwer, 'Die Lage der deutschen Arbeiter im Jahre 1898', *Neue Zeit*, 1898/99, vol. 17(11), pp. 554-63.

[68] R. Calwer, *Das Wirtschafts jahr 1908, Das Wirtschafts jahr 1909* (Jena, 1912).

[69] G. Bry, *Wages in Germany* (Princeton, 1960), pp. 73-4; J. Kuczynski, *Die Geschichte der Lage der Arbeiter unter dem Kapitalismus* (Berlin, 1966), vol. 5, pp. 161-80. For an opposing view see A. V. Desai, *Real Wages in Germany* (Oxford, 1968), pp. 34-40.

[70] Spethmann, *Ruhrgebiet*, pp. 554-8; W. Neumann, *Die Gewerkschaften im Ruhrgebiet* (Köln, 1951) p. 31; R. Hundt, *Bergarbeiterwohnungen im Ruhrgebiet* (Berlin, 1902), pp. 4-5.

[71] Croon and Utermann, p. 44.

[72] Neumann, pp. 32-5; W. Düwell, 'Werkwohlfahrtseinrichtungen', *Neue Zeit*, 1907/8, vol. 26(2), pp. 833-42.

[73] Pieper, p. 205.

[74] Croon and Utermann, p. 19.

[75] Ibid., p. 81.

[76] Spethmann, *Ruhrgebiet*, pp. 561-3.

[77] Koch, p. 72.

[78] H. U. Wehler, 'Die Polen im Ruhrgebiet', *VfSW*, 1961, vol. 48, p. 233. Wehler suggests that the Poles in the Ruhr were the major reason for the *Reichsvereinsgesetz*.

[79] See, for example, Brepohl, *Aufbau*, p. 18.

[80] STAM, OBA, 1808, Bl.33.

[81] STAM, OBA, 1808, LA Recklinghausen to government president Münster 29.7.1914.

[82] R. Eberstadt, *Rheinische Wohnungsverhältnisse und ihre Bedeutung fur das Wohnwesen in Deutschland* (Jena, 1903), p. 21. R. Kuczynski, *Post War Labour Condition* (Washington, 1925) gives the number of people living in *Mietskasernen* as 0.3 per cent in Essen, 0.8 percent in Düsseldorf but 71 per cent in Berlin, 40 per cent in Breslau.

[83] In 1910 the average figures of persons per house were Düsseldorf 19.12, Dortmund 20.9, Essen 18.1, Berlin 75.9, Hamburg 38.7. Compare this also with Sheffield 4.8, Manchester 5.0 or Brussels 9.03. Statistics from B. Heymann and K. Freudenberg, *Morbidität und Mortalität der Bergleute im Ruhrgebiet* (Essen, 1925), pp. 26-8; *Beiträge zur Statistik der Stadt Essen*, no. 2, p. 29; O. Most, *Die Grundbesitz und Wohnungsverhältnisse in Düsseldorf* (Düsseldorf, 1912), pp. 16ff.

[84] Heymann and Freudenberg, p. 27; Most, p. 16.

[85] Heymann, pp. 26-7.

[86] HSTAD, 24792, 24793 and 24809. This is of course provided that the inspectors were willing to make a conscientious effort. If they stayed within the letter of the law they would have indeed found little to complain of. The law did not speak of overcrowding unless six or more persons were living in one room or eleven in two rooms. Thus the inspector in Oberhausen for example found fault only with 127 of the 5,564 flats inspected. By contrast Essen: 1,580 out of 3,409; HSTAD, 24809.

[87] D. Wiedtfeldt, *Das Aftermietwesen in der Stadt Essen* (Essen, 1906), p. 2. See also F. Enke, *Genossenschaftliche und Städtische Wohnungspolitik in Essen* (Stuttgart, 1912), especially pp. 150-60.

[88] STAM, OBA, 2488/9.

[89] Hundt, p. 33.

[90] P. Quante, *Die Flucht aus der Landwirtschaft* (Berlin, 1939).

[91] Köllmann, 'Industrialisierung', pp. 60–2.

[92] 'Übersicht über die Förderung des Arbeiterwohnungswesen in den Jahren 1911 und 1912', HSTAD, 24786; ZStA, M'burg, Rep. 120, BB, VII, 1, no. 11, vol. 17, pp. 55–6.

[93] A. Brust, *AfSS,* 1904/5, vol. 20, pp. 480–506.

[94] Koch, pp. 77–108; Kirchhoff, pp. 137–59.

[95] Their interpretation was upheld in a recent essay: A. Gladen, 'Die Streiks der Bergarbeiter im Ruhrgebiet in den Jahren 1889, 1905, 1912', in J. Reulecke, *Arbeiterbewegung an Rhein und Ruhr* (Wuppertal, 1974), pp. 111–48.

[96] 1904 reports of the *Landräte* to government president, HSTAD, 15916.

[97] Note for example ibid., Bl.7.

[98] See p. 11.

Chapter 2

[1] On the background: W. Köllmann, *Sozialgeschichte der Stadt Barmen* (Tübingen, 1960), and 'Soziale Frage und Soziale Bewegungen', in W. Först (ed.), *Das Rheinland in Preussischer Zeit* (Köln, 1965), pp. 145–64; E. Stursberg, *Remscheid und seine Gemeinden* (Remscheid, 1969); H. Rosenthal, 'Betriebsgrösse Solinger Firmen', *Die Heimat,* vol. 20 (1954), pp. 3–7.

[2] Rosenthal, p. 3. On growth rate in Remscheid: Stursberg, pp. 175–8.

[3] Rosenthal, p. 3.

[4] Stursberg, p. 198; J. Reulecke, Die wirtschaftliche Entwicklung der Stadt Barmen von 1910–1925 (Phil. Diss., Bochum, 1972), p. 6.

[5] Rosenthal, pp. 4–7; Reulecke, p. 6f; Stursberg, p. 66. Also *Landrat* Lennep to Government President 2.12.1914 (HSTAD, 15058, Bl. 10) and lord mayor Remscheid to latter 8.12.1914 (Bl. 27). On housing: Köllmann, *Sozialgeschichte,* p. 150.

[6] See p. 23.

[7] Election details: HSTAD, 9028, 9040, 9042; H. Herberts, *Zur Geschichte der SPD im Wuppertal* (Wuppertal, 1963).

[8] Herberts, p. 118; HSTAD, 9059, 42809.

[9] HSTAD, 9041, Bl. 411.

[10] *Landrat* Solingen to Government President, 29.8.1908. HSTAD, 42810.

[11] Herberts, p. 152 and Dittman, 'Memoirs', unpublished manuscript at the IISG, p. 245.

[12] E.g. *Landrat* Solingen to government Düsseldorf, HSTAD 42810, Bl. 26–31.

[13] On Düsseldorf's background: O. Most, *Geschichte der Stadt Düsseldorf,* vols. 1 and 2 (Düsseldorf, 1921); H. A. Lux, *Düsseldorf* (Düsseldorf, 1925); H. Weidenhaupt, *Kleine Geschichte der Stadt Düsseldorf* (Düsseldorf, 1968). Also STA Düsseldorf, XXII, 220.

[14] C. Hugo, 'Wohnungsfrage und Sozialdemokratie', *Neue Zeit,* 1899/1900, vol. 18(2), p. 810.

[15] O. Most, *Die Grundbesitz und Wohnungsverhältnisse in Düsseldorf, 1912* (Düsseldorf, 1912), p. 16.

[16] P. Gerlach, 'Die Arbeiterbewegung in Düsseldorf', in *Lux,* p. 131; P. Berton, *Lebenslauf eines einfachen Menschen* (Düsseldorf, 1958), pp. 81–5.

[17] Berton, p. 95.

[18] Berton, pp. 97–105.

[19] See the annual report of the Düsseldorf administration to government president, HSTAD, 42809, 42811, 42812, 15918. E.g. 42809, Bl. 299–304.

[20] HSTAD, 9041, Bl. 406.

[21] For a most recent description: O. Hemmer, 'Die Bergarbeiterbewegung im Ruhrgebiet unter dem Sozialistengesetz', in Reulecke, p. 99.

[22] Reports to government Münster, STAM, Reg. Münster, VII, 43, vol. 3.

[23] Ritter, p. 70.

[24] Friedrich Naumann tried to establish a Lutheran counterpart to the Catholic workers' association in the early 1890s. He and his supporters, however, were soon severely cautioned by the church hierarchy and they decided to give up the attempt. J. Christ, *Staat und Staatsraison bei Friedrich Naumann* (Heidelberg,1969).

[25] HSTAD, 9040, Bl. 300ff. Also articles on election in local party newspapers.

[26] For statistical material on 1907 and 1912 Reichstag elections, *Statistik des deutschen Reichs*, vol. 315(1–6). In Essen the *Zentrum* scored 37.7 per cent at the 1912 Reichstag election, the SPD 35.7. Being first past the post did not mean winning the seat. For this a candidate had to score more than 50 per cent of the vote. Normally the middle-class parties united for the *Stichwahl* and their total could often defeat the socialist candidate.

[27] H. Wetzler, 'Die Grosstadt Bochum', *Kommunale Praxis*, 1907, vol. 38/39, p. 894.

[28] H. Croon, 'Studien zur Sozial- und Siedlungsgeschichte der Stadt Bochum' in *Bochum und das mittlere Ruhrgebiet*, pp. 85–114.

[29] R. Lützenkirchen, *Der sozialdemokratische Verein für den Reichstagswahlkreis Dortmund-Hoerde* (Dortmund, 1970), pp. 14–15.

[30] Ibid., pp. 48–50.

[31] HSTAD, 9041, Bl. 258.

[32] STA Dortmund, Bestand Do n 263, Bl. 171.

[33] STAM, Reg. Münster, VII, 82.

[34] Lützenkirchen, pp. 82–4.

[35] Lützenkirchen, pp. 85–6. Also STA Dortmund, Bestand 3 Do n 263.

[36] On the history of the Free Union movement in Germany: H. J. Varrain, *Freie Gewerkschaften, Sozialdemokratie und Staat* (Düsseldorf, 1956); S. Nestriepke, *Die Gewerschaftsbewegung* (Stuttgart, 1922), 2 vols.

[37] J. A. Moses, 'The Trade Union Issue in German Social Democracy', *IWK*, 1973, vol. 19/20, pp. 1–19

[38] Beside these larger unions there were the yellow associations, (*wirtschaftsfriedliche Verbände*, unions run by the employers) and the Hirsch-Duncker Union. The latter participated very actively in industrial conflicts but their membership was very low (3,000 in the Ruhr in 1913; 'Sozialpolitische Chronik', *AfSS*, vol. 36, p. 683). This was even less than that of the Rhenish-Westphalian Workers Association, a Protestant grouping, which in 1906 was accredited with 7,244 members; STAM, Reg. Arnsberg, I, 104, vol. I. The figures for the real yellow unions which were set up by the industrialists between 1907 and 1910 were never clearly established. K. J. Mattheier's figure of 21,000 seems very high. His source, a study commissioned by the mine owners' association is not very convincing. 'Werkvereine und wirtschaftsfriedlich-nationale (gelbe) Arbeiterbewegung im Ruhrgebiet', in Reulecke, *Arbeiterbewegung*, p. 188.

[39] On the *Gewerkverein:* Imbusch, pp. 190–200; Koch, pp. 59–62; Varrain, pp. 40–3.

[40] This is based on the results of the elections for the position of safety officers *(Sicherheitsmänner)*, STAM, OBA, 1851, Bl. 61ff.

[41] Note, for example, the low percentage of colony houses in the strongly Catholic Oberhausen; 'Zusammenstellung der im Bezirk des OBA im Besitz der Zeche befindlichen Wohnungen', STAM, OBA, 1838.

[42] Wehler, pp. 203–35.

[43] On the history of the *Alte Verband:* W. Neumann, *Die Gewerkschaften im Ruhrgebiet* (Köln, 1951).

[44] Note the court cases in STAM, Reg. Münster, VII, Nr. 84. Politically the unions had to be strictly neutral. Hence, if at any union branch meeting comments with political undertones were made or if participation of non-members could be established, charges could be laid for having omitted to register as a political institution.

[45] E.g. *Landrat* Ruhrort to Government President, 30.11.1906, HSTAD, 15934.

[46] *Leipziger Volkszeitung*, 1905, no. 43.

[47] STA Dortmund, *Bestand* 3, Do n 263, Bl. 184.

[48] Neumann, p. 25.

[49] Koch, pp. 121–29.

[50] Gladen, pp. 146–48.

[51] Above p. Compare also food prices listed in *Statistische Korrespondenz*, 1906, vol. XXXII, no. 3; 1912, vol. XXXVIII, no. 18; *Jahresbericht der Handelskammer für den Kreis Essen, 1909, 1910*, food prices of the *Kruppsche Konsumanstalt*, pp. 73–5.

[52] See p. 16.

[53] HSTAD, Praesidialbüro, 846, Bl. 6, 8,75–8, 106–7.
[54] Ibid., Bl. 28.
[55] HSTAD, 15939, Bl. 42, e.g. Scharnhorst, Kaiserstuhl I + II.
[56] Praesidialbüro, 851, Bl. 6.
[57] Ibid.
[58] HSTAD, 15939, Bl. 28ff.
[59] Ibid.
[60] Ibid.
[61] In 1912 about two-thirds of the workforce belonged to a union (270,000 out of 400,000). If the Catholic Union members and the members of the *Dreibund* unions who did not participate are deducted only 50 per cent of the strikers belonged to a union.
[62] STAM, OBA, 1857.
[63] Ibid.
[64] HSTAD, 15939, Bl. 180–2.
[65] HSTAD, Praesidialbüro, 851, Bl. 35–7.
[66] Ibid., Bl. 46.
[67] Police president Essen to government president, 17.3.1912, HSTAD, 15944.
[68] HSTAD, 15943.
[69] On 19 March the vote was taken. 349 voted to continue the strike, 215 opposed this. As a two-third majority was necessary to continue with the strike the union leaders could call it off.
[70] HSTAD, 15945, e.g. Bl. 4, 24, 35.
[71] Quoted in Legien, p. 16.

Chapter 3

[1] Referred to below as AK.
[2] For a recent work on German Society during the war see Jürgen Kocka, *Deutsche Sozialgeschichte 1914–1918* (Göttingen, 1973).
[3] Schieck, p. 7.
[4] Ibid.
[5] G. D. Feldmann, *Army, Industry and Labor in Germany, 1914–1918* (New Jersey, 1966), pp. 52–63.
[6] Ibid., pp. 97ff.
[7] Reports to Government President, HSTAD, 15058.
[8] Ibid. Also WWA, IHK Bochum, 2, no. 22, for example Bl.73–4.
[9] HSTAD, 15058. See, for example, the reports from Hamborn and Essen.
[10] M. Sogemeier, *Die Entwicklung und Regelung des Arbeitsmarkts im rheinisch-westfälischen Industriegebiet* (Jena, 1922), p. 21.
[11] Note the decree of the Prussian Minister for Trade and Commerce of 22.3.1915, STA Dortmund, Bestand 5, Do 144.
[12] By October 1917 there were 71,000 prisoners of war in the collieries. Sitting of the demobilisation commission of 20.1.1919, STAM, Reg. Münster, 2969.
[13] HSTAD, 15058, Reports from Düsseldorf, Solingen and Remscheid. On the textile cities Wuppertal and Barmen: Reulecke, *Barmen*, pp. 26–47.
[14] Sogemeier, p. 52; see also STA Remscheid, W II/3 Bl. 10.
[15] Reulecke, pp. 46/7.
[16] C. Lorenz, 'Die gewerbliche Frauenarbeit während des Krieges', in P. Umbreit (ed.), *Der Krieg und die Arbeitsverhältnisse* (Stuttgart, 1928), p. 345.
[17] W. Zimmerman, pp. 350–1.
[18] On the Belgian workers: HSTAD 15001 and 15048.
[19] For example lawyers Rosenberg and Westfeld to Düsseldorf government, 6.8.1915, HSTAD 15045.
[20] *Nordwestliche Gruppe* to Government President, 3.10.1915, Decree of AK, 1.11.1915; HSTAD 15005.
[21] Ibid.

[22] Krupps work Rheinhausen to Düsseldorf government, HSTAD 15057.

[23] Circular letter AK, 5.11.1915, HSTAD 15057.

[24] HSTAD 15005 and 15057. See also STA Castrop-Rauxel, Amt Bladenhorst, 24.

[25] Zimmermann, pp. 348–51.

[26] von Oertzen, *Betriebsräte*, p. 274.

[27] E.g. *WAVZ*, 19.1.1918; *BAZ*, 3.2.1918; *VBB*, 30.7.1918.

[28] E.g. *BAZ*, 3.2.1918 and 1.6.1918.

[29] *BAZ*, 12.1.1918 and 3.2.1918.

[30] *BAZ*, 23.3.1918.

[31] E.g. *WAVZ*, 2.1.1918.

[32] Thiele, 'Der Gesundheitsstand unter den Arbeitern', in F. Bumm (ed.), *Deutschland's Gesundheitsverhältnisse* (Stuttgart, 1928), vol. 1, pp. 131–47.

[33] At the rolling mill Heckmann in Duisburg the 56-hour week was introduced in July 1918 (*VBB*, 30.7.1918). For Solingen: *BAS*, 12.8.1918; HSTAD 9081, e.g. Bl. 382.

[34] E.g. ibid., Bl. 359–74.

[35] *BAZ*, 23.3.1918.

[36] *BAZ*, 5.11.1918.

[37] The food problem in Germany during the war is covered in A. Skalweit, *Die deutsche Kriegsernährungswirtschaft während des Krieges* (Stuttgart 1927); F. Aeroboe, *Der Einfluss des Krieges auf die landwirtschaftliche Produktion* (Stuttgart, 1927); F. Bumm, *Deutschlands Gesundheitsverhältnisse unter dem Einfluss des Krieges* (Stuttgart, 1927).

[38] Bumm, vol. 2, pp. 2–7.

[39] Sogemeier, p. 13.

[40] Aeroboe, pp. 50–2; Skalweit, *Kriegsernährungswirtschaft*, pp. 92–8.

[41] STAM, LA Recklinghausen, no. 11, Bl. 82.

[42] The distribution of meat was undertaken originally by the private proprietors, the *Viehhandelsverbände*. When this did not prove reliable the government established the meat board.

[43] See for example J. Lange, Die Lebensmittelversorgung der Stadt Essen während des Krieges (Diss., Erlangen), p. 51; Skalweit, *Die Nahrungsmittelwirtschaft grosser Städte* (Berlin, 1917), pp. 29–37; B. Brand, 'Der Weltkrieg, seine Entwicklung auf Bevölkerung und Wirtschaft', typescript at STA Wanne-Eickel, Sections 14–30.

[44] The reports of the meetings are in HSTAD 14914–14917.

[45] Skalweit, *Grosse Städte*, p. 5.

[46] STA Düsseldorf, Bestand XXIII, 22.

[47] Skalweit, *Grosse Städte*, pp. 5–9; A. Oehler, *Düsseldorf im Weltkrieg* (Düsseldorf, 1927), pp. 255–8. For complaints about the Dortmund procurement association see *Verwaltungsbericht Gelsenkirchen 1903–1921* (Gelsenkirchen, 1921), p.148.

[48] In his study on the food economy of big cities during the war, Skalweit listed three basic factors which influenced the situation. The difficulties of storage and distribution increased with the size of the population. Secondly it was important whether the city was surrounded by rural hinterland. Finally the composition of its population was vital, since a high percentage of manual labour demanded more food than non-manual employees. On all points, the city chosen from the Ruhr, Dortmund, was most unfavourably placed (*Grosse Städte*, pp. 2–4).

[49] Figures worked out from the official weekly food distribution as advertised in all local daily newspapers.

[50] E.g. *WAVZ*, 8.7.1918, 13.7.1918; *VBB*, 18/19.6.1918, 12.7.1918; also STA Lünen, 11/22.

[51] Correspondence between the *Landrat* in Recklinghausen, the Government President of Münster and the *Reichsgetreidestelle*, STAM, LA Recklinghausen, No. 11.

[52] Brand, section 22a.

[53] Ibid., section 14; STA Castrop-Rauxel, Stadt Castrop, 165.

[54] *Landräte* to Arnsberg government, STAM 1307 II; ZStA M'burg, Rep. 197 A, Tit. I, o, no. 1 e.g. Bl. 1,11,64,123ff.

[55] Spethmann, *Zwölf Jahre*, vol. 1, ch. 1.

[56] STA Dortmund, Bestand 5, no. 143, Bl. 61, ZStA, M'burg, Rep. 197 A, Tit. I, No. 1, Bl. 121 and 182.

[57] Ibid., Bl. 177 and 148.

[58] Ibid., Bl. 168; *VZD*, 2.1.1919, 16.1.1919.

[59] *VZD*, 2.1.1919, 16.1.1919.

[60] *VBB*, 31.10.1918.

[61] *VZD*, 21.2.1919, 24.2.1919, 3.5.1919, 7.5.1919, 5.6.1919; STA Düsseldorf, Bestand VII, 561, government president to Düsseldorf administration, 16.9.1918; Bestand III, 18072, copy of charges levelled by the Düsseldorf USP chairman Schmidt against mayor Knopp; *Stenographische Verhandlungen der Stadtverordnetenversammlungen zu Düsseldorf*, 1919, p. 212.

[62] *AZE*, 13.5.1919; STAM, Oberstaatsanwalt Hamm, 17.

[63] *WAVZ*, 23.1.1918, 29.1.1919, 7.3.1919, 31.7.1919.

[64] *VZD*, 5.2.1919, 20.2.1919.

[65] See, p. 46.

[66] STA Düsseldorf, Bestand XXIII, 18.

[67] *VBB*, 5.9.1918.

[68] See, for example, the arguments around the story 'Give the child a necklace' in *RWZ*, 15.1.1918, *WAVZ*, 20.1.1918. Also Bumm, pp. 70, 80; Günther, p. 225. The hardest hit were no doubt the recipients of social services payments, the old-age and war-invalid pensioners and the families who lost their breadwinner. Their income remained far behind the rising prices.

[69] J. Kuczynski, *Die Geschichte der Arbeiter unter dem Kapitalismus* (Berlin, 1966), vol. 4, pp. 349–51.

[70] *WAVZ*, 17.7.1918.

[71] *BAZ*, 28.9.1918.

[72] See the industrial files at the HSTAD (15307–45), e.g. 15326 (Harkott), 15327 (Krupp), 15328 on five Stinnes mines.

[73] On the strikes in the coal-mining industry, Spethmann, pp. 18–36. 12 Jahre, pp. 338–47; in the mining industries HSTAD 9081, e.g. Bl. 92–3, 109–13, 299–301, 328 and 33590, vols. 1 and 2.

[74] *BAS*, 28.1.1918.

[75] *VBB*, 8.10.1918.

[76] *WAVZ*, 9.3.1918; STA Düsseldorf, Bestand XXII, 27.

[77] The word *hamstern* is not easy to translate. Dictionaries offer 'hoarding' which is not a good translation. The process of *hamstern* involves more than just the hoarding of food. The task of reaching the countryside, the illegal bartering with the farmers, the difficult process of returning with the goods which often had to be hidden (the image of hiding food in the clothes and big pockets brings in the notion of *Hamsterbacken*), all this suggest that scrounging is probably a better translation.

[78] See the article 'EineHamsterfahrt', *VBB*, 13.7.1918.

[79] STA Düsseldorf, Bestand VII, 561.

[80] *VZD*, 27.11.1918; the discoveries at the *Rheinische Metallwarenfabriken* were the largest made, but considerable food stocks were also found at other factories for several weeks.

[81] In 1917, to combat the black market, the Düsseldorf Government President wrote to major companies about possible co-operation in the procurement of food. The answers of the firms were not encouraging and the project was shelved. HSTAD, Industrial files e.g. 15327.

[82] Documents quoted in Spethmann, *Zwölf Jahre*, pp. 338–9.

[83] Feldman, p. 256.

[84] *WAVZ*, 6.7.1918; Brand, p. 32.

[85] In Düsseldorf and Bochum, for example, the contributions did not reach 50 per cent of the expected figure. *RWZ*, 2.9.1918, 5.9.1918; *VBB*, 23.6.1918.

[86] *VZD*, 23.1.1919.

[87] Thiele, pp. 137–8.

[88] H. Hennig, Die Situation der deutschen Kriegswirtschaft im Sommer 1918 (Diss., Hamburg, 1957), pp. 70–2.

[89] *WAVZ*, 28.5.1918; *RWZ*, 2.9.1918, 9.9.1918.

[90] In Solingen for example the number of medical practitioners decreased from 23 to 8. In Ohligs, near Solingen, a town of 30,000 inhabitants, there was in 1915 only one G. P. left. HSTAD 38865.

[91] 'Kriegsgesundheitsbericht für den Bezirk Düsseldorf', in HSTAD 8148.

[92] Ibid., pp. 19–28.

[93] *VBB*, 20.7.1918.

[94] HSTAD, *Praesidialburo* 1078.

[95] *BAZ*, 27.7.1918.

[96] WWA, IHK, K2, File 1015.

[97] *BAS*, 16.8.1918.

[98] *WAVZ*, 12.9.1918.

[99] Ibid.

[1] *WAVZ*, 13.9.1918.

[2] *VBB*, 8.7.1918.

[3] Meerwarth, pp. 50–2. There is no overall account of the total number in the region but the figures given in the Düsseldorf health report suggest a death toll of about 15,000 (HSTAD, 8148).

[4] *VBB*, 16.1.1918; *WAVZ*, 5.10.1918.

[5] STA Dortmund, Best. 3, Do r 12, for reports of Landräte, STAM, 1307 II; of Supreme President, DZA Merseburg, Tit. 1059, no. 3 Beiheft II, vol. 3.

[6] STA Dortmund, Police *Stimmungsbericht* Dortmund, 4.11.1918, Bestand 3, Do r 123.

Chapter 4

[1] These were the *Bergische Arbeiterstimme* in Solingen and its subsidiary in Remscheid, the *Bergische Volkstimme*, the *Niederrheinische Volksstimme* in Duisburg, the *Volkszeitung* in Düsseldorf, the *Arbeiterzeitung* in Essen, the *Volksblatt* in Bochum and the *Arbeiterzeitung* in Dortmund. There was also the weekly periodical of the *Alte Verband*, the *Bergarbeiter-Zeitung*.

[2] E. Teuber, 'Beiträge zur neueren Geschichte der Arbeiterbewegung', *Sozialistische Politik und Wirtschaft*, vol. 4, 1926, no. 31.

[3] Circular no. 1 of the branch leadership to the local branches, HSTAD 14924.

[4] STA Duisburg, 306/309, branch meeting of 23 August 1914.

[5] For example his speech in Oberhausen, *Oberhausener Volkszeitung*, 31.1.1915, quoted in Teuber, no. 31.

[6] Note Woczek's complaint that the VBB 'in its enthusiasm for the war goes so far [that it wants] to eliminate the Prussian Landtag and the Reichstag, . . . [and advocates] that the army should rule'. STAM, Reg. Münster, VII, 43, vol. 2.

[7] E.g. *WAVZ*, 22.1.1918.

[8] *WAVZ*, 26.1.1918.

[9] *WAVZ*, 22.1.1918; *BAZ*, 19.1.1918.

[10] STA Dortmund, Bestand 15,174, Bl. 15–20.

[11] E.g. STA Dortmund, Bestand 5, Nr. 144, Bredenbeck's correspondence about the article 'Wenn wir Nachtschicht haben'.

[12] *WAVZ*, 23.1.1918.

[13] *WAVZ*, 1.1.1918, 22.1.1918.

[14] *WAVZ*, 22.1.1918.

[15] Dittmann, p. 806.

[16] *WAVZ*, 12.8.1918.

[17] Quoted in Varrain, pp. 77–8.

[18] STAM, Reg. Münster, VII, 58, vols. 2–4; STA Dortmund, Bestand 3, Do r 118, e.g. staff meeting of the mine Hansa, 15.9.1918; STA Duisburg 306/303.

[19] *MB*, 2.6.1918, 7.7.1918; *BAS*, 10.6.1918, 18.6.1918, 21.6.1918, 11.7.1918, 13.7.1918; *WAVZ*, 8.6.1918, 18.6.1918.

[20] For detailed discussion of the ASL: Feldmann, pp. 197–249.

[21] On Hindenburg program: ibid., pp. 150–68.

[22] HSTAD, 9077.

[23] *Protokolle über die Verhandlungen des Würzburger Parteitages der Sozialdemokratischen Partei* (Berlin, 1917), pp. 115–17.

[24] Feldmann, p. 247. Note also Feldmann's discussion of paragraph 9 of the ASL, pp. 308–16.

[25] STAM, OBA, 1814, Kruse to von Gayl, 24.12.1915.

[26] Ibid., Bl. 101.

[27] Ibid., Bl. 115–16.

[28] Ibid., mine owners' association to von Gayl, 10.8.1915.

[29] Feldmann, p. 204.

[30] HSTAD, 33556, Bl. 43–50.

[31] Ibid., Bl. 6–8.

[32] Ibid., Bl. 97.

[33] E.g. STA Gelsenkirchen, XVIII, 9/3.

[34] VBB, 31.7.1918.

[35] STA Dortmund, Bestand 5, r 201 and 231.

[36] STA Essen, Rep.102, Abt.I, 1084, von Gayl to Essen administration, 7.1.1916, 21.9.1916.

[37] STAM, OBA, 1408, *Verwaltungsberichte* Münster and Arnsberg 1917.

[38] This refers only to the Ruhr region, the Lower Rhine branches on the left bank of the Rhine stayed with the SPD.

[39] See pp. 61–3.

[40] On the conflict about the party newspapers in Germany: K. Koszyk, *Zwischen Kaiserreich und Diktatur, die sozialdemokratische Presse 1914–1933* (Heidelberg, 1958).

[41] Ibid., pp. 48–54.

[42] HSTAD, 14922-25. Preventive censorship meant that the manuscript had to be read before the printing.

[43] *NVS*, 13.4.1916.

[44] *Der Kampf*, 1916, vol. 1, nos. 1–3.

[45] HSTAD, 14924–5.

[46] Herberts, p. 149.

[47] *MB*, 21.4.1918, 28.4.1918, 19.5.1918; *BAS*, 19.4.1918, 20.4.1918, 22.4.1918, 24.4.1918, 1.5.1918, 11.5.1918; *WAVZ*, 18.4.1918.

[48] Berlau, p. 148.

[49] STAM, Reg. Münster, VII, 61, vol. 4, Correspondence Windau; *MB*, 1.4.1917, 3.6.1917, 28.10.1917.

[50] Dittmann, pp. 641–2.

[51] STAM, Reg. Münster, VII, 43, vol. 2, Woczek to Hue, 31.10.1915.

[52] Berton, p. 145.

[53] Ibid., p. 146.

[54] HSTAD, 14936.

[55] Berton, p. 148.

[56] HSTAD, 14939.

[57] IISG, Rocher Memoiren, unpublished transcript, vol. 2, p. 22.

[58] See the report of a lecture on left-wing activities to police officers in Düsseldorf on 14.4.1918. HSTAD, 9086.

[59] STA Remscheid, Akte Issel.

[60] On Minster: Kurt Kozsyk, 'Das abenteuerliche Leben des sozial-revolutionären Agitators Carl Minster', *AfS*, 1965, vol. 5, pp. 194–5.

[61] STA Duisburg, 306/309.

[62] *Der Kampf*, no. 1, 1917.

[63] Ibid., no. 13.

[64] Ibid., no. 30.

[65] Walther and Engelmann, p. 126.

[66] The sub-branches Neudorf-Duissern and Hamborn placed regular advertisements.

[67] Koszyk, 'Minster', p. 199.

[68] *Das Werk des Untersuchungsausschusses der deutschen verfassungsgebenden Nationalversammlung und des Deutschen Reichstags,* fourth series, vol. 4, pp. 190–2.

[69] STA Duisburg, 306/455, Police Düsseldorf to AK, 11.4.1917.

[70] Walther and Engelmann, p. 185.

[71] HSTAD, 9086. Krohn's lecture to police, 14.4.1917, p. 6.

[72] Note her speech given at the Neuenkamp sub-branch against Schluchtmann, STA Duisburg, 306/303.

[73] ZStA, Po, M.d.I. 124–73, Bl. 204/205.

[74] STAM, Büro Kölpin, 173.

[75] *Archivalische Forschungen zur Geschichte der deutschen Arbeiterbewegung,* vol. 4,1–4, *Die Auswirkungen der Grossen Sozialistischen Oktoberrevolution* edited by F. Stern (Berlin, 1959), Document 561, pp. 1349–51.

[76] Walther and Engelmann, p. 172; Reulecke, *Arbeiterbewegung,* p. 229.

[77] H. M. Bock, *Syndikalism and Linkskommunismus* (Meisenhein, 1969), pp. 23–34.

[78] HSTAD, 42781, police report Düsseldorf 1910; 42809, Bl.110 and 333; 42812, 42813 especially police reports from Düsseldorf.

[79] STAM, Reg. Münster, VII, 82.

[80] Ibid. E.g. Bochum police president to government Münster, 18.10.1910, 26.10.1910.

[81] Ibid. Police Hamborn to government Düsseldorf, 8.1.1912, HSTAD 42785.

[82] In 1913 their number was estimated at 1,263 in the government district of Düsseldorf (HSTAD, 42809, Bl. 336). There are no corresponding figures for the Westphalian part of the Ruhr. To judge from the documents in STAM, Reg. Münster, VII, 82, membership here would have been several hundred.

[83] The police chief in Düsseldorf, Robert Lehr, for example, writes that the war reduced the police force to one-third of its normal size. Duties on the other hand rose with the increase of war measures (STA Düsseldorf, Nachlass Lehr, Nr.57). Not surprisingly, Lehr made major mistakes, like for example listing the moderate Majority Socialist Gerlach among the dangerous left-wing section of the Düsseldorf party branch (HSTAD, 14923). Interesting too is the fact that the regional police president in Bochum was not able to control the Polish settlements. His main officers who were able to speak sufficient Polish had been drafted into the army. By 1918 the Bochum police president had to admit that he had no information at all about the Polish settlements. And in those places were the 'backward and non-organised workers', which, Rosa Luxemburg had forecast in 1906, would show themselves as the most radical in times of revolution. (Note the correspondence between the Bochum police president, the government in Münster, the ministry of the interior and the war ministry, ZStA, M'burg, Rep.77, Tit.437a, Nr. 29, vol. 2.)

[84] *Archivalische Forschungen,* Doc.441, b, pp. 1156/7; Gauer's report on the USP and other left-wing dissenters, HSTAD, 14974.

[85] ZStA, Rep. 120, B.B., VII, 1, 3, vol. 29, Bl. 96; HSTAD, 9081, Bl. 359–74.

[86] Lord mayor Hamborn to Düsseldorf government, 9.11.1918, HSTAD, 15279.

[87] Bock, p. 136.

[88] Dittmann, p. 414.

[89] *FPE,* 4.8.1914, in HSTAD, 14922.

[90] HSTAD, 14922, police Düsseldorf 25.8.1914.

[91] Ibid.

[92] Dittmann, p. 444.

[93] Ibid., p. 475.

[94] *Verbandstag der Metallarbeiter,* 1915, pp. 20–4.

[95] Ibid.

[96] Walther and Engelmann, p. 89.

[97] ZStA, Po, MdI, 1395/10, Bl. 96, quoted in Walther and Engelmann, p. 95.

[98] Düsseldorf, Lennep-Remscheid, Solingen, Hagen and now also Elberfeld-Barmen left the SPD immediately after the foundation of the USP at Gotha.

[99] Henri and Engelmann, p. 125.

[1] HSTAD, 15708.

[2] *MB,* 1.4.1917; HSTAD, 14974, Gauer's report.

[3] Ibid.

[4] Files on censorship: HSTAD, 14922–34.

[5] Quoted in W. Först, *Robert Lehr* (Düsseldorf, 1962), pp. 19–20.

[6] E.g. Lehr to AK, 27.2.1915, 24.4.1915, HSTAD, 14923.

[7] HSTAD, 14932.

[8] Landrat Benrath to government Düsseldorf, 21.6.1915, HSTAD, 14932.

[9] E.g. von Gayl to Solingen police, 7.6.1915, HSTAD, 14925.

[10] Both papers were printed in Solingen. The front page with the national items was the same in both papers. The regional parts were printed separately.

[11] HSTAD, 14941 , Bl. 77–85.

[12] HSTAD, 14937.

[13] Ibid. Jarres to Düsseldorf government, 24.10.1918.

[14] Reports on strikes in HSTAD, 9081, *ZStA,* M'burg, Tit. 500, no. 52, Beiheft 10; documents quoted in Spethmann, *Zwölf Jahre,* pp. 334ff.

[15] See p. 59.

[16] HSTAD, 9081, Bl. 6–8.

[17] Ibid., Bl. 162.

[18] ZStA, M'burg, Tit. 500, no. 52, Beiheft 10, Bl. 44.

[19] ZStA, M'burg, Rep. 77, Tit. 500, no. 52, vol. 1. Government president Arnsberg to MdI, 12.5.1917.

[20] Documents in Walther and Engelmann, vol. 2, pp. 18–43; HSTAD, 14936; ZStA, M'burg, Rep. 77, Tit. 437a, no. 29, vol. 2, Bl. 171–184; Rep. 197A, Tit.I, O, no. 8, vol. 1, Bl. 96–99; *Archivalische Forschungen,* Documents 332, 374, 419, 445 and 459.

[21] Henri and Engelmann, vol. 2, pp. 30–43; Spethmann, *12 Jahre,* pp. 52–64.

[22] HSTAD, 9081, Bl. 537–538, 548–550; ZStA, Rep. 120, BB VII, 1, vol. 29, Bl. 71, 99, 100, 109.

[23] *BAS,* 6.2.1918.

[24] *VZD,* 3.12.1918.

[25] ZStA, Po, M.d.I., 124–73, Bl. 335.

[26] HSTAD, 14974 Gauer's report.

[27] Ibid.

[28] Circular letter of Police President Essen, STA Castrop-Rauxel, Stadt Kastrop, 11; STA Gelsenkirchen, IV/1/19, p. 5.

[29] *BAS,* 19.7.1918.

[30] *MB,* 8.12.1918. 'Und immer wieder gegen die Unabhängigen'.

[31] *Archivalische Forschungen,* p. 1607.

[32] STA Castrop-Rauxel, Stadt Kastrop, 11, letter police Essen.

[33] Del Tedesco, pp. 87–92; G. D. Feldmann, The Origins of the Stinnes-Legien Agreement, *IWK* 1973, vol. 9, 19/20, pp. 45–103.

[34] As stressed for example by Metzmacher, pp. 259–62. Reulecke, *Arbeiterbewegung,* pp. 237–8.

Part III

[1] For a detailed account of the establishment of Workers' and Soldiers' Councils see U. Kluge, 'Militärrevolte und Staatsumsturz. Ausbreitung und Konsolidierung der Räteorganisation im rheinisch-westfälischen Industriegebiet', in Rürup, *Arbeiter-und Soldatenräte,* pp. 39–82.

[2] On von Gayl: E. Schulte, *Münstersche Chronik zu Novemberrevolte und Separatismus* (Münster, 1936), pp. 34–8; also see pp. 72.

[3] *AZE,* 9.11.1918; *VZD,* 11.11.1918.

[4] *WAVZ,* 11.11.1918.

[5] Metzmacher, p. 153.

[6] Dittmann, p. 851.

[7] Note, for example, the reaction to the Underberg incident, G.A. Duisburg, 23.10.1918, also HSTAD, 9086, government Düsseldorf to Underberg.

[8] E.g. Dittmann, p. 851.

Chapter 5

[1] The reform of the voting system after the revolution abolished the voting for one candidate in one electorate but introduced regional lists. The list for Bochum and Dortmund was the district western Westphalia. The old party structures, however, survived for some time.

[2] See pp. 23–5.

[3] See pp. 55.

[4] *WAVZ*, 10.10.1918.

[5] *WAVZ*, 28.10.1918.

[6] STA Gelsenkirchen, IV/1/19, p. 2; Brandt, 'Bericht Wanne', section 42.

[7] The *General-Anzeiger* Press was politically not committed, but had a general trend towards the liberals.

[8] *GA* Dortmund 24.10.1918, 26.10.1918, 30.10.1918.

[9] 1.11.1918.

[10] *BAZ*, 9.11.1918.

[11] *VBB*, 10.11.1918; H. W. Bimbel, 'Bochum zur Jahreswende 1918/19', *Der Bochumer Wanderer*, 1968, vol. 4, pp. 3–7.

[12] STA Gelsenkirchen, IV/1/19, pp. 5–10.

[13] Von Gayl to Eichhoff, 7.7.1917. STA Dortmund, Bestand 5, Do, 144.

[14] STA Dortmund, Bestand 5, 235, Bl. 25.

[15] *WAVZ*, 11.11.1918, Bestand 5, Nr. 234.

[16] *VBB*, 12.11.1918.

[17] E.g. Brandt, 'Bericht Wanne', section 42; *Bericht über die Entwicklung und den Stand der Gemeindeangelegenheiten der Stadt Herne vom 1. April 1897-1. April 1922*, pp. 15–17; STA Castrop-Rauxel, Amt Rauxel, 17.

[18] STA Gelsenkirchen, IV/1/19, pp. 10–13.

[19] *Lüner Anzeiger*, 13.11.1918.

[20] *WAVZ*, 14.11.1918; *VBB*, 14.11.1918.

[21] STA Dortmund, Bestand 3, Do n 126, Bl. 1.

[22] Brandt, Bericht Wanne, section 44.

[23] *VBB*, 26.11.1918, 2.12.1918.

[24] *WAVZ*, 4.12.1918.

[25] STA Gelsenkirchen, IV/1/19, pp. 53–60; *VBB*, 12.11.1918.

[26] STA Dortmund, Bestand 5, 234. These were the rates as paid in Dortmund. However, pay of the other security guards differed little.

[27] STA Dortmund, Bestand 3, Do n 288; STA Lünen 11/68.

[28] *Bericht Herne*, p. 17.

[29] STA Bochum 4010.

[30] STA Dortmund, Bestand 5, 234.

[31] *WAVZ*, 21.11.1918.

[32] STA Dortmund, Bestand 3, Do r 64; *GAZ*, 14.12.1918; 'Bericht Wanne', section 45.

[33] See pp. 43, 93.

[34] Article VII of the Armistice of 11 November 1918 demanded that large quantities of locomotives and railway rolling stocks be handed over to the Allies.

[35] *WAVZ*, 29.11.1918.

[36] *VBB*, 16.12.1918.

[37] WWA/IHK Bochum, K2, Nr. 920.

[38] For detail on the *Wirtschaftliche Demobilmachungsamt* and Koeth's work, see Feldmann's paper to the Internationale Symposium, 'The Economic and Social Consequences of the German Demobilization', Bochum 1973, published as 'Wirtschafts-und sozialpolitische Probleme der deutschen Demobilmachung' in H. Mommsen (ed.), *Industrielles System und politische Entwicklung in der Weimarer Republik* (Düsseldorf, 1974), pp. 618–47.

[39] 11.11.1918, WWA, IHK, Bochum, K2, Nr. 920.

[40] STA Dortmund, Bestand 3, Do r 47.

[41] STA Gelsenkirchen, XVIII/11/2, Bl. 200; STA Bochum, 10013, Bl. 23.
[42] For the dealings of the Bochum demobilisation board: WWA, IHK Bochum, K2, 667.
[43] *Bericht Herne*, pp. 15–17.
[44] STA Bochum, Stadt Bochum 4009.
[45] STA Herne, the 'Protokollbuch des Arbeiter-und Soldatenrates Sodingen' is a good document on the working of a smaller Workers' and Soldiers' Council.
[46] STA Gelsenkirchen, XXI/15/20.
[47] ZStA, M'burg, Rep. 77, Tit. 1373a, no. 5.
[48] STA Gelsenkirchen, IV/1/19.
[49] Circular telegram, 14.11.1918, STAM, Reg. Münster, 4204.
[50] See p. 82.
[51] HSTAD, Reg. Düsseldorf 15708.
[52] *WAVZ*, 28.11.1918, 3.12.1918.
[53] Ibid.
[54] Western Westphalia sent fourteen delegates to the National Congress: ten SPD and four USP.
[55] E.g. *WAVZ*, 28.11.1918, 4.12.1918.
[56] See p. 107.
[57] Printed in *WAVZ*, 9.1.1918.
[58] STA Dortmund, Bestand 5, 235.
[59] Ibid.; also STA Dortmund n 124, *GA* Dortmund to Workers' and Soldiers' Council, 11.1.1919.
[60] *VZD*, 19.12.1918.
[61] STA DortmuBestand 5, 236, Bl. 89–93.
[62] *AZE*, 8.1.1919.
[63] HSTAD, 15708.
[64] *WAVZ*, 9.1.1919.
[65] STA Dortmund, Bestand 5, 235; also *Bericht des Untersuchungsausschusses über die Ursachen und Verlauf der Unruhen im Rheinland und Westfalen in der Zeit vom 1. Januar bis 19. März 1919*, pp. 5585–90.
[66] STA Dortmund, Bestand 5, 236, Bl. 56.
[67] Schulte, *Novemberrevolution*, pp. 230–7.
[68] *WAVZ*, 4.1.1919.
[69] *WAVZ*, 15.1.1919, 23.1.1919.
[70] E.g. Schulte, *Spartakismus/Separatismus*, pp. 15/16.
[71] *VBB*, 20.1.1919.
[72] *WAVZ*, 20.1.1919.
[73] *BAZ*, 27.4.1918.
[74] See p. 65.
[75] *Lüner Zeitung*, 8.1.1919, 30.1.1919.
[76] *WAVZ*, 20.1.1919.
[77] Spethmann, p. 167; *RWZ*, 15.1.1919.
[78] STA Dortmund, Bestand 3, n 286; report Workers' and Soldiers' Council Dortmund, 15.1.1919.

Chapter 6

[1] *Archivalische Forschungen*, IV, p.1611.
[2] *BVS*, 22.10.1918.
[3] STA Duisburg, 51/1; *WZ*, 9.11.1918.
[4] Metzmacher, pp. 211–13; HSTAD 15279.
[5] Metzmacher, p. 216; *WZ*, 11.11.1918: *BAS*, 11.11.1918, 12.11.1918.
[6] STA Remscheid, N/K/I, 3; *BVS*, 11.11.1918, 12.11.1918. For a recent comprehensive history of the revolution and workers radicalism in Remscheid see E. Lucas, *Arbeiterradikalismus* (Frankfurt, 1976).
[7] *BVS*, 18.11.1918.

[8] SPD archive, Bonn, Nachlass Dittmann, Kasette I, Dokument 57.

[9] *BVS*, 2.12.1918, 4.12.1918, 5.12.1918, 20.12.1918.

[10] Vohwinkel, for examplSPD-USP, Workers' and Soldiers' Council. HSTAD, Reg. Düsseldorf, 15279, Bl. 132.

[11] *BAS*, 21.11.1918, STA Solingen N/5, 17, vol.1, II, 121, vol. 1.

[12] *RWZ*, 16.11.1918.

[13] *BVS*, 17.12.1918; *WZ*, 13.12.1918.

[14] *BAS*, 16.12.1918; *BVS*, 20.12.1918; *WZ*, 16.12.1918.

[15] *Freiheit* (Berlin), 14.3.1919; *BVS*, 10.2.1919 (Beilage).

[16] ZStA, M'burg, Rep.77, 1373 a, Nr.17, Bl.10–14.

[17] STA Remscheid, N/K/I,3.

[18] STA Bottrop, BI, 1078, Bl. 27.

[19] *VZD*, 23.11.1918.

[20] *BVS*, 23.11.1918.

[21] Brass was placed no. 2 on the ticket for the district Düsseldorf East (behind Lore Agnes) and was elected.

[22] H. Lambers, *Die Revolutionszeit in Hagen* (Hagen, 1963); H. U. Knies, 'Wuppertal', *passim*, in R. Rürup, *Arbeiter und Soldatenräte*, pp. 83–153.

[23] Short secondary descriptions of the revolution in Düsseldorf are found in Weidenhaupt, pp. 158–9; E. Hoffmann, *Dr. Francis Kruse* (Leipzig 1937), pp. 178–80. Note also W. Zensen, 'Politische Unruhen in Düsseldorf' (Staatsexamensarbeit, Neuss, 1969).

[24] *MB*, 21.7.1918.

[25] STA Düsseldorf, Nachlass Lehr, 57.

[26] STA Düsseldorf, XXI, 332.

[27] HSTAD, 15279, Bl. 22.

[28] HSTAD, 15081, Bl. 40.

[29] Ibid. Bl. 67.

[30] Ibid. Bl. 43.

[31] Ibid. Bl. 67.

[32] *Freie Presse*, Düsseldorf, 2.12.1918.

[33] STA Düsseldorf, XXI, 332.

[34] The terms of the armistice did not allow for soldiers to be stationed on the eastern bank of the Rhine. Hence the word 'Soldiers' had to be dropped from the name.

[35] See the records of the Workers' and Soldiers' Council's and Workers' Council's meetings. STA Düsseldorf, XXI, Akte 333.

[36] *VZD*, 27.11.1918.

[37] Oehler, p. 55.

[38] *VZD*, 27.11.1918.

[39] *VZD*, 11.12.1918.

[40] *VZD*, 5.12.1918.

[41] D. Mitchell, *1919—Red Mirage* (London, 1970), p. 93.

[42] *VZD*, 13.1.1919, 2.2.1919, 29.2.1919, 7.5.1919; STA Düsseldorf, III, 18072 (Schmitt v. Knopp).

[43] E.g. *VZD*, 26.11.1918.

[44] *VZD*, 28.11.1918, 14.12.1918, 2.1.1919; STA Düsseldorf, XXI, 333, negotiations with Stadtsekretär Herings (2.1.1919); STA Düsseldorf, XXI, 334.

[45] *VZD*, 2.1.1919.

[46] Ibid.

[47] *VZD*, 28.11.1918, 29.11.1918.

[48] Ibid.

[49] HSTAD, Reg. Düsseldorf, 15279, Bl. 25ff.

[50] *VZD*, 22.11.1918, 25.11.1918, 27.11.1918, 4.12.1918.

[51] Quoted in H. Habedank, *Um Mitbestimmung und Nationalisierung während der November Revolution und im Frühjahr, 1919* (Berlin, 1968), p. 153.

[52] *VZD*, 27.11.1918, 27.12.1918; see also Ochel's account in *Vorwärts und nicht vergessen* (Berlin, 1958), pp. 480–8; see also, pp. 56–7.

[53] *VZD,* 8.1.1919.

[54] Lucas, *Märzrevolution,* p. 252.

[55] E.g. HSTAD, 15279, Bl. 30, 32.

[56] HSTAD, Glaubach'sche Sammlung, RWZ No.65.

[57] Oehler, p. 637; Demobilization board to lord mayor Essen, 7.4.1919, STA Essen, Rep. 102, Abt. I/1087.

[58] STA Düsseldorf, XXI, 333, negotiations with *Stadtsekretär* Hering, 2.1.1919.

[59] HSTAD, 33557, Düsseldorf trade inspectors to Government President, 22.8.1918.

[60] HSTAD, 15132, Fachausschuss für Lokomotiven to Kriegsamtstelle Münster, 18.1.1919.

[61] G. D. Feldman, 'Wirtschafts -und sozialpolitische Probleme der deutschen Demobilmachung 1918/19', in H. Mommsen *et. al., Industrielles System* (Düsseldorf, 1974), pp. 618–36.

[62] E.g. HSTAD, 15132, Fachausschus für Lokomotiven to war board Münster, 18.1.1919.

[63] STA Düsseldorf, XXI, 332, e.g. Lücke's report about his visit to Hamborn; minutes of the Workers' and Soldiers' Council sitting of 3 December 1918; Sogemeier, p. 97.

[64] HSTAD, 15135, circular letter of the Economic Demobilization Board, 24.3.1919.

[65] STA Düsseldorf, XXI, 333.

[66] Ibid.

[67] IISG, Rocher Memoiren part II, p. 22.

[68] Ochel, pp. 484–5.

[69] STA Düsseldorf, XXI, 333, minutes of the Workers' Council sitting of 9.1.1919; *VZD,* 10.1.1919.

[70] Oehler to Stadtverordnete, 11.1.1919, HSTAD, 15974, Bl. 59.

[71] Först, *Lehr,* pp. 28–9; Weidenhaupt, pp. 158–9.

[72] Paul Siebel, 'Meine revolutionären Erlebnisse', STA Düsseldorf, XXIII, 40.

[73] HSTAD, 14971, Bl. 282.

[74] The procedures of the court case are reported comprehensively in the November issues of the *Düsseldorf Nachrichten; VZD,* 10.1.1918, 11.1.1918, 13.1.1918, 14.1.1918, 15.1.1918.

[75] *Düsseldorfer Nachrichten,* 8.11.1919, 11.11.1919, 18.11.1919.

[76] See e.g. Kolb, p. 307.

[77] *VZD,* 20.1.1919.

[78] *BVS,* 21.1.1919.

[79] *WZ,* 20.1.1919, 21.1.1919.

Chapter 7

[1] Lucas, *Ursachen,* pp. 2–23; A. Vogel, Die Auswirkungen der Industrialisierung auf die sozialpolitische Struktur Hamborn's in der Zeit von 1870–1914 (Staatsexamensarbeit, 1968), pp. 16–36.

[2] Vogel, p. 36.

[3] K. Freundlieb, *Allgemeine und wirtschaftliche Entwicklung der Stadt Hamborn am Rhein* (Würzburg, 1930), p. 73, quoted in Lucas, *Ursachen,* p. 11.

[4] See pp. 28–9.

[5] STA Duisburg, 51/75, report of the *Beigeordnete* Schweitzer, 13.4.1919.

[6] Spethmann, *Zwölf Jahre,* p. 85.

[7] Record of the sitting of the mine owners' executive, 14.10.1918 in G. D. Feldmann, 'The origins of the Stinnes-Legien agreement', *IWK,* 1973, 19/20, pp. 53–6.

[8] Mine owners' association to *Alte Verband,* 15.10.1918, ibid., p. 57.

[9] Del Tedesco, p. 87.

[10] Even this concession was only made provisionally. The mine owners' association in a circular letter a few days later claimed that the wage increases were made subject 'to the condition that nothing unusual was going to happen such as shortage of waggons, fall in production etc. . . . ' With the demobilisation of course difficulties were bound to ensue. The unions did not mention this to their followers. Ibid., p. 89.

[11] Ibid.

[12] Lucas, *Ursachen,* p. 32.

[13] Minister for Trade and Commerce to Government President, 14.11.1918, STAM, OBA. 1793.

[14] *Volkszeitung* (Bottrop), 11.11.1918.

[15] STAM, OBA. 1793, Bl. 275–279, 306–310.

[16] STA Duisburg 51/75.

[17] Ibid.

[18] *Bericht Untersuchungskommission*, p. 5649.

[19] Lucas, *Ursachen*, p. 35.

[20] STAM, OBA. 1793, Bl. 244.

[21] Lucas, *Ursachen*, p. 38.

[22] Ibid., p. 40.

[23] Ibid., p. 46.

[24] *Bericht Untersuchungskommission*, p. 5649. STAM, OBA. 1793, Bl. 248–50; Lucas, *Ursachen*, pp. 45–6.

[25] Record of meeting at Hamborn Altmarkt, 10.12.1918, STA Duisburg, 51/75.

[26] Ibid.

[27] The rise was not specified but when announced it was 50 per cent.

[28] Lucas, *Ursachen*, pp. 57–8.

[29] Ibid, p. 63; HSTAD, 15032, Bl 17–19.

[30] See p. 132–4.

[31] Lucas, *Ursachen*, p. 80.

[32] 'Stenographischer Bericht der Verhandlung mit der Streikkommission', STA Duisburg, 51/75.

[33] Ibid.

[34] Ibid.

[35] Ibid.

[36] STAM, Reg. Münster, Nr. 17, vol. 2, e.g. Bl. 158, 159, 163; HSTAD 15032, Bl. 65; Lucas, *Ursachen*, pp. 47–50.

[37] Protocol of the Mülheim conference in HSTAD, 15032 and in Lucas, *Ursachen*, pp. 107–14.

[38] A similar agreement was reached with the management of Neumühl and Concordia in Oberhausen, although at these mines the sum paid was slightly lower.

[39] On the November Revolution in Mülheim: I. Steinisch's, 'Linksradikalismus und Rätebewegung im westlichen Ruhrgebiet. Die revolutionären Auseinandersetzungen in Mülheim an der Ruhr' in Rürup, *Arbeiter-und Soldatenräte* pp. 239–97.

[40] See pp. 130, 135–6.

[41] They were accused of having conspired with the Belgium Army Command. The incident was widely reported in the newspapers, e.g. *WAVZ*, 5.12.1918, 10.12.1918, 11.12.1918. The charges could not be substantiated.

[42] *BAS*, 5.12.1918; Koszyk, *Minster*, p. 203; on Minster's background see also pp. 57–9.

[43] See for example Völker's speech of 10 December, above, p. 104.

[44] STA Duisburg 51/75, 'Stenographischer Bericht', 24.12.1918; Strecker was dismissed from office when Hamborn was occupied by government troops in late February 1919.

[45] STAM, Reg. Münster, VII, Nr. 17, vol. 2, Bl. 159f. Lucas, *Ursachen*, pp. 71–2.

[46] HSTAD, 15033, Bl. 91; *VZD*, 28.12.1918; Lucas, pp. 85–6.

[47] *VBB*, 28.12.1918.

[48] HSTAD, 15033, GDK to government Düsseldorf, December 1918.

[49] *Freiheit* (Mülheim), 31.12.1918.

[50] F. Mogs, Die sozialgeschichtliche Entwicklung der Stadt Oberhausen zwischen 1850–1933, (Diss., Köln, 1956), pp. 28–9, 88.

[51] Ibid., p. 92.

[52] Ibid., p. 142.

[53] Ibid., pp. 197–8; STA Oberhausen, Stadt Oberhausen, Nachkriegsakten, 3.

[54] *GA* Oberhausen, 31.12.1918.

[55] Mogs, p. 197.

[56] *700 Jahre Stadt Dorsten* (Dorsten, 1951), p. 35.

[57] STA Dorsten, B 2560.

[58] *Volkszeitung Dorsten*, 2.1.1919; *Volkszeitung Bottrop*, 3.1.1919; STA Dorsten 2560.

[59] Ibid.; *Volkszeitung Dorsten*, 16.1.1919.

[60] Chmielecki, p. 21.

[61] See p. 23.

[62] See pp. 135–7; for detail on the Bottrop Workers' Council see Rosenfelder, Die revolutionären Ereignisse in Bottrop, *passim*.

[63] See pp. 135–7.

[64] Rosenfelder, pp. 28–30.

[65] *Bericht Untersuchungskommission*, pp. 5597–8.

[66] *Freiheit* (Mülheim), 8.1.1919.

[67] *GA* Oberhausen, 17.1.1919.

[68] *BVS*, 6.1.1919.

[69] *Freiheit* (Mülheim), 18.1.1919.

[70] *NVS*, 10.11.1918.

[71] STA Duisburg, 51/6, e.g. records of sittings on 16, 23 and 28 November.

[72] See pp. 57–8.

[73] *Rhein-Ruhr Zeitung*, 12.1.1919; HSTAD, 15974, Bl. 365/6.

[74] Averdunk and Ring, *Geschichte der Stadt Duisburg* (Ratingen, 1949), p. 236.

[75] HSTAD, 15974, Bl. 57.

[76] Lucas, *Ursachen*, p. 100.

[77] HSTAD, 15277, Bl. 228.

Chapter 8

[1] Von Oertzen stresses the concept of 'Sozialization plus Councils' which he considers reached its highest level of development in the Essen model. He argues that the model had the support of the vast majority of the workers, a support strong enough to silence any dissatisfaction and KPD and SPD leaders (p. 248). Only 'a small . . . minority . . . of hopeless utopians . . . who could have been dealt with by the local police' (p. 262) opposed the model.

[2] Traditional West German historians reject the attack by 'third way' historians upon the SPD leadership and allege that they underplay the 'bolshevist danger' in 1918/1919. (Note for example A. Herzfeld's review of *Vom Kaiserreich zur Republik*, in *IWK*, 1974, vol. 10, Heft 1, pp. 109–110.) East German historians have refuted the argument that there was a 'third way' or an alternative to communism, although they credit von Oertzen with having gone the furthest of western historians in his criticism of SPD policies.

[3] Lucas especially points to the fact that three SPD representatives on the commission of nine were leading officials of the *Alte Verband*. He sees this as having been a step back from the position reached by the Hamborn miners. To him the Essen model was only a diversion *(Verschleierung)*. *Ursachen*, pp. 103–4. Kluge criticises Lucas's analysis for ending at the moment the Essen model began to make its impact (p. 59). However, Lucas limited the aim of his *Ursachen* to the gap in von Oertzen's article. A more thorough discussion of the relation of the Hamborn miners to the overall situation in the Ruhr and in Germany will have to await Lucas's planned work on the November Revolution in the Ruhr. (Announced in *Märzrevolution*, p. 5.)

[4] Kluge, p. 65.

[5] 'Die grossen Streik', pp. 248–9.

[6] H. Mommsen, 'Die Bergarbeiterbewegung in der Ruhr', in Reulecke, *Arbeiterbewegung*, pp. 291–2.

[7] H. Luther, *Zusammenbruch und Jahre nach dem ersten Weltkrieg* (Essen, 1958), p. 34.

[8] Note the discrepancies in population density between the various suburbs: *Beiträge zur Statistik der Stadt Essen*, 1902, no. 2, pp. 13, 25.

[9] The support for the socialists was strongest in the north of the city and the northern suburbs such as Altenessen and Stoppenberg. Support in the south, e.g. Kupferdreh, Rellinghausen, Stehle or Überruhr, was small, HSTAD, 12171.

[10] Police report Essen 1910, HSTAD 42781.

[11] Mattheier, pp. 180–4.

[12] The strength of this organisation in the pre-war years was estimated at between two and three thousand. Neumann, p. 145.

[13] Protokolle über die Verhandlungen des Parteitages der Sozialdemokratischen Partei, Deutschlands in Würzburg vom 14 bis 20 Oktober 1917, pp. 9–10.

[14] *MB*, 1.4.1917.

[15] On the revolution in Essen: *Chronik der Stadt Essen, 1912-1919*, pp. 129–40; STA Essen, Rep. 102, Abt. I, 1093; Luther, *Zusammenbruch und Jahre nach dem ersten Krieg*, pp. 34–9; F. Baade, 'Die November Revolution von 1918', *Die Heimatstadt Essen*, 1960, vol. 12, pp. 52–4; P. Brandi, *Essener Arbeitsjahre* (Essen, 1959), pp. 80–1. Secondary literature: H. E. Kromberg, Politische Strömungen und Wahlen im Stadt-und Landkreis Essen (Diss. Bonn, 1968); F. Mause, 'Der Einfluss der Arbeiter und Soldatenräte auf die Kommunalpolitik in Essen während der November Revolution 1918/1919', *Staatsexamensarbeit* (Münster, 1973).

[16] According to Luther (p. 24), Baade had initially intended to study theology and had joined the USP because of his pacifist beliefs. After the revolution Baade pursued a long and successful career as professor at Kiel University and the presidency of the university's institute of world economics *(Universitätsinstitut für Weltwirtschaft).*

[17] *AZE*, 10.11.1918, 11.11.1918.

[18] *AZE*, 11.11.1918.

[19] *AZE*, 13.12.1918.

[20] Luther, pp. 24–5.

[21] The only exception was a demonstration at the office of the *RWZ* on 3 December 1918. This followed an article by this paper which was directed against the Workers' and Soldiers' Councils.

[22] STA Essen, Rep. 102, Abt. I, 1093, Bl. 94–124; lord mayor Düsseldorf to lord mayor Essen, 7.4.1919. STA Essen, Rep. 102, Abt. I, 1087.

[23] Ibid., HSTAD, 1531.

[24] STA Essen, Rep. 102, Abt. I, 1093, Bl. 83.

[25] Lucas, p. 71.

[26] *AZE*, 13.12.1919.

[27] Ibid.

[28] *Illustrierte Geschichte*, pp. 317–18.

[29] Von Oertzen, 'Die grossen Streiks', p. 249; Mommsen, pp. 291–2.

[30] M. Brinton, *The Bolsheviks and Workers Control* (London, 1970). Von Oertzen points to the absence of concrete ideas in the German Socialist movement on how 'the emancipation of the working class' would look in practice (p. 236). But there is no evidence for his claim that the German workers themselves remedied this absence in the Essen model. None of the strikes which are said to have led the Essen Workers' and Soldiers' Council to attempt the socialisation of the coal-mining industry were for anything beyond wage demands. Nor did the course of events ever hint that the great bulk of the miners were prepared to sink their party loyalties in their pursuance of the council system. (See pp. 125–7).

[31] *BAZ*, 1.2.1919. The article errs here, the date was 9 January.

[32] Mommsen, p. 291.

[33] *Der Zentralrat der Deutschen Sozialistischen Republik*, edited by E. Kolb (Leiden, 1968), p. 689.

[34] Quoted in Spethmann, *Zwölf Jahre*, p. 150.

[35] See p. 123.

[36] Note extract quoted above, p. 121.

[37] Quoted in Spethmann, *Zwölf Jahre*, p. 151.

[38] C. D. Krohn, 'Steuerpolitik and Industrie in der Stabilisierungsphase', in H. Mommsen *et. al.*, *Industrielles System*, p. 428.

[39] Krombach, p. 56.

[40] *AZE*, 14.1.1919.

[41] VBB, 14.1.1919; Spethmann, *Zwölf Jahre*, p. 155.

[42] The Christian delegates later claimed that they had no right to vote, still they could have spoken up (von Oertzen, p. 249).

[43] These were the elections to the pit foremen's district council *(Steigerrevierräte)*, mine councils *(Zechenräte)*, district councils *(Revierräte)* and the supreme mines council *(Zentralzechenrat)*. VBB, 14.1.1919; Spethmann, *Zwölf Jahre*, p. 155.

[44] Quoted in Spethmann, p. 378.

[45] von Oertzen, 'Die grossen Streiks', p. 249.

[46] Julius Karski (Marchlewski), an economics graduate of Polish origin, was a leading member of the Spartacists. Like other co-founders of the KPD he left Berlin during the revolution to agitate for the communists throughout the rest of Germany. For an analysis of Karski's thoughts: H. Habedank, *Um Mitbestimmung und Nationalisierung während der November Revolution und im Frühjahr 1919* (Berlin, 1969), pp. 240–7; note also Karski's arguments in the *Broschüre Neuner-kommission*, which was written by him and his speech to the conference of 5 March. There is a printed copy of this speech at the STA Essen.

[47] Reproduced in Spethmann, *Zwölf Jahre*, p. 156.

[48] The policies of the people's delegates and their background have been extensively researched into. For a comprehensive account see the works of Schieck and Elben. For more recent and shorter articles see G. Feldmann, E. Kolb, R. Rürup, 'Die Massenbewegungen der Arbeiterschaft am Ende des ersten Weltkrieges (1917–1920)'; R. N. Hunt, 'Friedrich Ebert and the German revolution', in L. Krieger and F. Stern (eds.), *The Responsibility of Power* (New York, 1971). For a critical study of the orthodox USP, especially of Kautsky, Habedank, pp. 115–16; on the relations between the government and the army see Sauër and Kluge.

[49] Dörnemann, p. 37.

[50] *Der Zentralrat der Deutschen Sozialistischen Republik, 19.2.1918–8.4.1919*, edited by E. Kolb and R. Rürup in the series *Quellen zur Geschichte der Rätebewegung in Deutschland*, vol. 1 (Leiden, 1968), pp. 522–3.

[51] *BAZ*, 1.2.1919.

[52] *VBB*, 14.1.1919.

[53] Ibid.

[54] *WAVZ*, 15.1.1919.

[55] *AZE*, 14.1.1919. Italics added.

[56] Quoted in *Broschüre Neunerkommission*, p. 10.

[57] *Broschüre Neunerkommission*, p. 10

[58] Quoted in Dörnemann, p. 39.

[59] *NVS*, 23.1.1919.

[60] STA Dortmund, Bestand 5, File 145, Bl. 323–326.

[61] STA Lüner, 68 Hauprakte Bl.131–3, *Lüner Zeitung* 8.1.1919.

[62] STA Dortmund, Bestand 3.n286: report Workers' and Soldiers' Council, Dortmund, 15.1.1919.

[63] Rosenfelder, p. 78.

[64] STA Essen, Rep. 102, Abt. I, 1093, Bl. 235–261. 'Bericht über die dritte Konferenz der Arbeiter-und Soldätenrate 6. Februar 1919 im städtischen Saalbau Essen'.

[65] Third conference, p. 1.

[66] Ibid., p. 2.

[67] Ibid., p. 3.

[68] Ibid., p. 4.

[69] Ibid., p. 5.

[70] Ibid., p. 6.

[71] Ibid., p. 6.

[72] Ibid., p. 7.

[73] Ibid., p. 8.

[74] Ibid., p. 10.

[75] Ibid., p. 9.

[76] Ibid., p. 27.

[77] *Broschüre Neunerkommission*, pp. 13–18.

[78] Ibid.; also Dörnemann, pp. 42–3.

[79] Elben, p. 168.

[80] STAM, files of the Büro Kölpin.

[81] In the first month of the November Revolution the Kölpin office did not function so efficiently. In fact the documents of its early activities have little value at all although they do throw light upon the mental climate of the world of secret agents. This is illustrated for example by the January report of the Düsseldorf agent which was so highly confidential that it could be passed on only from hand to hand. The agent claimed to have been working in close co-operation with the Düsseldorf KPD leader Schmittgen and to be in possession of the latter's plan for a West German Republic. The plan amounted to little more than gossip. The 'highly valuable information' was hardly a secret.. An independent socialist West German Republic was a topic of discussion at a meeting of left-wing leaders held early January in Brunswick and was mentioned in the daily press. There was nothing behind it. A united North-West German left staging a major uprising against the Berlin government was never a serious possibility.

[82] *Darstellungen aus den Nachkriegkämpfen Deutscher Truppen*, vol. 9, 'Errettung des Ruhrgebiets' (Berlin, 1943), p. 7.

[83] *Bericht Untersuchungsausschuss*, p. 5594.

[84] *Darstellungen*, pp. 20–1.

[85] For details see F. L. Carsten, *The Reichswehr and Politics* (Oxford, 1966), p. 18.

[86] Schulte, *Spartakismus*, pp. 324ff.

[87] *WAVZ*, 14.2.1919.

[88] Dörnemann, pp. 44–5.

[89] *Dokumente und Materialien*, 2nd series, vol. 3, pp. 149–50.

[90] *Bericht Untersuchungsausschuss*, pp. 5599–612.

[91] Ibid., pp. 5602–5.

[92] STAM, Reg. Münster, 4264, report *Amtmann* Wulfen, 27.2.1919.

[93] Note, for example, his speech at the third conference, above, p. 126.

[94] HSTAD, Landgericht Essen G, 52,VI.

[95] STAM, Reg. Münster, 4264, script of his resignation of 12.3.1919; *Darstellungen*, p. 27.

[96] Ibid., pp. 27–30.

[97] *Rhein-Ruhr Zeitung*, 24.2.1919.

[98] *VBB*, 27.2.1919, STA Dorsten B 2560.

[99] Quoted in Krombach, p. 62.

[1] *Broschüre Neunerkommission*, p. 23.

[2] Lucas, *Märzrevolution*, p. 43; Habedank, pp. 248–52.

[3] The USP leadership in Düsseldorf, for example, was highly critical of the Mülheim decision (*VZD*, 17.2.1919). However, the majority of the workers went on strike immediately.

[4] *AZE*, 17.2.1919, 19.2.1919; *WAVZ*, 19.2.1919; *Broschüre Neunerkommission*, pp. 23–4.

[5] Ibid.

Chapter 9

[1] Dörnemann, p. 50.

[2] *RWZ*, 21.2.1919.

[3] *VZD*, 21.2.1919.

[4] *NVS*, 18.2.1919.

[5] Ibid.

[6] Ibid.

[7] GA Oberhausen, 19.2.1919.

[8] Spethmann refers to thirty-one cases altogether. In five of these even Spethmann does not mention any outside interference or minority action which prevented the shifts from descending (Prosper 2/3, Arenberg Fortsetzung, König Ludwig, Ver. Carolinenglück, Prinz Regent). At a further six mines the strike was called by one or two speakers whereupon the miners went home. (Prosper I, Nordstern 3/4, Bergmannsglück, Brassert, Ver. Salzer and Neuack.) At five more collieries work was brought to a halt by a full demonstration from a neighbouring mine (Auguste Viktoria, Holland 1/2, Hannibal I, Wickern, de Wendel).

[9] *VBB*, 8.5.1919, 9.5.1919.

[10] ZStA, Po, *Informationsstelle der Reichsregierung*, 31.
[11] *VBB*, 22.2.1919; *GA Gelsenkirchen*, 20.2.1919, 22.2.1919.
[12] *VBB*, 22.2.1919.
[13] Ibid.
[14] *GA Gelsenkirchen*, 22.2.1919.
[15] Ibid.
[16] Ibid., 28.2.1919.
[17] Woczek to lord mayor Gelsenkirchen, 6.3.1919, STA Gelsenkirchen, XVIII/5.20.
[18] See p. 149.
[19] For details see the author's Ph.D. thesis, pp. 254–6.
[20] See pp. 110–11.
[21] Knies, pp. 103ff.
[22] *Freiheit* (Mülheim), 24.1.1919.
[23] *Bericht Untersuchungsausschuss*, p. 5654.
[24] *Freiheit* (Mülheim), 21.1.1919.
[25] The battle of Bottrop is still remembered in big memorial services held every five or ten years. All the city's dignitaries attend, especially the local politicians, and stirring speeches are made, in which historial reality is lacking but rhetoric is powerful. The services are held to honour fourteen members of the Bottrop Workers' and Soldiers' Council and security guard who, on 19 February 1919—as it was put at the most recent commemoration—'were murdered by the communists . . . while defending democracy and freedom'. In these speeches mourning for the victims is overshadowed by polemics and by references to the state of present day politics in Germany.
[26] Rosenfelder, p. 53.
[27] Spethmann, *Zwölf Jahre*, p. 221; Darstellungen, p. 33.
[28] *Bericht Untersuchungsausschuss*, p. 5613.
[29] HSTAD, *Landgericht Essen*, Rep.G 53 I and II; the court procedures were also described in detail in the *AZE* from 21.7.1919 to 24.8.1919; *VZD*, 19.2.1919; note Ochel's speech at the meeting in the Apollo theatre.
[30] *Bericht Untersuchungsausschuss*, pp. 5612–18; *AZE*, 26.7.1919; note also the pleadings of the public prosecutor (*AZE*, 21.8.1919) the counsels for the defence (*AZE*, 23.8.1919) and the publication of the judgment (*AZE*, 24.8.1919); *Freiheit* (Mülheim), 21.2.1919.
[31] *Illustrierte Geschichte*, p. 72; *Darstellungen*, p. 34; this seems certainly too high.
[32] Spethmann, pp. 244–5.
[33] *NVS*, 26.2.1919.
[34] HSTAD, 15974, Bl. 162–3.
[35] Quoted in Rosenberger, p. 35.
[36] *AZE*, 24.2.1919; *Volkszeitung* (Bottrop), 25.2.1919.
[37] HSTAD, 15974, Bl. 199.
[38] Ibid., Bl. 200.
[39] *Bericht Untersuchungsausschuss*, pp. 5654–6.
[40] Ibid., p. 5644.
[41] *RWZ*, 26.2.1919.
[42] *GA Oberhausen*, 3.2.1919; *Bericht Untersuchungsausschuss*, pp. 5644–7; HSTAD, 15974, Bl. 370; Mogs, pp. 197–201.
[43] *NVS*, 19.1.1919, 20.1.1919.
[44] HSTAD 15974, Bl. 366.
[45] *Rhein-Ruhr Zeitung*, 27.2.1919; *NVS*, 27.2.1919; HSTAD, 15974, Bl. 366.
[46] *NVS*, 12.3.1919; HSTAD, 15974, Bl. 367; *Bericht Untersuchungsausschuss*, pp. 5652–3.
[47] *GA Oberhausen*, 28.2.1919; *NVS*, 28.2.1919.
[48] *GA Oberhausen*, 1.3.1919.
[49] STA Duisburg, 51/71.
[50] Spethmann, *Zwölf Jahre*, p. 250.
[51] Quoted in *VZD*, 21.6.1919.
[52] Schulz, *Ein Freikorps im Ruhrgebiet* (no date and place of publication). I. Steinisch, *passim*.
[53] *Darstellungen*, pp. 35, 36; HSTAD, 15974, Bl. 369.

[54] See pp. 97–8.

[55] 15.1.1919.

[56] STA Düsseldorf, Bestand XXI, 333, Workers' Council sitting of 17.1.1919.

[57] STA Düsseldorf, 333, notice of 22.1.1919.

[58] A. Oehler, 'Meine Beziehungen zur Revolution in Düsseldorf', in HSTAD, 15974. The couple had left their home in Oberkassel across the river Rhine where they had taken up residence after their escape from Düsseldorf and were casting their vote at a Düsseldorf polling booth. They were recognised, arrested and kept for several hours at the headquarters of the executive Council until their request to be taken to relatives at the Rhenish country town of Wesel was granted. The road to Wesel, about 100 km to the north of Düsseldorf, was closed outside Hamborn because of clashes between troops and workers around the Lohberg mine. The couple were then brought to Mülheim where they were held for several days in an hotel on the charge of collaborating with the Allies. As the charges could not be substantiated they were dismissed on 23 February, whereupon they moved to relatives in central Germany.

[59] STA Düsseldorf, Bestand XXI, 334.

[60] *VZD*, 6.2.1919; *Düsseldorfer Nachrichten*, 6.2.1919.

[61] See pp. 93.

[62] E.g. *VZD*, 28.1.1919.

[63] STA Düsseldorf, Bestand XXI, 334, February sitting of district advisory board for economic demobilisation.

[64] STA Düsseldorf, 332, sitting of 23.12.1918. *VZD*, 4.12.1919, 13.2.1919.

[65] *VZD*, 11.2.1919.

[66] Quoted in *VZD*, 14.2.1919.

[67] Quoted in *VZD*, 26.2.1919.

[68] Ibid.

[69] Treasurer to Schmittgen, 24.2.1919; STA Düsseldorf, Bestand XXI, 334.

[70] Ibid.

[71] Council sitting 4.2.1919, STA Düsseldorf, 334.

[72] STAM, Büro Kölpin, Nr. 19, Bl. 39. According to the report the Allies would not deal with the Spartacists.

[73] Sitting of 12.2.1919; STA Düsseldorf, 334.

[74] Ibid.; *VZD*, 21.2.1919.

[75] *VZD*, 25.2.1919, 26.2.1919; STA Düsseldorf, Bestand XXI, 335, Leyser's report.

[76] Ibid.

[77] *Darstellungen*, pp. 38–40.

[78] *RWZ*, 1.3.1919.

[79] *VZD*, 3.3.1919, 4.3.1919.

Chapter 10

[1] *WAVZ*, 24.2.1919.

[2] *BAZ*, 8.3.1919.

[3] *BAZ*, 15.3.1919.

[4] *WAVZ*, 3.3.1919.

[5] *VBB*, 3.3.1919.

[6] *GA* Duisburg, 12.3.1919.

[7] ZStA, Po, Informationsstelle der Reichsregierund, 31, Bl. 90.

[8] Ibid.

[9] E.g. 'Report Wanne', section 23 g; *GA* Duisburg, 28.3.1919; *WAVZ*, 28.3.1919.

[10] STA Dortmund, Bestand 3, Do n 90.

[11] IISG, *Zentralrat*, B 3; report about meeting of 4.3.1919.

[12] *AZE*, 21.2.1919; note also the complaint of the *Nordische Ein-und Ausfuhrgesellschaft*, 25.1.1919, *Zentralrat*, B 3.

[13] ZStA, Rep. 77, Tit. 1373 a, Nr. 7, Bl. 9.

[14] Ibid., Bl.18.

[15] E.g. *WAVZ*, 21.3.1919, *RWZ*, 10.3.1919, *AZE*, 18.3.1919.

[16] Sogemeier, p. 107.
[17] *AZE*, 8.3.1919.
[18] *WAVZ*, 25.3.1919.
[19] *VBB*, 11.3.1919.
[20] *Darstellungen*, pp. 40–2.
[21] HSTAD, 16009, Bl. 1.
[22] Quoted in W. Oehme, *Die Weimarer Nationalversammlung* (Berlin, 1962), p. 237.
[23] Ibid.
[24] Note *BAZ*, 25.1.1919; Bachmann's role in the battle for Bottrop, *VZD*, 10.3.1919.
[25] *Ruhrwacht* (Duisburg), 6.6.1919.
[26] WC Gelsenkirchen to *Zentralrat*, 11.3.1919, B 12; STA Gelsenkirchen XVIII/12/23.
[27] The Workers' Council in Duisburg, for example, resigned on 21 March, STA Duisburg, 51/45.
[28] *WAVZ*, 8.3.1919.
[29] *WAVZ*, 4.3.1919.
[30] *NVS*, 7.3.1919.
[31] Ibid.
[32] *WAVZ*, 13.3.1919.
[33] Ibid.
[34] Ibid.; *AZE*, 3.3.1919.
[35] *VBB*, 3.3.1919.
[36] *VBB*, 3.3.1919.
[37] *NVS*, 3.3.1919.
[38] See pp. 139–40.
[39] For the results in Mülheim: *RWZ*, 31.1.1919; Düsseldorf: *VZD*, 17.3.1919; Hagen: *WAVZ*, 3.3.1919; Essen: *Essener Chronik*, p.20. The *Zentrum* or combined middle-class tickets scored well in these elections. E.g. 21,000 out of 47,000 votes in Düsseldorf, half of the 42,000 votes in Essen. However, the most generous interpretation of the term worker, which allowed white-collar workers and other middle-class professions to vote too, helped their fortunes considerably.
[40] G. D. Feldman, 'Wirtschafts-und sozialpolitische Probleme', *passim*.
[41] The first time the six-hour shift received a mention was in the *NVS* on 10.3.1919.
[42] *RWZ*, 18.3.1919.
[43] Mainly in the west, although some mines were as far east as Castrop; *Castroper Zeitung*, 31.3.1919.
[44] 'Die Sozialisierung des Bergbaus', p. 17.
[45] *GA* Duisburg, 5.3.1919.
[46] STA Witten, 1/11/13, 'Verwaltungsbericht 1915–1919'.
[47] *VBB*, 26.3.1919; *Wittener Volkszeitung*, 16.7.1919.
[48] *Wittener Volkszeitung*, 20.3.1919.
[49] Note the evidence given by Beltzer during the trial at the Bochum court, *Wittener Volkszeitung*, 15.7.1919.
[50] O. Plesken to administration, 13.4.1919, STA Witten 1/16/1.
[51] *VBB*, 26.3.1919; records on court procedures 15–20.7.1919, *Wittener Volkszeitung*.
[52] *WAVZ*, 27.3.1919, 28.3.1919; *VBB*, 28.3.1919.
[53] *Wittener Volkszeitung*, 20.7.1919.
[54] Tampke, thesis, pp. 296–7.
[55] HSTAD, 15034, Bl. 53.
[56] *Dokumente und Materialien*, Second Series, vol. 3 (Berlin, 1958), pp. 343–4.
[57] See chapter 1.
[58] *Illustrierte Geschichte*, p. 329.
[59] Strike statistics in Spethmann, *Zwölf Jahre*, p. 280.
[60] Dörnemann, p. 63.
[61] E.g. *Dokumente und Materialien*, p. 349; *Volksrecht* (Frankfurt), 4.4.1919, 5.4.1919, 6.4.1919, 7.4.1919, 8.4.1919.
[62] See pp. 157.
[63] 10.4.1919.

[64] *WAVZ*, 2.4.1919.
[65] Quoted in Dörnemann, pp. 61–2.
[66] *Darstellungen*, p. 48.
[67] Ibid.
[68] HSTAD, 15034, Bl. 156.
[69] *AZE*, 20.4.1919.
[70] *Essener Chronik, 1919*, p. 74.
[71] C. Severing, *1919/1920 im Wetter-und Watterwinkel* (Bielfeld, 1927), pp. 138–9.
[72] Quoted in Dörnemann, p. 67.
[73] *WAVZ*, 29.3.1919.
[74] STA Dortmund, Bestand 3, Do, n, 312.
[75] STAM, Reg. Arnsberg, I, Pa, 342, Police President Gelsenkirchen to 7.AK, 21.4.1919.
[76] *WAVZ*, 22.4.1919.
[77] H. Teuber, 'Beiträge zur neueren Geschichte der Arbeiterbewegung im Ruhrgebiet', *Sozialistische Politik und Wirtschaft*, 1926, vol. 4, no. 39; *BAZ*, 3.5.1919; *VZD*, 29.4.1919.
[78] *Darstellungen*, p. 49; *Illustrierte Geschichte*, p. 331; Schulz (Major), *Ein Freikorps im Ruhrgebiet* (Mülheim, 1922).
[79] HSTAD, 15034, Bl. 220–1.
[80] Tampke, thesis, pp. 305–7.
[81] *Illustrierte Geschichte*, p. 332; Dörnemann, p. 67f; *Essener Chronik*, p. 66.
[82] See e.g. *VBB*, 3.4.1919.
[83] Spethmann, *Zwölf Jahre*, p. 280; Dörnemann, p. 69.
[84] *Volksrecht* (Frankfurt), 19.4.1919.
[85] *Freiheit* (Berlin), 5.4.1919.
[86] *Volksstimme* (Hagen), 14.4.1919.
[87] *VZD*, 4.4.1919.
[88] Tampke, thesis, pp. 309–12.
[89] Spethmann, *Zwölf Jahre*, p. 280.

Conclusion

[1] STAM, Büro Kölpin, 140; HSTAD, 15346, 15524, 15972.
[2] For the May election 1924 see *Statistik des Deutschen Reichs*, vol. 315, pp. 1–6
[3] G. D. Feldman, E. Kolb, and R. Rürup, 'Die Massenbewegung der Arbeiterschaft in Deutschland am Ende des ersten Weltkrieges (1917–1920)', *Politische Vierteljahresschriften* vol. 13, 1972, p. 96.
[4] Ibid.
[5] See chapter 6.
[6] See chapter 5.
[7] Note, for example, Krishnar Kumar, *Revolution* (London, 1970) and Hannah Arundt, *On Revolution* (London, 1963).
[8] Helga Grebing, 'Konservative Republik oder Soziale Demokratie?', in E. Kolb, *Kaiserreich*, p. 394.
[9] Ibid., p. 395.
[10] See chapter 7.
[11] *Soldatenräte.*
[12] For a discussion of the work of the socialisation commission see H. Schieck, 'Die Behandlung der Sozialisierungsfrage in den Monaten nach dem Staatsumsturz', in Kolb, *Kaisserreich*, pp. 138–64.
[13] Ibid., p. 149.

Bibliography

[1] For a detailed list of all the archive material consulted for this work see the bibliography of my Ph.D. thesis 'The Ruhr and Revolution' (Australian National University, 1975). A copy of this thesis has been deposited at all archives and libraries which are listed in the acknowledgments.
[2] Note the full list of newspapers on pp. 199–200.

Bibliography

I. *PRIMARY SOURCES*

A. *Note on Archive material*[1]

The sources at the *Hauptstaatsarchiv* in Düsseldorf-Kalkum and the *Staatsarchiv* in Münster are invaluable for the economic, social and political history of the Rhenish-Westphalian Industrial Region up to 1918. The correspondence between the government presidents and the local administrators provides detailed material on population growth, industrial development and its impact, average income and prices, standard of health and housing statistics. In these two archives are also the records of the political police and the large number of administrative files covering the war years. Additional interesting material on all these aspects is also to be found at the *Zentrale Staatsarchiv, Historische Abteilung 2* in Merseburg.

As far as the November Revolution of 1918 and the Workers' and Soldiers' Councils are concerned the holdings of these archives are less impressive. For the time between November 1918 and April 1919 it is necessary to consult the sources held at the regional *Stadtarchive.* Most valuable for this period are also the local newspapers[2] which are generally found in the town archives of their place of publication.

B. *Personal accounts and contemporary publications*

Baade, F. 'Die November Revolution von 1918', in *Die Heimatstadt Essen,* 1960, vol.12.

Bericht der Sozialisierungskommission über die Frage der Sozialisierung des Kohlenbergbaus (Berlin, 1920).

Berton, P. *Lebenslauf eines einfachen Menschen* (Düsseldorf, 1958).

Brandi, P. *Essener Arbeitsjahre* (Essen, 1959).

Luther, H. *Zusammenbruch und Jahre nach dem ersten Krieg in Essen* (Essen, 1958).

Marchlewski, (Karski) J. *Die Sozialisierung des Bergbaus* (1919).

Meinberg, A. 'Aus dem Wetter und Watterwinkel', *Westfälischer Kämpfer,* 1927, vol. 3.

Neunerkommission für die Vorbereitung der Sozialisierung des Bergbaus im Rheinisch-Westfälischen Industriegebiet, *Die Sozialisierung des Bergbaus und der Generalstreik im Rheinisch-Westfälischen Industriegebiet* (Essen, 1919).

Ochel, E. 'Rote Volkswehr schlug den Bürgerspuk auseinander' in *Vorwärts und nicht vergessen. Erlebnisberichte aktiver Teilnehmer der November-Revolution 1918/19,* edited by the Institut für Marxismus-Leninismus (Berlin, 1958).

Ruben, E. *Geschichte der Essener Sozialisierungsbewegung* (1919).

Schulz (Mayor) *Ein Freikorps im Ruhrgebiet* (Mülheim, 1922).

Severing, C. *Im Wetter-und Watterwinkel* (Bielefeld, 1927).

_____ *Vom Schlosser zum Minister* (Köln, 1950).
Teuber, H. 'Beiträge zur neueren Geschichte der Bergarbeiterbewegung im Ruhrgebiet', *Sozialistische Politik und Wirtschaft,* vol. 4, Nr. 30, 32, 35, 36, 37, 38, 39, 40.
Wilbrandt, R. *Sozialismus* (Jena, 1919).

C. *Administrative and other official publications, union publications, annual reports, yearbooks and statistical publications*

(i) Administrative publications

Amtsverwaltung Wanne, *50 Jahre Amt Wanne* (Wanne, 1925).
Bericht über die Entwicklung und den Stand der Gemeindeangelegenheiten der Stadt Herne vom 1.April 1897-1.April 1922, (Herne, 1922).
Bericht über die Verwaltung der Stadt Gelsenkirchen April 1903-März 1920 (Gelsenkirchen, 1921).
Bericht über die Verwaltung und den Stand der Gemeindeangelegenheiten der Stadt Duisburg in den Rechnungsjahren 1912-1924 (Duisburg, 1924).
Chronik der Stadt Essen, 1912–1919.
Handbuch für die Kriegsfürsorge und Volksernährung der Stadt Bochum, 1917, 1918.
Jahresbericht der Handelskammer zu Dortmund.
Jahresbericht der Handelskammer für den Kreis Essen, 1909, 1910.
Erstes Jahrbuch der Stadt Bottrop, 1919–1920.
Stenographische Berichte über die Verhandlungen des deutschen Reichstags, vol. 247.
Stenographische Verhandlungsberichte der Stadtverordnetenversammlungen zu Düsseldorf, 1919 (Düsseldorf, 1919).
Verwaltungsbericht der Stadt Bochum, 1913–1924.
Verwaltungsbericht der Stadt Castrop, 1914–1926.
Verwaltungsbericht der Stadt Dortmund, 1918–1919.
Verwaltungsbericht der Stadt Düsseldorf, 1912–1919.
Verwaltungsbericht der Bürgermeisterei Sterkrade, 1910–1912.

(ii) Union publications

Deutscher Metallarbeiterverband, *Die Arbeitszeiten in der Eisenindustrie und Metallindustrie Deutschlands* (Stuttgart, 1911).
Generalkommission der Gewerkschaften Deutschlands, *Rechenschaftsbericht,* 1.6.1914–31.5.1919 (Berlin, 1919).
Industriegewerkschaft Metall, *Fünfundsiebzig Jahre Industriegewerkschaft, 1891-1966* (Frankfurt, 1966).
Jahr-und Handbuch des Deutschen Metallarbeiterverbandes, 1913–1918.
Protokolle der Generalversammlungen des Deutschen Metallarbeiterverbandes, 1905–1917.
Protokolle der Generalversammlungen des Verbandes der Bergarbeiter Deutschlands, 1911–1920.
Protokolle der Reichskonferenz der Sozialdemokratie Deutschlands vom 21, 22 und 23 September 1916.
Protokolle über die Verhandlungen des Parteitages der Sozialdemokratischen Partei Deutschlands, in Würzburg vom 14 bis 20 Oktober 1917.
Verband der Bergarbeiter Deutschlands, *Was leistete der Verband während der Krieges?* (Bochum, 1917).

Vorstand des Verbandes der Bergarbeiter Deutschlands, *Verhandlungen und Vereinbarungen der vier Bergarbeiter-Verbände mit dem Zechenverband von Oktober 1918 bis Juli 1919* (Bochum, 1919).

(iii) Statistics

Beiträge zur Statistik der Stadt Essen, Nr. 7, 'Das Aftermietwesen in der Stadt Essen' (Essen, 1900, 1902).

Feig (Dr) 'Erhebungen von Witschaftsberechnungen minderbemittelter Familien im Deutschen Reich', Kaiserliches Statistisches Amt, 2. Sonderheft zum *Reichsarbeitsblatt,* Berlin 1909.

Reichsarbeitsblatt, vols. 12–17.

Statistik des Deutschen Reichs, vols. 207, 209, 217, 218, 250 (1–2), 315 (1–6). Old series: 57, 240 (1).

Statistische Amt der Stadt Essen, *Beiträge zur Statistik der Stadt Essen,* Nr. 2, 'Die Wohnungsverhältnisse in der Stadt Essen nach der Aufnahme vom 1.12.1900'.

Statistische Korrespondenz, vols. 31–38.

Statistisches Jahrbuch der Stadt Essen, vols. 5 and 6.

Statistische Tabellen der Stadt Essen, 1908.

Statistisches Jahrbuch für das deutsche Reich, vols. 40 and 41.

D. *Printed Collections of Documents*

Dokumente und Materialien zur Geschichte der Deutschen Arbeiterbewegung, Second series, vol. 3 (Berlin, 1958).

Quellen zur Geschichte der Rätebewegung in Deutschland, vol. 1, *Der Zentralrat der Deutschen Sozialistischen Republik, 19.12.1918–8.4.1919.* Edited by E. Kolb and R. Rürup (Leiden, 1968).

Quellen zur Geschichte des Parlamentarismus und der Politischen Parteien, vol. 3, parts one and two, *Die Reichstagsfraktion der deutschen Sozialdemokratie —1918.* Edited by W. Conze and E. Matthias (Düsseldorf, 1966). Vol. 6, part one and two, *Die Regierung der Volksbeauftragten, 1918/1919,* edited by E. Matthias (Düsseldorf, 1969).

Quellen und Forschungen zur Geschichte der Stadt Münster, vol. 7, *Münstersche Chronik zu Novemberrevolution,* edited by E. Schulte (Münster, 1936); vol. 10, *Münstersche Chronik zu Spartakismus und Separatismus,* edited by E. Schulte (Münster, 1939).

Ursachen und Folgen vom deutschen Zusammenbruch bis zur staatlichen Neuordnung in der Gegenwart, edited by H. Michaelis and E. Schaepler (Berlin) vols. 1–3.

II. *SELECTED SECONDARY SOURCES*

A. Books

Angress, W.T. *Stillborn Revolution* (Princeton, 1963).

Aereboe, F. *Der Einfluss des Krieges auf die landwirtschaftliche Produktion in Deutschland* (Stuttgart, 1927).

Altkemper, J. *Die Landwirtschaft der Kreise Recklinghausen und Gelsenkirchen unter dem Einfluss der Industrie* (Bonn, 1905).

Averdunk/Ring *Geschichte der Stadt Duisburg* (Ratingen, 1949).

Baumgarten, O. *Geistige und sittliche Wirkungen des Krieges in Deutschland* (Stuttgart, 1927).
Berlau, A.J. *The German Social Democratic Party, 1914–1921* (New York, 1949).
Bock, H.M. *Syndicalismus und Linkskommunismus 1918–1923* (Meisenheim, 1969).
Brepohl, W. *Der Aufbau des Ruhrvolkes im Zuge der Ost-West Wanderung* (Recklinghausen, 1948).
______ *Industrievolk im Wandel von der agraren zur industriellen Daseinsform dargestellt am Ruhrgebiet* (Tübingen, 1957).
Bry, G. *Wages in Germany 1871–1945* (Princeton, 1960).
Bumm, F. *Deutschlands Gesundheitsverhältnisse unter dem Einfluss des Weltkrieges* (Stuttgart, 1928).
Chmielecki, S. *Die Bevölkerungsentwicklung im Landkreis Recklinghausen.*
Coper, R. *Failure of a Revolution* (Cambridge, 1955).
Croon, H. and Utermann, K. *Zeche und Gemeinde* (Tübingen, 1958).
Darstellungen aus den Nachkriegskämpfen Deutscher Truppen und Freikorps. Edited by the Kriegsgeschichtliche Forschungsanstalt des Heeres, vol. 9 (Berlin, 1943).
Desai, A.V. *Real Wages in Germany* (Oxford, 1968).
Dix, A. *Wirtschaftskrieg und Kriegswirtschaft* (Berlin, 1920).
Eberstadt, R. *Rheinische Wohnungsverhältnisse und ihre Bedeutung für das Wohnungswesen in Deutschland* (Jena, 1903).
Elben, W. *Das Problem der Kontinuität in der deutschen Revolution* (Düsseldorf, 1965).
Enke, E. *Genossenschaftliche und Städtische Wohnungspolitik in Essen* (Stuttgart, 1912).
Feldmann, G.D. *Army, Industry and Labour in Germany 1914–1918* (New Jersey, 1966).
Först, W. *Robert Lehr als Oberbürgermeister* (Düsseldorf, 1962).
______ (ed.) *Das Rheinland in Preussischer Zeit* (Köln, 1965).
______ (ed.) *Politik und Landschaft* (Köln, 1965).
______ (ed.) *Rheinische Lebensbilder* (Düsseldorf, 1968).
Gesellschaft für Geographie und Geologie Bochum *Bochum und das Mittlere Ruhrgebiet* (Padderborn, 1965).
Graf, H. *Die Entwicklung der Wahlen und politischen Parteien in Gross-Dortmund* (Hanover and Frankfurt, 1958).
Habedank, H. *Um Mitbestimmung und Nationalisierung während der November Revolution und im Frühjahr 1919* (Berlin, 1969).
Hartl, K. *Die wirtschaftliche und soziale Entwicklung der Landkreises Recklinghausen* (München, 1909).
Herberts, H. *Zur Geschichte der SPD im Wuppertal* (Wuppertal, 1963).
Hesse, F. *Die deutsche Wirtschaftslage von 1914–1923* (Jena, 1923).
Heymann, B. and Freudenberg, K. *Morbidität und Mortalität der Bergleute im Ruhrgebiet* (Essen, 1925).
Hinkers, H.W. *Die geschichtliche Entwicklung der Dortmunder Schwerindustrie seit der Mitte des 19. Jahrhunderts* (Dortmund, 1925).
Hoegner, W. *Der politische Radikalismus in Deutschland, 1919–1933* (München, 1966).
Hoffmann, E. *Dr. Francis Kruse* (Leipzig, 1937).
Hunt, R.N. *German Social Democracy, 1918–1933* (New Haven and London, 1964).

_____ 'Friedrich Ebert and the German Revolution of 1918', in L. Krieger and F. Stern (eds.), *The Responsibility of Power* (New York, 1971).
Hue, O. *Die Bergarbeiter* (Stuttgart, 1910), two volumes.
_____ *Die Sozialisierung der Kohlenwirtschaft* (Berlin, 1921).
Hugo, C. *Die Deutsche Städteverwaltung* (Stuttgart, 1901).
Hundt, R. *Bergarbeiterwohnungen im Ruhrrevier* (Berlin, 1902).
Illustrierte Geschichte der Deutschen Revolution (Berlin, 1970).
Imbusch, H. *Arbeitsverhältnis und Arbeiterorganisation im Deutschen Bergbau* (Essen, 1908).
Jahn, R. *Essener Geschichte* (Essen, 1957).
Joniak, N. *Das Arbeiter-Wohnungselend im Rheinisch-Westfälischen Industriebezirk* (Frankfurt, 1908).
Jüngst, E. *Festschrift zur Feier des 50 jährigen Bestehens des Vereins für die Bergbaulichen Interessen im Oberbergamtsbezirk Dortmund in Essen* (Essen, 1908).
Kirchhoff, H.G. *Die staatliche Sozialpolitik im Ruhrbergbau, 1871-1914* (Köln, 1958).
Klein, P. *Separatisten an Rhein und Ruhr* (Berlin, 1961).
Kleinow, G. *Der Polizeiführer in den Nachkriegsjahren* (Lübeck, 1939).
Kluge, U. *Soldatenräte und Revolution* (Göttingen, 1975).
Koch, M.J. *Die Bergarbeiterbewegung im Ruhrgebiet zur Zeit Wilhelm II (1888-1914)* (Düsseldorf, 1954).
Köllmann, W. *Sozialgeschichte der Stadt Barmen* (Tübingen, 1960).
Könnemann, E. *Einwohnerwehren und Zeitfreiwilligenverbände* (1969).
Kolb, E. *Die Arbeiterräte in der deutschen Innenpolitik, 1918-1919* (Düsseldorf, 1962).
_____ 'Räte-Ideologie in der deutschen Revolution von 1918/19' in H. Neubauer (ed.), *Deutschland und die Russiche Revolution* (Stuttgart, 1968).
_____ (ed.) *Vom Kaiserreich zur Weimarer Republik* (Köln, 1972).
Kocka, J. *Klassengesellschaft im Krieg 1914-1918* (Göttingen, 1973).
Kuczynski, J. *Die Geschichte der Lage der Arbeiter unter dem Kapitalismus,* vols. 4 and 5 (Berlin, 1966).
Kuczynski, R.R. *Postwar Labour Conditions in Germany* (Washington, 1925).
Küppers, Paul *Die Kriegsarbeit der Stadt Bochum* (Bochum, 1926).
Lambers, Hanno *Die Revolutionszeit in Hagen* (Hagen, 1963).
Lindemann, A.S. *The Red Years. European Socialism versus Bolshevism,* 1919-1921 (Berkeley, 1974).
Lindemann, H. *Die deutsche Stadtgemeinde im Krieg* (Tübingen, 1917).
Lucas, E. *Arbeiterradikalismus* (Frankfurt, 1976).
_____ *Märzrevolution im Ruhrgebiet, Marz/April 1920,* 2 vols. (Frankfurt, 1973/1974).
_____ *Ursachen und Verlauf der Bergarbeiterbewegung in Hamborn und im Westlichen Ruhrgebiet 1918/19* (Duisburg, 1971). Duisburger Forschungen, vol. 15.
Lützenkirchen, R. *Der sozialdemokratische Verein für den Reichstagswahlkreis Dortmund-Hörde* (Dortmund, 1970).
Lux, H.A. *Düsseldorf* (Düsseldorf, 1925).
Matthias, E. 'Die Rückwirkungen der russischen Oktoberrevolution auf die deutsche Arbeiterbewegung', in H. Neubauer (ed.), *Deutschland und die Russiche Revolution* (Stuttgart, 1968).
_____ *Zwischen Räten und Geheimräten* (Düsseldorf, 1970).
Meerwarth, R., Günther, A. and Zimmerman, W. *Die Einwirkungen des Krieges*

auf die Bevölkerungsbewegung, Einkommen und Lebenshaltung in Deutschland (Stuttgart, 1932).
Mitchell, D. *1919—Red Mirage* (London, 1970).
Morgan, D.W. *The Socialist Left and the German Revolution* (London, 1975).
Mommsen, H., Petzina, D., Weisbrod, B. *Industrielles System und Politische Entwicklung in der Weimar Republik* (Düsseldorf, 1974).
Most, Otto *Die Grundbesitz-und Wohnungsverhaltnisse in Düsseldorf und ihre Entwicklung seit 1903* (Düsseldorf, 1912).
______ *Geschichte der Stadt Düsseldorf*, vols. 1 and 2 (Düsseldorf, 1921).
Müller, R. *Vom Kaiserreich zur Republik* (Wien, 1924).
______ *Der Bürgerkrieg in Deutschland* (Berlin, 1925).
Nestriepke, S. *Die Gewerkschaftsbewegung* (Stuttgart, 1922) two volumes.
Neumann, W. *Die Gewerkschaften im Ruhrgebiet 1918* (Köln, 1951).
Oehler, A. *Düsseldorf im Weltkrieg* (Düsseldorf, 1927).
Oeckel, H. *Die Revolutionäre Volkswehr, 1918/1919* (Berlin, 1968).
Oehme, W. *Die Weimarer Nationalversammlung* (Berlin, 1962).
Oertzen, F.W. von *Die deutschen Freikorps 1918–1923* (München, 1936).
Oertzen, P. von *Betriebsräte in der November Revolution* (Düsseldorf, 1963).
Opel, F. *Der Deutsche Metallarbeiterverband während des ersten Weltkrieges und der Revolution* (Frankfurt, 1973).
Pieper, L. *Die Lage der Bergarbeiter im Ruhrrevier* (Stuttgart and Berlin, 1903).
Pounds, N.J.G. *The Ruhr* (Bloomington, 1952).
Reulecke, J. (ed.) *Arbeiterbewegung an Rhein und Ruhr* (Wuppertal, 1974).
Ritter, G.A. *Die Arbeiterbewegung im Wilhelminischen Reich* (Berlin, 1959).
Roden, G. von *Geschichte der Stadt Duisburg*, vol.1 (Duisburg, 1970).
Rosenberg, A. *The Birth of the German Republic, 1871–1918* (Oxford, 1970).
Rürup, R. (ed.) *Arbeiter-und Soldatenräte im rheinisch-westfälischen Industriegebiet* (Wuppertal, 1975).
Schmidt-Pauli *Geschichte der Freikorps* (Stuttgart, 1936).
Schorske, C.E. *German Social Democracy, 1905–1917* (Cambridge, Massachusetts, 1955).
Schreiner, A. *Revolutionäre Ereignisse und Probleme in Deutschland während der Periode der Grossen Sozialistischen Oktoberrevolution 1917/18* (Berlin, 1957).
Skalweit, A. *Die Deutsche Kriegsernährungswirtschaft* (Stuttgart, 1927).
______ *Die Nahrungsmittelwirtschaft grosser Städte im Krieg*, printed in the series *Beiträge zur Kriegswirtschaft* (Berlin, 1917).
Sogemeier, M. *Die Entwicklung und Regelung des Arbeitsmarktes im rheinisch-westfälischen Industriegebiet im Kriege und in der Nachkriegszeit* (Jena, 1922).
Spethmann, H. *Das Ruhrgebiet im Wechselspiel von Land und Leuten, Wirtschaft, Technik und Politik* (Berlin, 1933).
______ *Zwölf Jahre Ruhrbergbau*, vols. 1 and 2 (Berlin, 1928).
Stern, L. *Der Einfluss der Grossen Sozialistischen Oktoberrevolution auf Deutschland und die Deutsche Arbeiterbewegung* (Berlin, 1958).
______ *Die Auswirkungen der Grossen Sozialistischen Oktoberrevolution auf Deutschland. Archivalische Forschungen zur Geschichte der deutschen Arbeiterbewegung*, Bd. 4/I–IV (Berlin, 1959).
Stockder, A.H. *History of the Trade Associations of the German Coal Industry* (New York, 1924).
Stollberg, O. (ed.) *Zehn Jahre Deutscher Geschichte* (Berlin, 1928).
Stursberg, E. *Remscheid und seine Gemeinden* (Remscheid, 1969).
Tormin, W. *Zwischen Rätediktatur und sozialer Demokratie* (Düsseldorf, 1954).

Umbreit, P. and Lorenz, C. (eds.) *Der Krieg und die Arbeitsverhältnisse* (Stuttgart, 1928).
Varain, H.J. *Freie Gewerkschaften, Sozialdemokratie und Staat* (Düsseldorf, 1956).
Vogel, Ilse *Bottrop, eine Bergarbeiterstadt in der Emscherzone des Ruhrgebiets* (Remagen, 1959).
Das Werk des Untersuchungsausschusses der Deutschen Verfassungsgebenden Nationalversammlung und des Deutschen Reichstags, Vierte Reihe, vol. 4–6.
Waite, R.G.I. *Vanguards of Nazism* (Cambridge, 1952).
Weidenhaupt, H. *Kleine Geschichte der Stadt Düsseldorf* (Düsseldorf, 1968).

B. *Articles*

Bimbel, H.W. 'Bochum zur Jahreswende 1918/19'. *Der Bochumer Wanderer*, Heft 4, 1968, pp. 3–7.
Croon, H. 'Die Einwirkung der Industrialisierung auf die gesellschaftliche Schichtung der Bevölkerung im rheinisch-westfälischen Industriegebiet'. *Rheinische Vierteljahresblätter*, vol. 20, pp. 301–17.
Dahn, K.W. 'German Protestantism and Politics, 1918–1939'. *JCH*, vol. 3, pp. 29–50.
Ekstein, M. 'Frankfurter Zeitung-Mirror of Weimar Germany'. *JCH*, 1971, vol. 6, no. 4, pp. 3ff.
Eliasberg, G. 'Der Ruhrkrieg 1920'. *AfS*, vol.X, pp. 291–377.
Kluge, Ulrich 'Essener Sozialisierungsbewegung und Volksbewegung im rheinisch-westfälischen Industriegebiet'. *IWK*, 1972, vol. 16, pp. 56–65.
Köllmann, W. 'Binnenwanderung und Bevölkerungstrukturen der Ruhrgebietsgrosstädte im Jahre 1907'. *Soziale Welt*, 1958, Heft 3–4, pp. 219–33.
______ 'Industrialisierung, Binnenwanderung, und "soziale Frage" '. *VfSW*, 1959, vol. 46, pp. 45–70.
______ 'Politische und soziale Entwicklung der deutschen Arbeiterschaft, 1850–1914'. *VfSW*, 1963, vol. 50, pp. 480–504.
Koszyk, K. 'Das abenteuerliche Leben des sozialrevolutionären Agitators Karl Minster's'. *AfS*, 1965, vol. V.
Lucas, E. and Del Tedesco, C. 'Zur Bergarbeiterbewegung in Hamborn 1918/19'. *Duisburger Forschungen*, vol. 22, 1975, pp. 141–68.
Oertzen, P. von 'Die grossen Streiks der Ruhrbergarbeiterschaft im Frühjahr 1919'. *Vierteljahreshefte für Zeitgeschichte*, 1958, vol. 6, pp. 231–63.
Rürup, R. 'Problems of the German Revolution'. *JCH*, 1968, vol. 3, Nr. 4, pp. 109–35.
______ 'Rätebewegung und Revolution in Deutschland 1918/19'. *Neue Politische Literatur*, 1967, vol. 12, pp. 303ff.
Wehler, H.U. 'Die Polen im Ruhrgebiet bis 1918'. *VfSW*, 1961, vol. 48, pp. 203–35.

III. *NEWSPAPERS*

Arbeiter-Zeitung, Essen, 1918/1919
Bergarbeiter-Zeitung, Bochum, 1918/1919
Bergische Arbeiterstimme, Solingen, 1918/1919
Bergische Volksstimme, Remscheid, 1918/1919
Bottroper Volkszeitung, 1918/1919
Castroper Zeitung, 1918/1919

Dorstener Volkszeitung, 1918/1919
Dortmunder General Anzeiger, 1918/1919
Düsseldorfer Freie Presse, 1918/1919
Düsseldorfer Nachrichten, 1919
Düsseldorfer Tageblatt, 1919
Duisburger Generalanzeiger, 1918/1919
Essener Allgemeine Zeitung, 1918/1919
Essener Volkszeitung, 1918/1919
Freiheit, Berlin, 1918/1919
Freiheit, Mülheim, 1919
Gelsenkirchener Allgemeine Zeitung, 1918/1919
Gelsenkirchener Zeitung, 1918/1919
Generalanzeiger für Sterkrade, Oberhausen, Osterfeld, Bottrop und Umgegend, 1918/1919
Der Kampf, Duisburg, 1916/1917
Lokal-Anzeiger für Dorsten, Hervest-Dorsten, Holsterhausen, Hervest, 1918/1919
Lüner Zeitung, 1918/1919
Mitteilungs-Blatt, Berlin, 1917/1918
Remscheider Zeitung, 1919
Remscheider General-Anzeiger, 1918
Die Republik, Berlin, 1918/1919
Rheinisch-Westfälische Zeitung, 1918/1919
Volksblatt, Bochum, 1918/1919
Volksrecht, Frankfurt, 1919
Der Volksverein, Mönchengladbach, 1912–1919
Volkszeitung, Düsseldorf, 1918/1919
Volksstimme, Hagen, 1919
Walder Zeitung, 1918/1919
Westdeutscher Herold, Volkszeitung für Aemter Wanne und Eickel, 1918/1919
Westfälische-Allgemeine Volkszeitung, 1918/1919
Wittener Tageblatt, 1919
Wittener Volkszeitung, 1919

Index